S0-AGE-437

COLLECTION OF
COOK BOOKS

If your bookseller does not have these titles, you may order them by
sending retail price, plus 10¢ for postage and handling to: MAIL SERVICE
DEPT., Pocket Books, Inc., 1 West 39th Street, New York, New York 10018.
Enclose check or money order—not responsible for orders containing cash.

THE
FRENCH
POCKET
COOKBOOK

GINETTE MATHIOT

Translated and Edited by
EILEEN B. HENNESSY

 A POCKET CARDINAL® EDITION published by
POCKET BOOKS, INC. • NEW YORK

THE FRENCH POCKET COOKBOOK

A Pocket *Cardinal* edition

1st printing........February, 1965

This original Pocket *Cardinal*® edition is printed from brand-new
plates made from newly set, clear, easy-to-read type.
Pocket *Cardinal* editions are published by Pocket Books, Inc.,
and are printed and distributed in the U.S.A. by Affiliated Publishers,
a division of Pocket Books, Inc., 630 Fifth Avenue, New York, N.Y. 10020.
Trademarks registered in the United States and other countries.

L

Table of Contents

Introduction

Show me a man who has never heard of the delights of French cuisine, and you'll probably be showing me a man who is blind, deaf, and lacking a tongue—in short, a man who is completely isolated from the world. For the creations of generations of French chefs have influenced the eating habits and the culinary practices and vocabulary of the entire Western world.

What is the secret of this popularity? What do the French have that the rest of us don't have? Actually, there are two "secrets," two vital building-blocks which form the foundation not only of French cuisine but, for that matter, of French civilization as a whole.

The first and most important ingredient of French success is careful and patient attention to details. Have you ever watched a Frenchwoman placing a pin at just the right angle on her blouse—making the final critical appraisal of her appearance before leaving her house? Have you looked at the careful cut and fit of French clothing, at the finishing details which are often lacking in even the most expensive American-made clothes? This attention to detail marks every aspect of French life, from language, art and literature through *haute couture* down to the cooking in even the most humble French home. The resulting perfection and elegance have made France the leader of the Western world in all those areas of life which concern the pleasures of the senses.

The second secret lies in the individualism and variety of France and her people. She is a land of many climates (from the lush green, rainy north to the sunburnt Mediterranean coast), many landscapes (from flat plains to rolling hills to barren mountain peaks), and many peoples (Celts, Germans,

Franks, Romans, Greeks, Phoenicians, Normans). Such diversity could have split this tiny country (it could be neatly fitted into our state of Texas, with a few miles to spare) into a million warring factions. Instead, the French have turned this very diversity into their greatest virtue. Two thousand and more years of national life together have resulted in a civilization and national character that are marked above all by moderation, balance, tolerance of individual foibles and peculiarities. "Nothing in excess" is one of the guiding principles of France, her people, her cuisine, her entire civilization. At the same time, each province has maintained its own regional mentality, customs and specialties, while contributing its special virtues (and vices) to the national character. For the lover of good food, this means not only that he can enjoy excellent "standard" French cooking anywhere in the country, but also that by driving a relatively short distance he can taste regional specialties varying from the tomato-garlic-olive-oil dishes of Provence to apples and butter in Normandy to sausages and sauerkraut in Alsace—to name only three provinces.

* *

How and what do the French eat? Let's look in on a typical French family as it sits down to its mid-day or evening meal.

First of all, the family is *together*. This is one of the most important clues to the French character. To the French, the family is the most sacred institution known to man, and nothing and no one—neither work, school, social activities or visiting foreigners—is permitted to break into it. This means that shops, factories, schools and offices close at noon and remain closed until two so that working people can go home for lunch (except, of course, in the very largest cities). The table is most likely set with a table *cloth* (here's one department of French life that the plastics industry has been slow to penetrate), and each member of the family has his *cloth* napkin neatly tucked into a napkin ring. There is the quart bottle of red "*vin de table*," the cheap, strong, often vinegary wine which the French drink with ordinary meals, and a bottle of water for those who prefer to dilute it. There is the long, crusty loaf of French bread, so fondly remembered by well-traveled Americans when faced with our over-processed and rather tasteless American bread.

The first dish arrives: the *hors-d'oeuvres* (or, if this is the evening meal, the traditional soup). This is a small tidbit, a "little nothing" to stimulate the appetite: perhaps a salad of sliced tomato or cucumber with a vinegar-and-oil dressing, or two or three slices of cold cuts, or a little mixed vegetable salad, and so on. This may be followed by a second light introductory dish (the *entrée*): croquettes, a meat pastry, a *Vol-au-vent* (a patty shell filled with creamed meat or fish). If the dinner is an important one the *entrée* may be more substantial: a fish or egg dish. If this course is skipped, the main course of meat, vegetables, and often a tossed green salad is served immediately after the *hors-d'oeuvre*. The meal ends with dessert, which is usually cheese, a piece of fresh fruit or a yogurt. At a more formal dinner, however, the fruit or cheese is followed by a sweet dessert or pastry. And finally, the coffee —a small cup of very strong "espresso" or filtered coffee, drunk at most with sugar, never diluted with cream. The Frenchman who has dined out in his favorite restaurant usually drinks his coffee, weather permitting, on the terrace of a café, where he can watch the passing show in the street, read his paper, write letters or simply relax. If it's a really special occasion, even the coffee has a final encore: a liqueur.

❖   ❖

Contrary to what many people believe, you *can* duplicate French cuisine right in your own kitchen. Admittedly our cream and butter are slightly different from the French products; it's true that French and American flour manufacturers follow different methods of milling, that French and American butchers don't see eye to eye on how a side of meat should be cut. But all these differences have been taken into account in preparing this cookbook, so the results should be practically identical with those obtained by the French housewife in her kitchen. All but two of the essential ingredients you need to cook *à la française* are obtainable anywhere in the U.S.A., and those two you yourself must contribute. For French cuisine is not a matter of materials, it's a matter of *attitude* and *method,* and it's difficult to say which is the more important.

First of all, you and your family must love yourselves and love life. At first blush this seems to have nothing at all to do with cooking. Actually, it makes all the difference in the world. We Americans love hard work and money far more than we love ourselves—an attitude derived, according to the sociologists, from our stern and ascetic Puritan forefathers. As a result we tend to view with suspicion anything that sounds like pampering our bodies: sitting down quietly for two hours to *enjoy* a really good dinner (as contrasted with nourishing ourselves for a day's hard work), relaxing for a half-hour with a glass of wine, sitting down for a while with a cup of coffee just to think or watch the world go by. Thus, our hard-working nation has developed business and technology to a very high degree, but our cuisine and eating habits, our dress—in short, our "civilization of the senses"—will need some time to catch up. We still have to learn to care about "just plain living" and our own bodies—the basis for creating and enjoying good cooking.

Assuming you and your family love yourselves enough to enjoy good food, the next point is method. THE method consists in paying close attention to each step in the preparation of a dish. There are no shortcuts in French cuisine. No adding cold milk to the sauce when it should be hot, "so that I won't have another dirty pot to wash." No adding three or four ingredients simultaneously when they should be added one by one. No skipping a step "to save a few minutes." The French are by temperament craftsmen, an animal which unfortunately has long since disappeared from the American scene. Either they take the time and care to do a thing well, or they don't do it at all. Either you and your family get into the habit of sitting down together and relaxing over your good meals, or you buy yourself a sturdy can opener and let it go at that.

But you and your family do appreciate good food and good living, otherwise you wouldn't have bought this book. So now you have all the ingredients you need to cook *à la française:*

love, patience and good will, and an excellent cookbook written by a Frenchwoman who was formerly an inspector of home economics courses in the Paris school system and who has several cookbooks to her credit.

Good luck and *bon appetit!*

The French Pocket Cookbook

A Word About Two Miracles:

WINE . . . .

One of the strangest things about us Americans is that we distrust wine and look down on those who drink it regularly as "winos"—yet we pour gallons of lethal cocktails into our digestive systems each year.

Let's not preach a sermon about the bad effect the cocktail habit can have on our bodies. Let's just consider the reason why the cocktail is the enemy of good cooking and good eating: to wit, the mixture of several strong alcoholic beverages that is a cocktail deadens your taste buds and clouds your senses so that often you hardly know what you're eating, still less can you appreciate the subtle blend of flavors that characterizes a well-cooked dish.

The cocktail is supposed to relax you. Actually, a glass of wine relaxes you far more and far better, because it doesn't make such a violent assault upon your brain and your senses. Wine stimulates, rather than deadens, your taste buds, so that a good meal tastes even better. It helps your digestive organs to perform their task properly. It contains body-building vitamins and minerals, iron- and bone-building phosphates. It gently warms and relaxes you, so that the friends or family with whom you're dining seem even more interesting and charming than usual. If a wine glass could replace the cocktail glass at business and social gatherings, the world might be in far better condition!

So now that you're going to become a Blue-Ribbon French

1

chef, encourage the (adult only, please!) members of your family to drink wine with their meals (in moderate quantities, of course). If your tired husband "absolutely has to have" a cocktail after his long, hard day at the office, try to persuade him to substitute a glass of Sherry, Vermouth, Port, Malaga or similar apéritif—it's better for his health.

Forget what you've heard about "rules" of wine-drinking —there are none. True, the French throw up their hands in despair when they see Americans drinking chilled Sherry with their roast beef. But that's simply because the French have found, after centuries of experience, that dry red wines served at room temperature best set off the flavor of hearty meat dishes, that chilled dry white wines enhance the more delicate dishes like fish, veal and chicken, that sweet wines like Sherry go best with desserts. However, we Americans seem to have a fondness for combining the sweet and the salty sides of life (pineapple with ham, mint jelly with lamb, cranberry sauce with turkey and so on), so if you really like to drink Sherry with your roast beef go ahead and do so—it's no one's business but your own!

The French have also found that wine is best served in a fairly large glass only half-full. The essences of the wine's "bouquet" gather in the remaining space and add to the delights of tasting and smelling a good wine. It doesn't have to be a fancy stemmed glass, either. The average Frenchman, when he is in the castle of his own home, drinks his wine out of an ordinary drinking glass. Experience has also shown that it's better to serve the wine right out of its bottle, shaking it as little as possible. If you pour it into a decanter the shaking-up changes its taste and perfume. For the same reason, don't drink from a bottle of wine immediately after you've jolted it home in the trunk of your car. Let it sit quietly for as long as possible so that it can catch its breath!

Experiment with various types of wine to see which ones you like best. Nowadays there's very little price difference between American and imported French wines (with a few exceptions), so if you can afford wine at all you can afford both.

Wine is a strange, subtle and complex miracle, the result of a unique interaction between the grapevine, the soil in which it's grown, the type and amount of rain and sunshine that fall upon it. Thus the same type of vine grown in two different regions will produce two quite different wines. If you don't believe it, compare our California "Burgundies," "Chiantis," "Rhine" wine, etc., with the original European vintages! (For this reason many purists wish that American vintners would invent new names for their wines.) Incidentally, try some of the New York State wines which have been developed from vines native to our country rather than imported from Europe. The gustatory results are always very interesting, and more often than not downright delightful!

When buying imported French wines, you might keep in mind that the words "Mise en bouteilles au Château" (i.e., bottled by the wine grower himself) on the label is a guarantee of good quality. Of course you'll also find many a good wine that isn't so marked, but there's a greater element of chance involved. As for the matter of "vintage years," a good general rule is that the odd-numbered years (since the Second World War, at least) have produced the best wines.

For cooking purposes, always use dry wine—11 to 12½% alcohol. For that matter, drink dry wine with your meals as well. As we noted above, dry wine enhances the flavor of meat, fish and vegetables much better than sweet.

Here is a *very* brief list of wines (you'll note that not all of them are French):

Red, Dry	*White*, Dry	Some *Sweet* Wines
The red Burgundies and Bordeaux	The white Burgundies and Bordeaux	Muscatel
Medoc	Chablis	Sherry
St. Julien	Sylvaner	Malaga
Beaujolais	Riesling	Port
etc.	Liebfraumilch	Sauterne
	Rhein Wine	
	etc.	

Don't forget the Rosé wines, which are light and refreshing (if perhaps a little bland) and go well with just about everything.

. . . . AND CHEESE

Cheese is as subtle a miracle as wine, and it's probably no accident that nothing sets off the flavor of a good cheese so well as a good red wine. It's as old a miracle, too—many writers of antiquity mention cheese in the same breath with wine, olives and bread.

As in the case of wine, the flavor of cheese results from a unique combination of the milk of a certain kind of animal with the grass of a certain piece of land, which in turn was the result of a certain amount of rain and sun and chemicals peculiar to that territory.

We Americans, as has been said before, seem to have a preference for sweet things, especially when it comes to desserts. To us, cheese is strictly for sandwiches and as an added ingredient in many dishes. But the cheese-for-dessert habit is a very pleasant one to get into, as any Frenchman or Italian will tell you. Cheese tastes best when eaten on a bit of unbuttered crusty French- or Italian-style bread. But if all you have in the breadbox is dear old American white, by all means run for the box of crackers!

One of the blessings of the Age of Technology is that we can now buy many foreign cheeses here, imported from just about every country in the world. If you have a gourmet or speciality shop nearby, try to buy imported Roquefort, Camembert, Munster or whatever-it-is, rather than American imitations of these European cheeses (which are sometimes quite competent, however, especially in the field of Cheddar). By the way, our "processed cheese spreads" can be called cheese only by the greatest courtesy and extension of the word.

For cooking purposes the French use Gruyère and Parmesan in dishes requiring grated cheese. Our Wisconsin Swiss cheese is a satisfactory substitute for Gruyère. Try if possible not to use ready-made grated cheese but to grate some as you need it. It tends to turn rancid and change flavor when kept for any length of time in those little cardboard containers.

Here is a list of a few dessert cheeses from various countries, and their relative strength of flavor:

Mild Cheeses—Gruyère, Emmenthal, Neufchâtel, Bel Paese, Port-Salut

Mild-to-strong Cheeses—Pont-l'Évêque, Brie

Quite strong Cheeses—Camembert, Stilton, Roquefort, Danish Blue

Very strong Cheese—Gorgonzola.

For Your Information

If shallots are not available in your neighborhood store, you may substitute either the white portion of green onions, minced, or very finely minced onion which has been dropped for one minute in boiling water, then rinsed and drained.

Imported canned truffles are at best a poor substitute for the fresh ones available to the French housewife. If you decide to use them nevertheless, rather than omit them, you can improve their flavor a little by adding one or two teaspoons of Madeira wine to the truffles about 30 minutes before using them.

Sticklers for perfection buy *imported* bay leaves. (American bay leaves have a slightly different flavor from the European variety, with the result that your version of a dish may not taste exactly the same as the one you ate in that delightful little Left-Bank restaurant! However, the difference is felt by only the most discriminating palate.)

For barding, larding, lining a pot or baking dish, and similar operations requiring fat, the French use a type of fat the American equivalent of which (fatback) is not readily available in many parts of the United States. You will see that the recipes in this book advise you to use the following substitutes:

(a) Fat salt pork, simmered for 10 min. in water to remove the salt.

(b) Fat trimmed from a fresh ham or a fresh pork loin.

(c) Bacon which has been blanched to remove the smoky flavor (otherwise your dish will taste of nothing but bacon). Place bacon strips in pan of cold water (1 qt. water to 4 oz. of bacon). Bring to simmer, then simmer for 10 min. Rinse bacon strips in fresh cold water. Dry before using.

6

Many of the recipes in this book call for grated Gruyère cheese. If it isn't available in your neighborhood store, our Wisconsin Swiss is a satisfactory substitute.

Use only *dry* wine (11 to 12½% alcohol) in recipes which call for wine.

To properly sauté and fry food, the butter or oil must be very hot, almost smoking, to seal in the juices and brown the food properly. For this reason clarified butter (see recipe 886) or a mixture of butter and oil is better for cooking than plain butter, which cannot be heated to a sufficiently high temperature. Remember, too, that the food must be absolutely dry if it is to brown properly.

What Does That Mean?

Here are a few words and terms which you may be meeting for the first time in this cookbook.

TO BARD: To cover a piece of meat with a thin slice of fat.

TO BIND: To add various ingredients to a sauce or soup in order to increase its consistency and smoothness. (See p. 11 for instructions.)

BOUQUET GARNI: A small packet of herbs and spices (2 sprigs parsley, ⅓ bay leaf, 1 spring thyme) much used for flavoring sauces and soups. Powdered thyme (about ⅛ tsp.) and parsley flakes (¾ tsp.) may be used; in this case, strain sauce carefully before serving.

TO BRAISE: To cook food slowly in a closed container, in its own juice or with a small quantity of additional liquid.

CROUTONS: Pieces of bread which have been diced, or cut in fancy shapes of various sizes, then fried in butter or oil. Much used in French cuisine as a garnish for soups and various dishes.

DEGLAZE: To pour a liquid into a pan in which meat has been roasted or sautéed, after pan has been degreased. Coagulated cooking juices are then scraped from bottom and sides of pan into liquid as it simmers.

DEGREASE: To remove grease from surface of a hot liquid.

FINES HERBES: Mixture of fresh parsley, chives, tarragon and chervil.

JULIENNE: Mixture of carrots, turnip, celery and white part of leek, cut in thin strips. **TO JULIENNE:** To cut food into very thin strips.

TO LARD: To introduce bits of fat under surface of piece of uncooked meat. This is done with a special larding needle.

MACEDOINE: A mixture of vegetables or fruit.

MACERATE: To soak fruit or vegetables in a liquid.

TO NAP: To cover food with a thin coating of sauce. (Any remaining sauce is served separately.)

TO REDUCE: To boil down a sauce or liquid in order to thicken it and reduce its volume.

SHALLOT: A plant closely related to the onion. Its leaves and bulbs **are** similar to but milder than garlic.

"SHIVER": The slow motion of a liquid when it is just beginning to boil.

TRUFFLE: An edible fungus, about 1 to 4 in. in diameter, which grows below the surface of the ground, close to tree roots. It grows wild in a number of European countries, and has never been successfully cultivated. It is usually hunted with dogs or hogs in France.

Table of Standard Measurements

Dash or few grains	less than ⅛ teaspoon
3 teaspoons	1 tablespoon
2 tablespoons	⅛ cup
4 tablespoons	¼ cup
5 tablespoons + 1 teaspoon	⅓ cup
8 tablespoons	½ cup
10 tablespoons + 2 teaspoons	⅔ cup
12 tablespoons	¾ cup
16 tablespoons	1 cup
2 cups	1 pint
4 cups or 2 pints	1 quart
4 quarts	1 gallon

All measurements are level and based on standard measuring spoons, cups, etc.

Sauces

HOW TO BIND A SAUCE

Binding with egg yolk: Use 1 egg yolk per pint of sauce. Beat yolk slightly with 1 tbsp. water. Stir in a small quantity of the sauce to be thickened; mix well, then pour into rest of the sauce, away from heat. Blend mixture thoroughly. Stir over very low flame or in top of double boiler until sauce has reached desired thickness. _Do not let sauce boil._

Binding with egg yolk and cream: Substitute 1 tbsp. cream for water.

Binding with butter and flour: Cream 1 tbsp. softened butter with 1 tbsp. flour. Form mixture into tiny balls; drop one by one into hot sauce. Let mixture simmer (_not boil_) for several minutes.

Binding with butter and starch: Substitute corn- or potato starch for flour. Simmer sauce 2 min.

Binding with flour: Use 1 tsp. flour to 2 cups sauce. Blend flour with ½ cup sauce until perfectly smooth. Stir into rest of the sauce; stir for a minute over low heat. Serve immediately.

Binding with starch (corn or potato): Mix 1 tsp. starch with 2 tbsp. water. Add a little hot sauce; blend thoroughly. Add to rest of sauce. Stir over low heat until sauce is very hot. Serve immediately.

1. GRAVY FOR ROAST (JUS DE RÔTI)

Pour small quantity of hot water or stock into roasting pan. Carefully scrape grease and coagulated juices of meat from bottom and sides of pan. Skim off grease, if necessary. Strain gravy, season to taste. If desired, add Madeira, Port or Sherry wine, or tomato purée. If gravy is very thin, bind with very small quantity of cornstarch blended with a little cold water; simmer 2 min.

2. "INSTANT" GRAVY

1½ cups Madeira wine   several bouillon cubes, meat extract, etc.

Place wine in bottle; place bottle, uncorked, in pot of water. Gradually heat water to boiling point. Remove ¾ cup wine from bottle; add bouillon cubes or highly concentrated meat stock to wine remaining in bottle. Cork bottle; let stand for 2 hours near heat source. This preparation is an excellent replacement for gravy and meat juices which have evaporated during roasting.

3. POOR MAN'S SAUCE

PREPARATION TIME: 5 MIN.   COOKING TIME: 5 MIN.

3 shallots, chopped   salt, pepper, bouquet garni
2 cups Stock (recipe 69)   chopped parsley
1 tbsp. vinegar or lemon juice

Boil all ingredients together for 5 min. Serve with very rich meats, game, leftovers.

4. MAÎTRE D'HÔTEL BUTTER

PREPARATION TIME: 5 MIN.

For each person:

2¼ tsp. butter   ¼ tsp. chopped parsley
    juice of 1 lemon   salt, pepper

Cream together all ingredients. Serve on broiled meat and fish, fried fish, boiled vegetables.

5. *RAVIGOTE BUTTER (CHIVRY BUTTER)*
PREPARATION TIME: 15 MIN.

For each person:

2¼ tsp. butter

1 sprig each chervil, tarragon, leek, watercress

Blanch herbs 3 min. in boiling water; chop finely. Cream together with butter. Rub through fine sieve. Use as garnish for cold hors-d'oeuvres, or in white sauces.

6. *BROWN BUTTER (BEURRE NOIR)*
PREPARATION TIME: 5 MIN.

4 tbsp. Butter (preferably clarified) (recipe 885)

½ tsp. vinegar

Heat butter in skillet until brown; pour over food to be served. Away from heat, pour vinegar into skillet; stir for a minute or two, then pour over butter. Serve on eggs, fish, boiled vegetables, brains, etc.

7. *COLBERT SAUCE*
PREPARATION TIME: 10 MIN.   COOKING TIME: 10 MIN.

¾ cup Meat Jelly (recipe 881) juice of 1 lemon

4 tbsp. butter chopped parsley

Heat Meat Jelly. Away from heat, add butter in small pieces, stirring constantly. Add lemon juice and chopped parsley. Serve with broiled fish and meat, vegetables.

WHITE SAUCES

8. *WHITE SAUCE I*
PREPARATION TIME: 10 MIN.   COOKING TIME: 20 MIN.

2 tbsp. butter 2 cups warm water

½ cup flour salt, pepper

Melt half the butter; blend in flour. Cook 2-3 min. Gradually add water, stirring constantly to prevent lumps. Simmer

10 min. Add remaining butter in small pieces. Season to taste.

9. WHITE SAUCE II

PREPARATION TIME: 5 MIN.   COOKING TIME: 20 MIN.

½ cup flour
3½ tbsp. butter
6 tbsp. cold water

2 cups boiling water
salt, pepper

Blend flour with cold water; pour into boiling water, stirring constantly. Season. Cook until sauce reaches desired consistency. Just before serving, add butter in small pieces. This sauce is easy to digest, easy to prepare, and tastes good!

10. BÉCHAMEL SAUCE

PREPARATION TIME: 10 MIN.   COOKING TIME: 20 MIN.

Follow either recipe for White Sauce, but use milk instead of water.

11. CREAM SAUCE

PREPARATION TIME: 10 MIN.   COOKING TIME: 20 MIN.

2 cups White Sauce
6 tbsp. cream

1 egg yolk

Add cream just before serving; bind with egg yolk. Remember that the addition of the cream will make the sauce thinner. Serve with vegetables, fish, eggs, poultry.

12. NORMAN CREAM SAUCE

PREPARATION TIME: 10 MIN.   COOKING TIME: 20 MIN.

1½ cups thick White Sauce I
6 tbsp. Fish Extract
(recipe 880)
6 tbsp. cream

6 tbsp. Mushroom Fumet
(recipe 883)
1 egg yolk

Add Fish Extract and Mushroom Fumet to sauce just before serving. Bind sauce with egg yolk and cream.

13. BUTTER SAUCE (SAUCE BÂTARDE)

PREPARATION TIME: 15 MIN.   COOKING TIME: 20 MIN.

2 cups White Sauce
2⅔ tbsp. butter

juice of one lemon
2 egg yolks, beaten

Add butter and egg yolks to sauce; thicken in top of double boiler. Add lemon juice just before serving. Serve with vegetables and boiled fish.

14. MORNAY SAUCE
PREPARATION TIME: 10 MIN. COOKING TIME: 20 MIN.

1½ cups White Sauce   ¾ cups grated Gruyère

Fold cheese into sauce. (Remember that this will thicken sauce.) Serve with eggs, vegetables, chicken.

15. POULETTE SAUCE
PREPARATION TIME: 10 MIN. COOKING TIME: 20 MIN.

1½ cups White Sauce   2 or 3 small onions
3½ tbsp. butter   juice of 1 lemon
6⅔ tbsp. dry white wine   1 egg yolk

Cook onions in sauce for 20 min. Remove onions; add lemon juice and wine. Bind sauce with butter and egg yolk just before serving. Serve with vegetables, poached variety meats.

16. SUPREME SAUCE
PREPARATION TIME: 25 MIN. COOKING TIME: 30 MIN.

¼ lb. mushrooms, cut in pieces   1½ cups White Sauce made with
6⅔ tbsp. cream   chicken stock

Simmer mushrooms in sauce for 30 min. Bind sauce with cream just before serving. Serve with eggs, poultry, vegetables, variety meats.

17. ENGLISH SAUCE
PREPARATION TIME: 5 MIN. COOKING TIME: 15 MIN.

2 cups White Sauce made with   3 tbsp. Mushroom Fumet (recipe
  chicken stock   883)
1 tbsp. Madeira wine   1 tbsp. Tomato Purée (recipe 876)

Combine all ingredients.

18. RICH SAUCE (DIPLOMAT SAUCE)
PREPARATION TIME: 10 MIN. COOKING TIME: 15 MIN.

1½ cups White Sauce
¼ lb. mushrooms, chopped
6 tbsp. brandy

1 truffle
pinch of Cayenne pepper

Combine all ingredients. Serve with fish.

19. SOUBISE SAUCE
PREPARATION TIME: 10 MIN. COOKING TIME: 35 MIN.

1 lb. onions, coarsely chopped
6⅔ tbsp. cream
6⅔ tbsp. white wine

6⅔ tbsp. Stock (recipe 69)
1½ cups White Sauce
2 tbsp. butter

Cook onions 10 min. in boiling water; drain. Simmer together onions, butter, wine, stock for 20 min. Rub mixture through sieve or food mill, add to White Sauce. Add cream; season to taste.

20. HORSERADISH SAUCE I
PREPARATION TIME: 10 MIN. COOKING TIME: 25 MIN.

2 cups Béchamel Sauce
6 tbsp. white wine

1 tbsp. horseradish

Combine all ingredients. Simmer 5 min.

21. HORSERADISH SAUCE II
PREPARATION TIME: 10 MIN. COOKING TIME: 25 MIN.

2 cups Béchamel Sauce
2 tbsp. horseradish

¼ cup blanched, crushed almonds
pinch of grated lemon rind

Combine all ingredients.

22. PRINTANIÈRE SAUCE (CHIVRY SAUCE)
PREPARATION TIME: 20 MIN. COOKING TIME: 2 MIN.

2 cups White Sauce II, without butter
¼ lb. butter

1 tbsp. each tarragon, chervil, parsley, leek

Blanch herbs in boiling water; drain, chop. Cream together butter and herbs; add to White Sauce. Serve with eggs and poultry.

23. ANCHOVY SAUCE
PREPARATION TIME: 15 MIN.   COOKING TIME: 15 MIN.

2 cups White Sauce   4 tbsp. anchovy butter (see p. 31)

Blend butter into sauce. If desired, add a few minced anchovy fillets. Serve with fish.

24. SHRIMP SAUCE
PREPARATION TIME: 1 HOUR   COOKING TIME: 20 MIN.

2 cups White Sauce, made with   ¼ lb. shrimp
court-bouillon or fish liquid   ¼ lb. butter

Make Shrimp Butter (see p. 31); add to White Sauce just before serving. Serve with fish.

25. MUSSELS SAUCE
PREPARATION TIME: 30 MIN.   COOKING TIME: 20 MIN.

2 cups White Sauce, made with   2 qts. Mussels, cooked (recipe 168)
court-bouillon (recipes 886 et   1 egg yolk
seq.) or fish liquid

Remove cooked mussels from shells; add to sauce together with water in which they were cooked. Bind with egg yolk. Serve with fish.

26. CARDINAL SAUCE
PREPARATION TIME: 15 MIN.

2 cups Béchamel Sauce   1 tbsp. crushed lobster coral
1 tbsp. crushed anchovies

Combine all ingredients. Serve with fillets of sole.

27. JOINVILLE SAUCE
PREPARATION TIME: 30 MIN.   COOKING TIME: 30 MIN.

Hollandaise Sauce (recipe 64)   3½ tbsp. Shrimp Butter (see p. 31)
3 tbsp. White Sauce   ¼ lb. shelled shrimp (tails only)

Combine all ingredients. Serve with fish.

28. CAPERS SAUCE
Add 4 oz. capers, drained, to 2 cups Béchamel Sauce. Serve with boiled fish.

29. *RAVIGOTE SAUCE*
PREPARATION TIME: 20 MIN.   COOKING TIME: 10 MIN.

2 cups White Sauce made with stock
½ tsp. minced shallot
2⅔ tbsp. butter
3 tbsp. vinegar

3 tbsp. white wine
1 tbsp. each chopped chervil and tarragon
1½ tbsp. chopped chives

Simmer together vinegar, wine and shallot until liquid is reduced by half. Add to White Sauce; simmer 6 min. Strain sauce. Add chopped herbs and butter just before serving. Serve with variety meats and poultry.

LIGHT BROWN SAUCES

30. *LIGHT BROWN SAUCE* (ROUX BLOND)
PREPARATION TIME: 10 MIN.   COOKING TIME: 20 MIN.

3½ tbsp. Butter (preferably clarified butter) (recipe 885)
¾ cup flour

2 cups hot stock or water
salt, pepper

Heat butter until very hot, almost smoking. Add flour; cook, stirring constantly, until flour turns a light brown color. Gradually add hot liquid, stirring constantly. Season to taste.

31. *TOMATO SAUCE*
PREPARATION TIME: 10 MIN.   COOKING TIME: 40 MIN.

1⅔ lbs. tomatoes, quartered
4 tbsp. butter
¾ cup Stock (recipe 69)
6 tbsp. flour

1 carrot; diced
1 onion
salt, pepper, thyme, bay leaf, parsley

Cook tomatoes without water for 5 min.; rub through sieve. Prepare a Light Brown Sauce with tomato purée, 2 tbsp. butter, flour. Stir in stock; add carrot, onion, seasonings, simmer 30 min. Add 2 tbsp. butter just before serving.

32. FINANCIÈRE SAUCE

PREPARATION TIME: 25 MIN. COOKING TIME: 25 MIN.

2 cups Light Brown Sauce, made
with chicken stock
1 Calf's Sweetbread, cooked
(recipe 337), cut in pieces
¼ lb. chopped mushrooms
salt, pepper

juice of 1 lemon or 6⅔ tbsp.
Madeira wine
salt, pepper
several Quenelles (recipe 871)
1¾ oz. cooked cockscombs, if
available

Combine all ingredients; simmer 6 min. Season to taste.
Serve with fish, timbales, mussels, Vol-au-vent, Bouchée à la
reine, etc.

33. RICHELIEU SAUCE

PREPARATION TIME: 15 MIN. COOKING TIME: 25 MIN.

2 cups Light Brown Sauce, made
with gravy from roast (recipe 1)
¼ lb. chopped mushrooms

2 tbsp. butter
truffles, if desired

Combine sauce, mushrooms and truffles; simmer 5 min. Add
butter just before serving.

34. BORDELAISE SAUCE

PREPARATION TIME: 15 MIN. COOKING TIME: 45 MIN.

2 cups Light Brown Sauce
¾ cup white Bordeaux wine
1 onion

1 mushroom
2 tbsp. olive oil
½ clove garlic

Chop finely onion, garlic, mushroom; cook 30 min. in olive
oil. Add sauce and wine; cook 5 min. Serve with broiled meat.

35. MARROW SAUCE

PREPARATION TIME: 10 MIN. COOKING TIME: 1 MIN.

1½ cups Bordelaise Sauce
½ lb. beef marrow, sliced

12 small slices bread, fried in
4 tbsp. butter

Blanch slices of marrow 1 min. in small quantity boiling
stock. Arrange on slices of fried bread croutons; nap with
sauce. Serve with broiled meats, vegetables, poached eggs.

36. MARINIÈRE SAUCE

PREPARATION TIME: 10 MIN. COOKING TIME: 20 MIN.

¾ cup flour
3½ tbsp. butter
¾ cup white wine

6 tbsp. Court-bouillon (recipe 866 et seq.) or fish liquid

Proceed according to recipe for Light Brown Sauce, substituting wine and court-bouillon for stock. Serve with fish, timbales, mussels, Vol-au-vent.

37. VELVET SAUCE

PREPARATION TIME: 10 MIN. COOKING TIME: 20 MIN.

Proceed according to recipe for Light Brown Sauce, but use 3 cups stock and cook longer, so that sauce will be thicker and more concentrated in flavor. Or use two cups concentrated meat stock and cook for same length of time as for Light Brown Sauce.

38. IVORY VELVET SAUCE

PREPARATION TIME: 10 MIN. COOKING TIME: 20 MIN.

2 cups Velvet Sauce

¾ cup cream

Reduce sauce by cooking to about two-thirds its original volume. Whip briskly with wire whisk, gradually adding cream. Serve immediately.

39. CHAUD-FROID SAUCE

PREPARATION TIME: 15 MIN. COOKING TIME: 40 MIN.

¾ cup Meat Jelly (recipe 881)
6⅔ tbsp. cream

4 egg yolks
Ivory Velvet Sauce

Slowly pour jelly into sauce; cook 20 min. over very low flame. Strain sauce; bind with egg yolks and cream, stirring constantly. Chill. When cold but not set, nap meat. Serve with white meats and poultry.

Omit cream if sauce is to be used for game.

DARK BROWN SAUCES

40. DARK BROWN SAUCE (ROUX BRUN)
PREPARATION TIME: 5 MIN. COOKING TIME: 20 MIN.

3½ tbsp. butter
¾ cup flour
1½ cups warm water or Stock
   (recipe 69)

1 small onion, quartered
2 oz. fatback, fresh pork fat or
   blanched bacon, diced
   bouquet garni, salt, pepper

Brown onion and diced fat in butter; remove. Re-heat butter to smoking; pour in flour in a rain and cook, stirring constantly, until brown. Gradually add stock, stirring constantly. Add onion and seasonings; cook 20 min. over low heat.

41. PIQUANT SAUCE
PREPARATION TIME: 10 MIN. COOKING TIME: 25 MIN.

2 cups Dark Brown Sauce
⅔ cup vinegar
¾ tsp. chopped shallot

sliced or finely chopped
gherkins

Cook vinegar with shallot over low heat until liquid is reduced to 3 tbsp. Add to sauce; simmer 5 min. Add gherkins. Serve with small cuts of meat and left-over meat dishes.

42. MADEIRA SAUCE
PREPARATION TIME: 5 MIN. COOKING TIME: 30 MIN.

Add 1¼ tsp. Madeira wine to 2 cups Dark Brown Sauce just before serving. Serve with small cuts of meat.

43. MUSHROOM SAUCE
PREPARATION TIME: 15 MIN. COOKING TIME: 20 MIN.

Simmer ¼ lb. small whole, peeled mushrooms for 20 min. in 2 cups Madeira Sauce. Add 1 tbsp. Madeira just before serving. Serve with small cuts of meat and sautéed poultry.

44. OLIVE SAUCE
PREPARATION TIME: 15 MIN.   COOKING TIME: 20 MIN.

Simmer 5 oz. pitted olives for 20 min. in 2 cups Madeira Sauce. Add 1 tbsp. Madeira wine just before serving.

45. PÉRIGUEUX SAUCE
PREPARATION TIME: 10 MIN.   COOKING TIME: 20 MIN.

Add 1 diced truffle to 2 cups Madeira Sauce. Serve with small cuts of meat, fowl; game; timbales, Vol-au-vent, etc.

46. CHATEAUBRIAND SAUCE

Add juice of 1 lemon and 1 tbsp. each chopped tarragon and parsley to 2 cups Dark Brown Sauce just before serving.

47. ITALIAN SAUCE
PREPARATION TIME: 10 MIN.   COOKING TIME: 20 MIN.

2 cups Dark Brown Sauce	¼ lb. mushrooms, chopped
1 tbsp. vinegar	chopped gherkins, if desired

Combine all ingredients.

48. PORTUGUESE SAUCE

2 cups Dark Brown Sauce	2 tbsp. Tomato Purée (recipe 876)
¾ cup Madeira wine	

Combine all ingredients; boil 1 min. Serve with eggs, fish, meat, poultry.

49. PEPPER SAUCE (SAUCE POIVRADE)
PREPARATION TIME: 5 MIN.   COOKING TIME: 45 MIN.

2 cups Dark Brown Sauce	1 small onion
6⅔ tbsp. vinegar	6⅔ tbsp. white wine
½ tsp. chopped shallot	salt, pepper, bay leaf, thyme
1 med. carrot, cut in pieces	

Simmer together all ingredients except wine and sauce, until reduced by half. Rub through sieve. Add mixture to sauce together with wine; simmer 40 min. Strain. Add pinch of pepper 5 min. before serving. Serve with meat and game.

50. ROBERT SAUCE
PREPARATION TIME: 10 MIN. COOKING TIME: 25 MIN.

2 cups Stock (recipe 69)
3½ tbsp. butter
1 small onion, finely chopped
¾ cup flour
6⅔ tbsp. dry white wine

1 tbsp. mustard
1 tbsp. Tomato Purée (recipe 876)
1 tbsp. vinegar
salt, pepper

Brown onion in butter. Add flour; cook, stirring, until brown. Add stock, wine, salt and pepper; simmer 20 min. Add mustard, vinegar and tomato purée just before serving. Serve with broiled meat, especially pork.

51. CHARCUTIÈRE SAUCE
PREPARATION TIME: 10 MIN. COOKING TIME: 25 MIN.

Add 2 or 3 sliced gherkins to Robert Sauce just before serving. Serve with broiled or sautéed pork.

52. GÉNEVOISE SAUCE
PREPARATION TIME: 15 MIN. COOKING TIME: 20 MIN.

2 cups Dark Brown Sauce made with fish stock
¾ cup red wine

¼ lb. mushrooms, chopped
chopped parsley and shallot
salt, pepper

Combine all ingredients (except ¼ cup wine); s. mer gently 15 min. Strain. Add remaining wine just before serving. Serve with fish, especially trout and salmon.

53. RED WINE SAUCE (SAUCE MATELOTE)
PREPARATION TIME: 10 MIN. COOKING TIME: 30 MIN.

¾ cup red wine
1½ cups water
½ cup flour
5⅓ tbsp. butter

½ tsp. brandy
salt, pepper, bouquet garni
garlic, shallot

Simmer together wine, water and seasonings for 20 min. over low flame. Strain. Use liquid to make a Dark Brown Sauce with flour and half the butter. Add brandy and remaining butter just before serving. Serve with eel and fish.

54. BLOOD SAUCE
PREPARATION TIME: 10 MIN.   COOKING TIME: 20 MIN.

liver of bird or animal, cooked, crushed in blood	1 small onion
3½ tbsp. butter	1½ cups red wine
¾ cup flour	¾ cup Stock (recipe 69)
3 oz. fatback, fresh pork fat or blanched bacon, diced	salt, pepper, *bouquet garni*

Brown diced fat and onion in butter, remove from pan. Sprinkle flour into pan; cook, stirring, until brown. Add wine, stock, seasonings, onion and diced fat; simmer 15-20 min. Away from fire, add crushed cooked liver and blood just before serving. Serve with game.

55. CHASSEUR SAUCE
PREPARATION TIME: 10 MIN.   COOKING TIME: 1½ HOURS.

1 qt. Marinade (recipe 856) gravy from roast	4 tbsp. butter
2 tbsp. currant jelly	⅔ cup flour

Cook marinade until reduced by half. Make a Dark Brown Sauce with marinade, flour, butter. Finish with jelly and a little gravy. Serve with small cuts of meat and sautéed fowl.

COLD SAUCES

56. VINAIGRETTE SAUCE
PREPARATION TIME: 5 MIN.

6⅔ tbsp. vinegar	salt, pepper, chopped *fines herbes*
1⅓ cups oil	

Dissolve salt in vinegar; add remaining ingredients. Mix thoroughly.

56A. RAVIGOTE SAUCE WITH OIL:
Add 1 tbsp. drained capers and 1 chopped onion to Vinaigrette Sauce.

57. MUSTARD SAUCE
PREPARATION TIME: 10 MIN.

3 tbsp. mustard
6⅔ tbsp. butter
1 tsp. cornstarch

6⅔ tbsp. warm water
salt, pepper

Heat mustard in top of double boiler. Add butter, stirring. When well blended add cornstarch and water, salt, pepper. Serve with grilled meat, especially pig's trotters St. Menehould.

58. RÉMOULADE SAUCE
PREPARATION TIME: 10 MIN.

2 tbsp. mustard
1 shallot, finely chopped

¾ cup oil
salt, pepper

Blend mustard with oil; add remaining ingredients.

59. GRIBICHE SAUCE
PREPARATION TIME: 10 MIN.

3 hard-boiled eggs
1⅓ cups oil
6⅔ tbsp. vinegar
1 tbsp. mustard

1 tbsp. chopped gherkins
salt, pepper, chopped fines herbes

Crush egg yolks; gradually add oil, mustard and vinegar and beat to a smooth paste. Add chopped gherkins and *fines herbes*, finely chopped egg whites. Serve with cold fish and shellfish.

60. MAYONNAISE
First Method   (PREPARATION TIME: 10 MIN.)

1 egg yolk
1 cup oil

1½ tsp. vinegar
salt, pepper

Egg and oil should be at a temperature of about 60° F. Beat egg yolk with wire whisk until creamy. Gradually add oil in small quantities, beating after each addition until perfectly blended. Add salt, pepper and vinegar when finished.

Second Method (PREPARATION TIME: 8 MIN.)

Place ingredients (except oil) in top of double boiler; beat constantly until thick. Gradually add oil as in first method, beating constantly. Water in bottom of double boiler should not reach boiling point.

60A. *MAYONNAISE MOUSSELINE*: Fold one stiffly beaten egg white into Mayonnaise. Serve with asparagus.

60B. *ANCHOVY MAYONNAISE*: Add 1 finely chopped shallot and 6 diced anchovy fillets to egg yolk before beating.

60C. *PRINTANIÈRE MAYONNAISE*: Add a few tbsp. of chopped *fines herbes* to completed Mayonnaise.

60D. *RED MAYONNAISE*: Add 3 tbsp. crushed lobster coral to Mayonnaise.

60E. *AILLOLI*: Add finely crushed clove of garlic to egg yolk before beating.

61. *PROVENÇAL AILLOLI*
PREPARATION TIME: 10 MIN.

3 cloves garlic, crushed
⅓ cup fresh bread crumbs, soaked in 6 tbsp. milk

2 cups oil
2 egg yolks
salt, vinegar, pepper

Combine garlic, bread crumbs (drained), egg yolks. Proceed as for Mayonnaise.

62. *GREEN SAUCE*

1 cup Mayonnaise
2 tbsp. capers, chopped

2 or 3 gherkins, chopped
1 tbsp. Herb Coloring (recipe 877)

Combine all ingredients.

62A. *VINCENT SAUCE*: Add pinch of finely chopped tarragon and 4 tbsp. cream to Green Sauce.

63. TARTARE SAUCE
PREPARATION TIME: 20 MIN.

1 cup Mayonnaise
2 tsp. mustard
1 small onion, chopped

chopped chives, chervil, tarragon,
    parsley
dash of Cayenne pepper
a few capers

Blend onion, herbs and mustard into Mayonnaise. Add capers and dash of pepper. Sauce should be very spicy.

64. HOLLANDAISE SAUCE
PREPARATION TIME: 10 MIN. COOKING TIME: 10 MIN.

3 egg yolks
¾ cup butter in small pieces
1 tbsp. cold water

juice of 1 lemon, warmed
salt, pepper

Place salt, egg yolks and water in top of doubler boiler; mix well. Remove from heat; gradually beat in butter. Place over heat and thicken sauce. Add lemon juice, salt, pepper. Serve immediately. Serve with vegetables, fish, eggs.

65. MOUSSELINE SAUCE
PREPARATION TIME: 15. MIN. COOKING TIME: 15 MIN.

Proceed as for Hollandaise, but omit water, use 2 egg yolks and ⅔ cup butter. Add 1 tsp. cornstarch to sauce before beating in butter. Finish with 4 tbsp. cream, and beat sauce well before serving. Serve with fish and boiled vegetables.

66. BÉARNAISE SAUCE
PREPARATION TIME: 15 MIN. COOKING TIME: 1 HOUR

¾ cup vinegar
2 shallots
1 branch tarragon

3 egg yolks
½ clove garlic
⅔ cup butter, in small pieces

Simmer together vinegar, shallots, garlic and tarragon 45 min. over very low heat. Rub through sieve. Place with egg yolks in top of double boiler. Gradually add butter, stirring constantly. Finish with 1 tbsp. chopped tarragon. Serve with broiled or sautéed meats, broiled fish.

If desired, vinegar and spices may be replaced by 1 tbsp. Béarnaise Extract (recipe 875).

67. *CRAPAUDINE SAUCE*
PREPARATION TIME: 10 MIN. COOKING TIME: 1 HOUR

¾ cup vinegar
2 shallots
½ clove garlic

1 branch tarragon
⅔ cup Meat Extract (recipe 880)
juice of 1 lemon

Simmer together vinegar, shallots, garlic and tarragon 45 min. over low heat. Rub through sieve. Beat in meat extract and lemon juice.

68. *DEVILED SAUCE* (SAUCE À LA DIABLE)
PREPARATION TIME: 15 MIN. COOKING TIME: 20 MIN.

6⅔ tbsp. white wine
6⅔ tbsp. vinegar
¾ cup stock (recipe 69)
1½ tsp. Meat Extract (recipe 880)
2 shallots, chopped

½ cup flour
4 tbsp. butter
salt, pepper, chopped chervil
and tarragon

Simmer together wine, vinegar and chopped shallots until liquid is reduced by half. Add stock; cook 8-10 min. Blend butter and flour; beat into hot liquid with wire whisk until mixture thickens. Add meat extract. Add herbs just before serving.

Hors-d'oeuvres

SUGGESTED HOT HORS-D'OEUVRES:

Croquettes—fish, poultry, meat
Eggs
Rissoles
Gnocchis
Shells
Vol-au-vent
Bouchée à la reine
Tarts
Cheese Delights
Mushroom Canapés
Quiche Lorraine

SUGGESTED COLD HORS-D'OEUVRES:

Cold cuts—cooked ham, bologna, sausage, etc.
Fish—sardines, tuna, salmon, marinated herring, anchovies,
etc., shrimp and mussel salads, cooked mussels, snails,
oysters, etc.
Vegetable salads.

SUGGESTED VEGETABLE HORS-D'OEUVRES:

Artichokes—Wash young, tender artichokes; cut off tips of
leaves. Serve with Vinaigrette Sauce (recipe 56).
Black Radishes—Peel radishes, slice thinly. Sprinkle with
salt; set aside for 30 min. Drain before serving.
Beets—Peel and slice chilled cooked beets. Marinate for 30
min. in mixture of Vinaigrette Sauce (recipe 56), sliced
onion, cloves, bay leaf, salt and pepper.

Cucumbers—Peel, slice thinly. Sprinkle with salt; set aside for 3 hours. Drain; wash in running cold water. Serve with cream or with a Vinaigrette Sauce (recipe 56).

Red Cabbage Salad—Chop cabbage finely. Place in flat dish; sprinkle with salt and set aside for 4 hours. Drain. Season with a Vinaigrette Sauce (recipe 56).

Tomatoes—Slice thinly and serve with a Vinaigrette Sauce. Peel if desired.

Macedoine—Mixed cooked vegetables served with a Vinaigrette Sauce, Mayonnaise (recipe 60) or Ravigote Sauce (recipe 56A). Suggestions:

1. Heap up diced cooked potatoes on serving dish. Surround with sliced beets; garnish each beet slice with a bit of chopped cooked meat. Season with sauce made of chopped *fines herbes,* mustard, oil, vinegar, salt and pepper.
2. Arrange thin slices of tomato on serving dish; top with sliced hard-boiled eggs, shelled cooked shrimp. Cover with Mayonnaise.
3. Place mixture of diced cooked carrots, string beans and potatoes in center of serving dish. Surround with hard-boiled eggs, garnish with truffle slices. Serve with Mayonnaise.

Mushrooms à la grecque—See recipe 608.

Stuffed tomatoes—See recipe 612.

BUTTERS

Hors-d'oeuvres are usually served with butter, often flavored or cut in fancy shapes, depending on the chef's imagination. Here are a few suggestions:

Vermicelli Butter—Place desired quantity of butter in sieve, strainer or colander with large holes. Force butter through holes, using wet wooden spoon or mortar.

Butter Shells—These are made with a special knife, soaked in hot water. An ordinary knife may also be used. Scrape surface of butter with knife blade, and fashion scraping into shape of a snail shell. Butter must be very hard and cold.

Shrimp Butter—Mix one part crushed cooked shrimp with one part butter. Or, crush shrimp together with butter; melt mixture in top of double boiler, then strain through wet strainer. Chill.

Sardine or Anchovy Butter—Remove bones and skin from sardines or anchovies. Make a paste of fish, chopped parsley and a little chopped chervil, 1 tsp. mustard. Mix thoroughly with equal amount of butter.

Coral Butter—Blend, in equal amounts, butter and cooked crushed lobster eggs.

Butter aux fines herbes—Cook together 6 leaves spinach, 1 tbsp. each chopped shallot, chives, chervil, tarragon, parsley for 5 min. in boiling salted water. Drain thoroughly. Crush with a mortar; blend in butter and mix until smooth.

CANAPÉS

Suggested spreads for canapés:

Anchovy—Cover one half of slice of toast with chopped white of hard-boiled egg; cover other half with crushed yolk. Between them place an anchovy fillet.

Radish—Place dab of Mayonnaise in center of slice of toast; surround with slices of radish and sliced gherkins.

Tarragon (Canapé Vieville)—Spread slice of toast with tarragon-flavored butter; top with slice of ham. Garnish with tarragon leaves.

No-no-Nanette canapé—Spread slice of toast with anchovy butter. Place slice of hard-boiled egg in center; surround with cooked shelled shrimp. Place dab of Mayonnaise on egg slice; sprinkle with chopped *fines herbes*.

Sardine—Spread slice of toast with butter. Spread cooked drained tomato on each end; cover center with Sardine Butter.

Shrimp—Halve rolls lengthwise; hollow out. Spread with Mayonnaise. Arrange cooked shelled shrimp at each end; garnish center with lettuce leaf.

Soups

N.B.: All recipes serve 6, unless otherwise indicated. For instructions on how to bind soups, see page 11.

69. MEAT STOCK or BOUILLON

PREPARATION TIME: 25 MIN.   COOKING TIME: 3½ HOURS.

1¾ lbs. any cut beef and bones
3 med. carrots
1 leek
¼ lb. turnip

1 parsnip
1 stalk celery
3 qts. water
3 tsp. salt

Clean and peel vegetables. Place meat, bones and salt in heavy pot; cover with cold water. Bring to boil; cook 15 min. Skim liquid. Add vegetables; bring liquid back to boil, then lower heat and simmer 3 hours. Strain and skim off grease. Use liquid in recipes calling for stock. If desired, cook small quantity of vermicelli or thin noodles in hot stock; serve as a soup.

Stock stored in refrigerator must be brought to boil every 3 or 4 days to prevent it from spoiling.

70. THICK SOUP

Blend 1½ cups flour or cream of rice in a little water; add to stock. Cook 20 min., stirring constantly. Bind with egg yolk, 2 tbsp. butter, or a little cream.

71. CONSOMMÉ

PREPARATION TIME: 25 MIN.   COOKING TIME: 4 HOURS.

9 cups water
2 lbs. any cut of beef
6 chicken giblets

same vegetables as for Meat
   Stock (recipe 69)
salt

Place meat in heavy pot; cover with cold water. Slowly bring to boil. Skim; add vegetables and salt. Simmer 3½ hours over low flame. Clarify liquid. May be served hot or cold.

72. VELVET SOUP
PREPARATION TIME: 15 MIN. COOKING TIME: 15 MIN.

2 qts. stock
½ cup tapioca

3½ tbsp. butter
1 egg yolk

Bring stock to boil. Gradually pour in tapioca in a rain. Cook 10 min. over low heat, stirring constantly. Bind with egg yolk and butter.

73. WATERCRESS SOUP
PREPARATION TIME: 20 MIN. COOKING TIME: 35 MIN.

7 cups boiling water
1 bunch watercress, washed, chopped
2 tbsp. butter

⅓ cup flour
¼ cup rice, washed
1 egg yolk

Cook watercress in butter until wilted and tender. Sprinkle in flour; stir in boiling water; cook 15 min. Add rice, season to taste; continue cooking 20 min. Just before serving, bind with egg yolk. Garnish with watercress leaves.

74. SORREL SOUP
PREPARATION TIME: 20 MIN. COOKING TIME: 1 HOUR

2 qts. water
½ lb. sorrel, washed and chopped
1 lb. potatoes, peeled, cut in pieces

2 tbsp. butter
1 egg yolk, beaten
salt, pepper
1 cup flour (optional)

Wilt sorrel in hot butter; add water, potatoes, seasonings. Cook 1 hour over low heat. Rub through sieve or food mill. Bind with egg yolk; add a little butter just before serving. If desired, sprinkle flour over sorrel before adding water.

75. *PARSLEY SOUP* (POTAGE CHOISY)

PREPARATION TIME: 20 MIN.   COOKING TIME: 1 HOUR.

small bunch of parsley, washed
1 bunch watercress, washed
2 tbsp. butter

1 lb. potatoes, peeled, cut in pieces
7½ cups boiling water
2 tsp. salt

Cook parsley, watercress and potatoes together in boiling salted water for 1 hour, over low flame. Rub through sieve or food mill. Add butter; garnish with chopped parsley.

75A.   *CHERVIL SOUP:* Substitute chervil for parsley.

76.   *HERB SOUP*

PREPARATION TIME: 20 MIN.   COOKING TIME: 1 HOUR.

8½ cups water
½ lb. sorrel (or watercress), finely chopped
½ lb. lettuce, finely chopped
½ leek, finely chopped

2 tbsp. butter
⅓ cup flour
⅓ cup tapioca
salt, pepper

Cook chopped greens in butter until tender. Add flour, water, seasonings; cook gently 1 hour. Twenty minutes before serving time, slowly pour in tapioca in a rain. Add butter just before serving.

77.   *LIÈGEOISE SOUP*

PREPARATION TIME: 20 MIN.   COOKING TIME: 45 MIN.

8 cups hot water
2 leeks
1 stalk celery
¼ lb. sorrel (or watercress)
1 lb. potatoes, peeled

2 tomatoes, crushed
5 tbsp. butter
1 tbsp. chopped chervil
salt, pepper, bay leaf

Wash and chop green vegetables; brown in 3½ tbsp. butter. Add hot water, seasonings; bring to boil. Add potatoes, cook 45 min. Rub through sieve or food mill. Add crushed tomatoes and remaining butter.

78.   *ASPARAGUS SOUP* (CRÈME D'ARGENTEUIL)

PREPARATION TIME: 25 MIN.   COOKING TIME: 45 MIN.

6 cups hot water
1 lb. asparagus
6 tbsp. butter

⅔ cup flour
¾ cup cream *or*
2 egg yolks

Scrape and dice asparagus stalks (reserve tips); scald 2 min. in boiling water. Melt 4 tbsp. butter; blend in flour; add hot water. Cook diced asparagus in liquid 45 min. Rub through sieve. Add tips, cook for 10 min. Just before serving, bind with remaining butter and cream or egg yolks.

79. CARROT SOUP (PURÉE CRÈCY)
PREPARATION TIME: 20 MIN.　COOKING TIME: 2 HOURS.

2 qts. water	2 med. onions, chopped
1 lb. carrots	3½ tbsp. butter
¼ lb. turnip, peeled	croutons fried in butter
1 lb. potatoes, peeled	salt, pepper

Cut vegetables in small pieces. Place in cold water; cook gently 1½ hours. Season to taste; rub through sieve or food mill. Cook onions 30 min. in butter. Add to soup; simmer 20 min. Serve with croutons.

80. GOOD WIFE'S SOUP
PREPARATION TIME: 20 MIN.　COOKING TIME: 45 MIN.

½ lb. carrots	1 lb. potatoes, peeled
3 or 4 leeks	6 cups boiling water
5 tbsp. butter	salt, pepper, bay leaf, cloves

Wash vegetables, cut in small pieces; brown in 3 tbsp. butter. Add water and seasonings; cook 45 min. Just before serving, add remaining butter (or a little cream, if preferred). Serve with pieces of vegetable left whole.

81. CELERY SOUP (CRÈME MARIA)
PREPARATION TIME: 15 MIN.　COOKING TIME: 35 MIN.

6⅓ cups stock	2 tbsp. cream of rice, blended
1 celeriac, sliced	with a little cold water
	1 egg yolk

Cook celeriac slices in stock for 30 min. Rub through sieve or food mill. Bring purée to boil; add cream of rice, cook 5 min. Just before serving, bind with egg yolk.

82. MUSHROOM SOUP (POTAGE RACHEL)
PREPARATION TIME: 30 MIN. COOKING TIME: 1½ HOURS.

½ lb. mushrooms
2 tbsp. cream of rice, blended with a little cold water
6⅓ cups water

3½ tbsp. butter
⅔ cup fresh bread crumbs
salt, pepper

Thinly slice three-quarters of the mushrooms. Chop remainder, sauté in butter. Simmer sliced mushrooms and bread crumbs in water for 1 hour. Rub through sieve or food mill. Bring purée to boil; add chopped cooked mushrooms, cream of rice, seasonings; continue cooking 10 min. Serve very hot.

83. CAULIFLOWER SOUP (CRÈME DUBARRY)
PREPARATION TIME: 30 MIN. COOKING TIME: 40 MIN.

6⅓ cups boiling water
1 med. cauliflower, separated into flowerets

6 tbsp. flour
2 tbsp. butter
2 egg yolks

Cook cauliflowerets 20 min. in boiling salted water; rub through sieve or food mill. Blend in flour, add cooking liquid; simmer 20 min. Just before serving, bind with egg yolks. Add butter and garnish with a few whole flowerets.

84. RED CABBAGE SOUP
PREPARATION TIME: 10 MIN. COOKING TIME: 1½ HOURS.

9½ cups hot water
1 red cabbage, coarsely chopped
1 lb. potatoes, peeled

1 small onion
6 tbsp. red Bordeaux wine (optional)

Cook cabbage 10 min. in boiling water. Place in pot with potatoes and onion; cover with 9½ cups hot water; cook 1 hour. Rub through sieve or food mill; add wine if desired. Continue cooking 30 min.

85. BRUSSELS SPROUTS SOUP (POTAGE BELGE)
PREPARATION TIME: 20 MIN. COOKING TIME: 1½ HOURS.

6 cups water or stock
1 lb. Brussels sprouts
6 tbsp. flour

3½ tbsp. butter
salt, pepper
croutons fried in butter

Cook sprouts 25 min. in boiling salted water; drain. Heat

butter, sauté sprouts. Sprinkle with flour; add hot water or stock, seasonings. Cook 1 hour. Rub through sieve. Serve with croutons.

86. CABBAGE SOUP
PREPARATION TIME: 20 MIN. COOKING TIME: 2½ HOURS.

½ lb. bacon
½ lb. ham
½ lb. lean pork with bones
1 med. cabbage, cut in half
2 med. potatoes

½ lb. turnip
3 med. carrots
1 small onion
thin slices bread

Place meat and bones in cold water; bring to boil, skim. Add vegetables; cook gently 2 hours. Reserve some of vegetables to serve separately with meat; rub remainder through sieve or food mill. Pour soup over thin slices of bread in individual soup bowls.

87. SPINACH SOUP (POTAGE FLORENTINE)
PREPARATION TIME: 30 MIN. COOKING TIME: 1¼ HOURS.

8½ cups water
1 lb. spinach, washed and chopped
1 cup flour

3½ tbsp. butter
salt, pepper
croutons fried in butter

Blend flour and butter; add water, cook 5 min. Add spinach and seasonings. Simmer 1 hour. Serve on croutons.

88. STRING BEAN SOUP (CRÈME MIMOSA)
PREPARATION TIME: 45 MIN. COOKING TIME: 45 MIN.

8 cups hot stock
½ lb. string beans
3 cups water
yolks of 3 hard-boiled eggs

2 tbsp. cream of rice, blended with a little cold water
2 tbsp. butter
salt, pepper

Cook string beans in salted water. Drain (reserve water) and cut into thin strips. Thicken stock with cream of rice; add cooking liquid from beans, cook 10 min. Add butter; season with salt and pepper. Force egg yolks through colander or sieve with large holes so that they fall in small balls into serving dish. Arrange string beans on top; pour in hot soup.

89. CREAM OF STRING BEAN SOUP
PREPARATION TIME: 1 HOUR.   COOKING TIME: 50 MIN.

2½ cups stock
1 lb. string beans
6⅔ tbsp. cream

2 tbsp. butter
salt, pepper
Béchamel Sauce (recipe 10)

Cook string beans 10 min. in boiling water. Reserve a few string beans for use as garnish; cook remainder in Béchamel Sauce for 30 min. over low flame. Season. Rub beans through sieve; add stock. Bind soup with cream and butter, and garnish with remaining beans cut in pieces.

90. JULIENNE SOUP
PREPARATION TIME: 45 MIN.   COOKING TIME: 2 HOURS.

8½ cups cold water
2 med. carrots
¼ lb. turnip, peeled
2 leeks
2 stalks celery
¼ lb. cabbage, chopped

2 tbsp. tapioca
¼ lb. fresh peas, shelled
1 head lettuce, finely chopped
2 med. potatoes, peeled
2 tbsp. butter
salt, pepper, chopped chervil

Cut carrots, turnip, leeks, celery, potatoes and cabbage into thin strips. Cover with water; cook 1½ hours. Add peas, chervil, lettuce and tapioca; continue cooking 1 hour. Add butter and seasonings just before serving.

91. SOUP À LA MÉNAGÈRE
PREPARATION TIME: 1½ HOURS.   COOKING TIME: 3½ HOURS.

8½ cups cold water
2 med. carrots
bone from leg of lamb or mutton
1 small onion

¼ lb. turnip, peeled
2 leeks
¼ lb. cabbage, chopped
2 tbsp. butter
salt, pepper, 3 cloves

Chop bone into sections, cook together with onion stuck with cloves, in salted water for 3 hours over very low flame. Cut vegetables in thin strips; cook 30 min. in butter. Add stock from mutton bone; simmer 1 hour. Rub through sieve before serving.

92. *TURNIP SOUP* (CRÈME FLAMANDE)
PREPARATION TIME: 20 MIN. COOKING TIME: 2 HOURS.

7 cups water
1 lb. turnip, peeled, cut in pieces
1 lb. potatoes, peeled, cut in pieces

1 bunch parsley, finely chopped
½ lb. stale bread
7 tbsp. cream
salt, pepper

Cover bread, vegetables and seasonings with cold water; cook 1½ hours over low heat. Rub through sieve or food mill. Bind with cream; garnish with chopped parsley.

93. *CHESTNUT SOUP*
PREPARATION TIME: 35 MIN. COOKING TIME: 1 HOUR.

8 cups stock
1 lb. chestnuts
3½ cups coarse fresh bread crumbs

4 tbsp. butter
croutons fried in butter
salt, pepper

Split chestnuts; blanch 5 min. in boiling water. Remove outer shell and skin. Cook chestnuts and bread crumbs in stock 30 min. Season; rub through sieve or food mill. Add butter; cook 10 min. Serve on croutons.

94. *ONION SOUP* (POTAGE PARISIEN)
PREPARATION TIME: 10 MIN. COOKING TIME: 20 MIN.

6⅓ cups warm stock
3 med. onions, sliced
4 tbsp. butter

1 cup flour
6 slices bread
salt, pepper

Cook onions in butter until golden. Sprinkle in flour; brown. Add stock; cook 10 min. Season to taste. Strain, if desired. Serve on slices of bread. Soup may be sprinkled with grated Gruyère and browned for 10 min. in very hot oven.

95. *SOUBISE SOUP*
PREPARATION TIME: 20 MIN. COOKING TIME: 1 HOUR.

4 cups stock
1 lb. onions, sliced
⅔ cup flour
2 cups warm milk

4⅔ tbsp. butter
1 egg yolk
salt, pepper

Blanch onion slices 5 min. in boiling water; drain. Melt 3⅓

tbsp. butter; cook onions until golden. Sprinkle in flour, add milk and seasonings; simmer 20 min. Rub through sieve. Add stock, continue cooking 20 min. Bind with egg yolk and 4 tsp. butter.

96. PARMENTIÈRE SOUP
PREPARATION TIME: 10 MIN. COOKING TIME: 45 MIN.

2 lbs. Mashed Potatoes (recipe 529)
3 tbsp. butter
1 med. onion, chopped

4 cups milk
4 cups hot water
salt, pepper, chopped parsley

Brown parsley and onion in butter; cover, cook 15 min. Add potatoes, water, enough milk to give soup a creamy consistency. Season. Continue cooking 10 min.

97. PUMPKIN SOUP (CRÈME D'OR)
PREPARATION TIME: 15 MIN. COOKING TIME: 30 MIN.

3 los. pumpkin, diced
4 cups milk
2 cups water

2 tbsp. butter
salt, pepper
croutons fried in butter

Cover pumpkin with cold water; cook until it crushes easily. Rub through sieve or food mill; add milk, salt, pepper, cook 10 min. Add butter. Serve over croutons.

98. AURORA SOUP
PREPARATION TIME: 15 MIN. COOKING TIME: 1 HOUR.

8 cups boiling water
1 lb. pumpkin, thinly sliced
½ lb. tomatoes, thinly sliced
1 egg yolk
4 tbsp. butter

2 tbsp. tapioca
½ lb. potatoes, peeled
3 tbsp. cream
salt, pepper

Brown pumpkin and tomato slices in butter. Add potatoes and boiling water, seasonings; cook 45 min. Rub through sieve or food mill. Bring to boil; add tapioca in a rain, cook 10 min. Bind with egg yolk and cream.

99. LEEK SOUP
PREPARATION TIME: 20 MIN. COOKING TIME: 1 HOUR.

5 cups water
3 leeks, diced
1 lb. potatoes, peeled, diced

2 tbsp. butter
2 cups warm milk
salt, pepper

Cook potatoes and leeks with seasonings in water for 1 hour. Rub through sieve or food mill; add milk and butter.

If desired, substitute ¼ cup rice for potatoes; cook with leeks in milk instead of water. Wash rice before cooking.

100. TOMATO SOUP I (POTAGE PORTUGAIS)
PREPARATION TIME: 10 MIN. COOKING TIME: 45 MIN.

6 cups stock
½ lb. potatoes, peeled, cut in pieces

1 lb. tomatoes, cut in pieces
finely chopped chervil
croutons fried in butter

Cook potatoes and tomatoes in stock for 45 min. Rub through sieve or food mill. Serve on croutons, garnish with chopped chervil.

101. TOMATO SOUP II (POTAGE ITALIEN)
PREPARATION TIME: 10 MIN. COOKING TIME: 40 MIN.

8½ cups warm stock
1 lb. tomatoes, cut in pieces
2 med. onions, thinly sliced
3½ tbsp. butter

⅔ cup flour
¼ cup rice, washed
½ cup grated Gruyère
salt, pepper

Brown tomatoes and onions in butter. Sprinkle in flour; add stock and seasonings, rice. Cook ½ hour. Pour over grated Gruyère.

102. GARLIC SOUP (POTAGE MARSEILLAIS)
PREPARATION TIME: 35 MIN. COOKING TIME: 1 HOUR.

7 cups hot water
1 lb. tomatoes, cut in pieces
8 cloves garlic
1 large onion
1⅓ tbsp. oil
2 tbsp. butter

⅔ cup flour
1 egg yolk
pinch of saffron
salt, pepper, parsley, thyme
croutons fried in butter

Cook together all ingredients except water, flour, oil and egg yolk for 30 min. Rub through sieve or food mill. Heat oil;

pour in purée. Add flour and hot water; cook 30 min. over low heat. Bind with egg yolk; pour over croutons.

103. CHAMPENOIS SOUP
PREPARATION TIME: 25 MIN. COOKING TIME: 1 HOUR.

13 cups water	2 tbsp. butter
1 large leek, coarsely chopped	1/3 cup grated cheese
1¾ lbs. potatoes, peeled, diced	salt, pepper
½ cup macaroni, broken in pieces	

Brown leek in butter. Add diced potatoes, water and seasonings; cook 45 min. Add macaroni; cook 15 min. longer. Pour over slices of bread sprinkled with cheese and browned in oven.

104. SPLIT PEA SOUP
PREPARATION TIME: 10 MIN. COOKING TIME: 2¼ HOURS.

½ lb. dried split peas	1 tbsp. chopped sorrel or
2 tbsp. butter	watercress
6 cups water	salt, pepper
	croutons fried in butter

Soak peas for several hours in 1 qt. water. Drain. Cook peas and sorrel gently in water for 2 hours. Season with salt and pepper; rub through sieve or food mill. Simmer 15 min. before serving on croutons.

105. PEA SOUP (CRÈME CLAMART)
PREPARATION TIME: 30 MIN. COOKING TIME: 50 MIN.

6 cups stock	salt, pepper
1⅔ lbs. peas, shelled	croutons fried in butter
½ cup cream	

Cook peas in stock 45 min. Crush. Add seasonings and cream. Serve on croutons.

106. SAINT-GERMAIN SOUP
PREPARATION TIME: 30 MIN. COOKING TIME: 50 MIN.

1 lb. fresh peas, shelled	6 cups water
½ leek, chopped	3 tbsp. cream
3 heads lettuce, coarsely	2 tbsp. butter
chopped	1 egg yolk

Cook vegetables in water 45 min. Mash. Bind soup with egg yolk and cream; add butter just before serving.

107. SOUP À LA FAUBONNE
PREPARATION TIME: 25 MIN. COOKING TIME: 2¾ HOURS.

¼ lb. sorrel or watercress	¾ lb. dried split peas
½ leek	3½ tbsp. butter
2 med. celery stalks	salt, pepper
2 small onions, cooked	croutons fried in butter
7½ cups water	

Soak peas for several hours in 1 qt. water; drain. Cook 2 hours in water. Coarsely chop celery, leek and sorrel; brown in butter, then add together with onions to the peas. Continue to cook gently for 30 min. Season; rub through fine sieve. Pour over croutons.

108. KIDNEY BEAN SOUP (POTAGE CONDÉ)
PREPARATION TIME: 10 MIN. COOKING TIME: 2½ HOURS.

1¾ lbs. dried kidney beans	2 tbsp. butter
10½ cups water	salt
2 med. onions, minced	croutons fried in butter
½ cup grated Gruyère	

Soak beans for several hours in some water; drain. Cook onions in butter until golden. Add onions and 10½ cups water to beans; cook 2½ hours, seasoning with salt after first hour of cooking. Rub through sieve or food mill; pour over croutons. Serve cheese separately.

109. WHITE BEAN SOUP (POTAGE RUSSE)
PREPARATION TIME: 15 MIN. COOKING TIME: 1¾ HOURS.

¾ lb. dried white haricot beans	½ head lettuce, chopped
4 cups water	salt, chopped chervil
½ lb. potatoes, peeled, quartered	croutons fried in butter
3 tbsp. butter	(optional)
¼ lb. sorrel or watercress	

Soak beans for several hours in some water; drain. Cook beans and potatoes in 4 cups water for 1½ hours. Rub through sieve or food mill. Add lettuce, chervil, salt to taste; continue cooking 15 min. Add butter. Serve over croutons, if desired.

110. *LENTIL PURÉE*
PREPARATION TIME: 10 MIN.   COOKING TIME: 3¼ HOURS.

10½ cups water	3 med. carrots
1 lb. lentils	salt, pepper
1 small onion	

Soak beans for several hours in some water; drain. Cook lentils and vegetables in 10½ cups water for 3 hours, stirring frequently. Season; rub through sieve or food mill. If purée is too thick, add a little hot stock. If it is too thin, add a little tapioca and cook 10 min.

111. *RICE SOUP I*
PREPARATION TIME: 5 MIN.   COOKING TIME: 25 MIN.

½ cup rice, washed	6⅔ tbsp. cream
6 cups boiling salted water	2 tbsp. butter
2 egg yolks	

Cook rice with water and butter 25 min. Bind with cream and egg yolks, stirring constantly.

112. *RICE SOUP II*
PREPARATION TIME: 25 MIN.   COOKING TIME: 2 HOURS.

8½ cups water	3 tbsp. chopped sorrel
1 large onion	2 tbsp. butter
1 large carrot	¼ cup rice, washed
½ lb. turnip, peeled	salt, pepper

Cover vegetables with water; cook 1 hour over low heat. Season; rub through sieve or food mill. Add rice; continue cooking for 25 min. Add butter just before serving.

113. *OX-TAIL SOUP*
PREPARATION TIME: 40 MIN.   COOKING TIME: 3½ HOURS.

6⅓ cups stock	3 ox-tails, cut in sections
4 tbsp. butter	¼ cup Madeira wine
½ cup flour	salt, pepper
2 tsp. tomato purée (recipe 867)	Veal Quenelles (recipe 871), cut in pieces
vegetables as for Meat Stock (recipe 69)	

Make a stock, following recipe 69, with ox-tails, vegetables, seasoning; simmer 3 hours. Remove ox-tails and vegetables. Make a light brown sauce (recipe 30) with 6⅓ cups stock, butter, flour; add Madeira, tomato purée, quenelles. Simmer 10 min.

114. LOBSTER BISQUE
PREPARATION TIME: 1½ HOURS. COOKING TIME: 55 MIN.

6 cups stock
8 tbsp. butter
2 tbsp. cream of rice
1 Lobster, cooked (recipe 164)
2 egg yolks

6 tbsp. warm cream
2 tbsp. oil
1 tbsp. vinegar
salt, pepper

Remove lobster meat from shell. Dice part of meat; marinate for 2 hours in mixture of oil, vinegar, salt and pepper. Finely chop remainder. With a mortar, grind lobster shell and debris into fine powder; blend in chopped lobster meat to form a paste. Melt 6 tbsp. butter; add cream of rice; cook, stirring constantly. Add stock, cream, lobster paste. Bind with egg yolks and remaining butter. Add diced marinated lobster just before serving.

115. SEAFOOD CREAM SOUP
PREPARATION TIME: 45 MIN. COOKING TIME: 30 MIN.

1 qt. Mussels, cooked, (recipe 168) with cooking liquid
12 oysters
¼ lb. mushrooms, peeled, thinly sliced

2 egg yolks
3 tbsp. tapioca
juice of 1 lemon
thyme, bay leaf, pepper

Remove mussels from shells. Open oysters; boil 3 min. in their own liquid plus lemon juice and dash of pepper. Drain. Add sufficient water to mussel and oyster liquid to make 6 cups. Cook mushrooms with seasonings and tapioca in liquid for 15 min. Bind with egg yolks; add mussels and oysters.

116. *FISHERMAN'S SOUP*

PREPARATION TIME: 25 MIN. COOKING TIME: 1 HOUR.

6⅓ cups hot water
½ leek
1 small onion, finely chopped
1 small clove garlic, finely
    chopped
1 tomato, cut in pieces

⅓ cup cream
    oil for frying
    bay leaf, thyme, salt, pepper
10 small or 2 large crabs
3 tbsp. cream of rice, blended
    in a little cold water

Brown leek, garlic and onion in small quantity of hot oil. Add tomato, seasonings, hot water; cook 20 min. Plunge in crabs; boil 30 min. Season to taste. Remove crabs; shell, dice meat. Rub soup through sieve; bring to boil. Add cream of rice; cook 10 min. Add diced crab meat and cream. Serve immediately.

117. *FISH SOUP*

PREPARATION TIME: 25 MIN. COOKING TIME: 40 MIN.

2 cups milk
4 cups water
1 small onion
3 med. cloves garlic
¾ cup cream
2 tbsp. butter

½ cup flour
3 lbs. fish scraps, trimmings,
    heads, etc.
    (or 3 lbs. fresh or frozen fish)
6 slices toast rubbed with garlic

Cook fish in water with onion and garlic. Blend flour and butter; moisten with milk and cooking liquid from fish, season to taste. Continue cooking 20 min. Bind with cream just before serving. Serve over toast.

Fish

Is it fresh?

A freshly caught fish has clear, bright eyes and red gills; its fins are whole and in good condition, its stomach flesh is firm and shining. Stay away from fish with sunken eyes, a spotty stomach, flesh which "gives" at the touch of a finger!

How to clean fish:

1. Scale it—Holding fish by the tail, scrape with flat knife (or special knife for scaling fish) from tail to head.
2. Skin sole and eel—Make an incision in the skin just above the tail. With a cloth, grasp skin and pull down hard from tail to head.
3. Insert finger in opening of gills and draw out intestines and gills. In the case of larger fish, make an incision in the stomach.
4. Wash fish in cold water. Do not soak it.
5. Trim off fins with old scissors.
6. Make short oblique incisions on back of fish.
7. Remove bone if desired. Flat fish: make an incision down center; slide knife blade between bone and meat. Larger fish: make an incision down center. Cut off head. Separate 4 fillets from bone.

118. BOILED FISH

Place cleaned and dressed fish in warm water or Court-bouillon (see recipes 866 through 870). If possible, use a special fish kettle with a removable rack. Bring to boil, then immediately lower heat so that water is barely "shivering." Simmer 10 min. per lb. for large fish, 8 min. per lb. for flat fish, 12 min. for small fish of ½ lb. or less.

To serve, remove skin, cut fillets into sections on the bias. Garnish with parsley, anchovies, capers, tomato slices, hard-boiled eggs, lemon slices, etc. Serve desired sauce separately.

If fish is to be served cold, chill it in the Court-bouillon before cutting.

119. FRIED FISH

Dry fish; dredge in flour. Place in smoking hot fat. Cook small fish for 5 min. Cook large fish for 10 min.; or cook for 6 min., then remove from fat, reheat fat to smoking, replace fish and brown for several minutes. Season with salt; garnish with chopped parsley and slices of lemon.

Small fish cooked in this way need not be cleaned out. Large fish should be cleaned out and scored.

120. BROILED FISH

Clean and dress a flat fish; dry thoroughly, brush with oil. Place in pre-heated broiler; broil 15 min. per lb., turning once to cook evenly. Season with salt; garnish with chopped parsley, lemon slices or quarters. Serve with melted butter, Maître d'hôtel Butter (recipe 4) or Béarnaise Sauce (recipe 66).

121. BAKED FISH

Marinate fish in vegetable oil for 2 hours, or wrap with slices of blanched bacon, fatback or fresh pork fat. Bake 15 min. per lb., basting occasionally. Season with salt; garnish with parsley, lemon slices or quarters. Serve with Maître d'hôtel Butter or any desired sauce.

122. SAUTÉED FISH (MEUNIÈRE)

Clean and dress fish (which should weigh no more than ½ lb.); dry thoroughly. Roll first in milk, then dredge in flour. In a skillet, heat sufficient quantity of butter to cook fish without completely covering it. Brown fish on one side, sprinkle with salt; turn and brown on other side, season with salt and pepper. Place fish on serving dish; sprinkle with lemon juice and cooking liquid remaining in pan. Garnish with chopped parsley, lemon slices or quarters.

Suitable sauces for fish:

Hot:

Anchovy (23)	Joinville (27)
Béarnaise (66)	Maître d'hôtel Butter (4)
Brown Butter (6)	Mornay (4)
Capers (28)	Mousseline (65)
Cardinal (26)	Red Wine (53)
Génevoise (52)	Shrimp (24)
Hollandaise (64)	Tomato (31)

Cold:

Deviled (68)	Ravigote (56)
Gribiche (59)	Ravigote Butter (5)
any Mayonnaise (60)	Rémoulade (58)
Mustard (57)	Vinaigrette (56)

N.B.: All recipes serve 6, unless otherwise indicated.

FRESH-WATER FISH

123. ANGLERFISH À L'AMÉRICAINE
PREPARATION TIME: 10 MIN. COOKING TIME: 50 MIN.

1 anglerfish, about 1¾ lbs.	flour
¾ cup olive oil	6 tbsp. Stock (recipe 69)
2 tbsp. tomato paste	6 tbsp. white wine
½ cup brandy	salt, pepper
onion and garlic as desired, chopped	1 clove
	1 tbsp. grated lemon rind

Clean and dress fish; cut in pieces, dredge in flour. Heat oil in a sauté pan; brown fish. Add 1 tbsp. brandy; ignite. Drain fish. Combine remaining ingredients in a casserole; cook 30 min. Add pieces of fish; continue cooking 15 min. Serve very hot.

124. CARP IN ASPIC
PREPARATION TIME: 20 MIN. COOKING TIME: 45 MIN.

Clean and dress carp; cut into pieces, reserving head, tail and roe. Cook in court-bouillon (see recipes 866 through 870) for 45 min.; drain. Add head, tail and roe, a little basil, to cooking liquid; boil until liquid is reduced by half. Remove skin from pieces of fish; arrange pieces on serving dish in shape of fish. Cover with liquid; chill overnight or until jelly is set.

If desired, gelatin may be added to liquid. Use 3 tbsp. gelatin, softened in a little water, for every 2 cups of liquid. Clarify (see recipe 882) before pouring over fish.

125. STUFFED CARP
PREPARATION TIME: 45 MIN. COOKING TIME: 45 MIN.

1 carp, about 2 lbs., cleaned and dressed	1 cup oil
Stuffing (recipe 864)	salt, pepper, thyme, bay leaf, parsley

Marinate fish for 45 min. in mixture of oil and seasonings. Stuff fish. Place in buttered baking dish; sprinkle with marinade. Bake 45 min. in moderate oven.

126. CODFISH STEAKS
PREPARATION TIME: 25 MIN. COOKING TIME: 10 MIN.

6 slices fresh cod	chopped parsley
6 tbsp. butter	lemon slices
1 egg, beaten	fine bread crumbs

Roll fish slices in beaten egg, then in bread crumbs. Heat butter until it begins to turn brown. Brown fish slices on both sides. Garnish with parsley and lemon slices.

127. SAUTÉED CODFISH STEAKS
PREPARATION TIME: 10 MIN. COOKING TIME: 1 HOUR.

6 slices fresh cod	juice of 1 lemon
6⅔ tbsp. butter	chopped chervil and parsley
½ cup flour	bouquet garni

Melt butter; place in fish slices, parsley, *bouquet garni*, lemon juice. Cook gently for 1 hour. Arrange fish on serving dish, bind sauce with flour and nap fish. Garnish with chopped chervil.

128. *EEL WITH RED WINE SAUCE* (ÀNGUILLE À LA MATELOTE)
PREPARATION TIME: 40 MIN.   COOKING TIME: 1½ HOURS.

2 lbs. eel, skinned, cut in sections
¼ lb. fatback, fresh pork fat or blanched bacon, diced
¾ cup Stock (recipe 69)
¾ cup red wine
1 med. onion, chopped
¼ lb. mushrooms
4 tbsp. butter
6 slices white bread
½ cup flour
6 crawfish (optional)
salt, pepper, *bouquet garni*

Brown onion and diced fat in 2 tbsp. butter; remove from skillet. Sprinkle in flour; cook until brown, stirring constantly. Add stock and wine, mushrooms, seasonings; simmer 30 min. Add pieces of eel; continue cooking 45 min. Fry bread in remaining butter; arrange on serving dish. Top with eel; nap with sauce. Garnish with cooked crawfish, if desired.

129. *EEL IN WHITE WINE*
PREPARATION TIME: 20 MIN.   COOKING TIME: 30 MIN.

2 lbs. eel, skinned, cut in sections
3 or 4 small onions
⅔ cup flour
2 cups white wine
2 small cloves garlic
⅔ cup butter
2 hard-boiled eggs, sliced
salt, pepper, *bouquet garni*

Brown onions in 4 tbsp. butter. Place pieces of eel in casserole; season with salt and pepper. Pour in wine; add garlic and *bouquet garni*. Cook for 30 min. Bind sauce with flour and remaining butter. Serve eel on platter, surrounded with sliced eggs. Serve sauce separately.

130. *PERCH À LA MEUNIÈRE*
PREPARATION TIME: 15 MIN.   COOKING TIME: 15 MIN.

1 perch, about 2½ lbs., cleaned and dressed
⅔ cup butter
½ cup flour
salt, pepper, chopped parsley

Season fish with salt; roll in milk, then dredge in flour. Heat butter in skillet; brown fish over high flame. Arrange on serving dish; sprinkle with chopped parsley. Nap with sauce made by cooking remaining butter until dark brown in color, then adding to butter in which fish has been cooked.

131. *PIKE AU BLEU*
PREPARATION TIME: 15 MIN. COOKING TIME: 15 MIN. PER LB.

Clean and dress pike. Plunge into 1 qt. boiling vinegar for 5 min. Poach in a court-bouillon (recipe 867 or 868), 15 min. per lb. Serve hot, with Maître d'hôtel Butter (recipe 4), or cold. If desired, rub fish with butter or oil and serve with Tartare Sauce (recipe 63).

132. *PIKE À LA CRÈME*
PREPARATION TIME: 15 MIN. COOKING TIME: ABOUT 30 MIN.

1 pike, about 2 lbs., cleaned and dressed	¾ cup cream
⅔ cup butter	salt, pepper, chopped parsley
	fine bread crumbs

Stuff fish with mixture of ½ cup butter blended with chopped parsley. Place fish in baking dish; dot with butter, season with salt and pepper. Bake 10 min. in hot oven. Baste with cream; continue cooking, basting with cream every 5 min. During last five minutes of baking, sprinkle with bread crumbs and chopped parsley.

133. *PIKE IN WHITE WINE*
PREPARATION TIME: 30 MIN. COOKING TIME: 30 MIN.

2 small pike, cleaned and dressed	1 egg yolk
⅔ cup butter	juice of 1 lemon
6⅔ tbsp. white wine	salt, pepper, thyme, parsley, bay leaf
1 med. onion, sliced	

Place pike in baking dish which has been buttered with 5 tbsp. butter. Cover fish with onion slices; add wine and seasonings. Bake 30 min. in moderate oven. Arrange fish on serving dish; keep warm. Make a sauce with cooking liquid, egg yolk, lemon juice and remaining butter; nap fish. Serve immediately.

134. SALMON GALANTINE
PREPARATION TIME: 25 MIN. COOKING TIME: 35 MIN.

1 salmon steak, about 1 lb.	1¾ cups fresh bread crumbs,
6 anchovy fillets	soaked in milk
¼ lb. mushrooms, cooked	salt, pepper, *fines herbes*
¼ lb. whiting, cooked	sliced gherkins
	Court-bouillon (recipe 868)

Remove bone from salmon; place steak on a piece of fine linen; garnish with anchovies, mushrooms, gherkins. Combine remaining ingredients; stuff opening left by bone. Secure fish with string; wrap in cloth. Cook 30-35 min. in barely "shivering" court-bouillon. Chill overnight in court-bouillon. Serve cold.

135. SALMON LOAF
PREPARATION TIME: 30 MIN. COOKING TIME (POTATOES and EGGS): 20 MIN.

1 1-lb. can salmon	2 hard-boiled eggs, sliced
2 med. potatoes	Mayonnaise (recipe 60)
4 tbsp. butter	chopped *fines herbes*

Steam potatoes or boil them in their jackets. Peel, mash; combine with salmon, butter, a handful of chopped *fines herbes*. Turn mixture into a buttered round mold; chill for 24 hours. Unmold; cover loaf with Mayonnaise, garnish with slices of egg.

136. SALMON SHELLS
PREPARATION TIME: 20 MIN. COOKING TIME: 20 MIN.

1 1-lb. can salmon	3½ tbsp. butter, melted
1¾ cups White Sauce	fine bread crumbs
(recipe 8 or 9)	

Open can of salmon and heat 10 min. in pan of water. Combine salmon and White Sauce; fill 6 shells or small baking dishes with mixture. Sprinkle with bread crumbs and melted butter. Heat 10 min. in very hot oven.

137. SHAD À LA CHARTREUSE

PREPARATION TIME: 45 MIN.   COOKING TIME: 2½ HOURS.

1 shad, about 2 lbs., cleaned
    and dressed
½ lb. carrots
1 head lettuce
1 lb. tomatoes
½ lb. sorrel

3 med. onions
¼ lb. ham, sliced
6⅔ tbsp. white wine
6⅔ tbsp. water
    salt, pepper, bay leaf

Chop vegetables and place in bottom of heavy pot. Top with fish. Add wine, water, seasonings. Cover and simmer over very low flame for 2½ hours.

SHAD MONTAGNARDE: See recipe 921.

TROUT À LA CRÈME: See recipe 906.

138. TROUT À LA SUPREME

PREPARATION TIME: 30 MIN.   COOKING TIME: 10 MIN.

6 small trout
4¼ tsp. oil, beaten with
1 egg

⅔ cup Anchovy Butter
    (see p. 31)
    fine bread crumbs
    shortening for frying

Slash trout down back; remove bone, clean fish. Roll in egg-and-oil mixture, then in bread crumbs; brown in hot shortening. Fill incision in trout with anchovy butter. Serve hot.

SALT-WATER FISH

139. FLOUNDER IN WHITE WINE SAUCE

PREPARATION TIME: 25 MIN.   COOKING TIME: 40 MIN.

2 lbs. flounder, cleaned and
    dressed
2 tbsp. butter
1 med. onion, finely chopped

1⅓ cups white wine
2 egg yolks
¼ cup flour
    chopped parsley, salt

Cut fish in pieces. Brown onion in butter; add fish, salt, wine. Cook 5 min. over high flame; lower heat, continue cooking for 35 min. Bind sauce with flour and egg yolks. Garnish with chopped parsley.

140. MARINATED HERRING

First Method: Use salted herring and roe. Wash fish; soak for 3 hours in cold milk. Remove head and skin, separate fish into fillets. Cook in court-bouillon (recipe 866). Make a sauce by crushing roe and mixing it with a little vinegar and oil. Arrange herring fillets on serving dish; cover with slices of carrot and lemon. Pour sauce over fish. Marinate for 4 days.

Second Method: Cook together ¾ cup vinegar, dash of pepper, *bouquet garni,* until liquid is reduced by one-third. Cool slightly. Make a sauce by adding finely crushed roe to lukewarm vinegar; add small quantity of oil, chopped parsley and chervil. Arrange fish fillets on serving dish; cover with slices of onion, and sauce. Marinate for 4 days.

141 HERRING ROLLMOPS

Separate boned herring into 2 fillets. Cook together ¾ cup vinegar, *bouquet garni,* dash of pepper. Roll up fillets; secure with toothpicks. (If desired, place a gherkin in center of each roll.) Place rolls in earthenware dish; cover with sliced onions and carrots, and sauce. Marinate for 8 days.

142. BOILED SALT COD

Place slices of salt cod on rack; place rack in pan, cover with cold water. Let stand for 12-15 hours, changing water once. Place fish in casserole, cover with cold water. Place over high flame; bring water to "shivering" point (*do not boil*). Remove casserole from heat; let stand 10-15 min. Drain fish, serve with any desired sauce.

BRANDADE OF SALT COD: See recipe 917.

143. BROILED COD

PREPARATION TIME: 10 MIN. COOKING TIME: 10 MIN.

Roll slices of boiled salt cod in beaten egg, then in bread crumbs. Brush with oil. Broil 5 min. on each side. Serve with Tartare (recipe 63) or Mustard (recipe 57) Sauce.

144. FRITOS
PREPARATION TIME: 20 MIN. COOKING TIME: 20 MIN.

½ lb. boiled salt cod
   batter for frying (recipe 884)
   shortening for frying

juice of one lemon
pepper
Tomato Sauce (recipe 31)

Cut cooked fish into pieces; sprinkle with lemon juice and pepper. Dip each piece into thick batter, and plunge into very hot shortening. Serve with Tomato Sauce.

145. SALT COD À LA PROVENÇALE
PREPARATION TIME: 20 MIN. COOKING TIME: 20 MIN.

1 lb. Salt Cod, cooked
   (recipe 142), flaked
1 lb. tomatoes, cut in pieces
1⅓ cups oil

1 large onion, finely chopped
½ clove garlic, minced
4 oz. black olives
pepper, parsley

Cook onion, garlic and tomatoes in oil. Add olives, parsley, pinch of pepper, flaked cod; cook gently for 10 min.

146. SALT COD IN MILK
PREPARATION TIME: 20 MIN. COOKING TIME: 1¼ HOURS.

1 lb. salt cod, soaked 15 hours
   in water
1 lb. potatoes, peeled and sliced

1 qt. milk
1 small onion, chopped

Place fish in deep baking dish; cover with potatoes and onion. Pour in milk. Bake in slow oven about 1¼ hours.

147. SALT COD À LA FLORENTINE
PREPARATION TIME: 20 MIN. COOKING TIME: 30 MIN.

1 lb. Salt Cod, cooked (recipe
   142)
2 lbs. spinach
   Béchamel Sauce (recipe 10)

4 tbsp. butter
¼ cup grated Gruyère
salt, pepper, nutmeg

Blanch spinach in boiling salted water. Drain, pressing to remove all water; chop coarsely. Cook slightly in butter; season with salt, pepper, nutmeg. Arrange spinach in buttered baking dish; top with pieces of fish. Cover with sauce; sprinkle with grated Gruyère. Brown about 10 min. in hot oven.

148. MARINATED MACKEREL
PREPARATION TIME: 15 MIN. COOKING TIME: 15 MIN.

several small mackerel,   ¾ cup olive oil
  cleaned and dressed   Marinade (recipe 857)

Soak fish for 5 min. in salted water seasoned with a dash of vinegar. Place fish in earthenware dish; cover with oil and boiling marinade. Place over heat; bring to boil. Remove from heat, cover tightly and chill. Serve with lemon slices.

149. STUFFED MACKEREL
PREPARATION TIME: 30 MIN. COOKING TIME: 25 MIN.

6 mackerel, cleaned and dressed   1 small onion, minced
1 cup fresh bread crumbs,   3½ tbsp. butter, melted
  soaked in small quantity milk   salt, parsley, fine bread
¼ lb. cooked, shelled shrimp   crumbs
¼ lb. mushrooms

Combine bread crumbs, shrimp, mushrooms, onion and chopped parsley; stuff each fish with mixture. Brush fish with melted butter, sprinkle with bread crumbs. Bake 25 min. in moderate oven. Mackerel may be broiled, if preferred; in this case, do not sprinkle with crumbs.

150. MACKEREL IN WHITE WINE
PREPARATION TIME: 15 MIN. COOKING TIME: 40 MIN.

6 mackerel, cleaned and   1 lemon, sliced
  dressed   3 tbsp. oil
6⅔ tbsp. vinegar   1 carrot, sliced
¾ cup white wine   1 onion, sliced
1 tbsp. coriander   salt, pepper, thyme, parsley,
  lemon slices   bay leaf

Boil together wine, vinegar, oil, carrot, onion and spices for 10 min. Place fish in buttered baking dish; cover with marinade, garnish with lemon slices. Cover with waxed paper. Bring to boil over high heat, then bake for 15 min. in hot oven. Place fish in earthenware dish and chill. May be kept for 2-3 days.

151. *MULLET WITH TOMATOES*
PREPARATION TIME: 20 MIN. COOKING TIME: 40 MIN.

2½ lbs. mullet, cleaned and
    dressed
1 large onion, chopped
1 small carrot
1 lb. tomatoes, cut in pieces
1 clove garlic
    chopped parsley

1 shallot
¾ cup dry white wine
4 tbsp. butter
6 tbsp. flour
    juice of 1 lemon
    salt, pepper, *bouquet garni*

Cut fish into pieces. Brown chopped onion and tomatoes in butter; add fish, seasonings and wine, cook 30 min. Bind sauce with flour; add chopped parsley and lemon juice. Serve fish in sauce.

152. *SKATE WITH CHEESE*
PREPARATION TIME: 20 MIN. COOKING TIME: 50 MIN.

1 skate, 2 lbs.
3 cups milk
2 cups White Sauce (recipe
    8 or 9)
1 cup grated Gruyère
    Court-bouillon (recipe 870)

5 tbsp. butter
1 shallot
1 clove garlic
    fine bread crumbs
    bouquet garni

Cook skate about 35 min. in court-bouillon with *bouquet garni*, shallot and garlic. Place in baking dish; sprinkle with grated Gruyère, nap with sauce and a little court-bouillon. Sprinkle top with bread crumbs, dot with butter. Brown 10-15 min. in hot oven.

153. *SAUTÉED SKATE*
PREPARATION TIME: 40 MIN. COOKING TIME: 25 MIN.

1 skate, 2 lbs.
2 cups Marinade (recipe 858)
⅔ cup flour

    lemon slices
4½ tbsp. butter

Separate fish into fillets; macerate in marinade 30 min. Dredge in flour, then brown in butter, 5 min. each side. Bake 15 min. in slow oven. Garnish with lemon slices.

154. SOLE BASQUE-STYLE
PREPARATION TIME: 30 MIN. COOKING TIME: 20 MIN.

3 med. sole, cleaned, dressed, boned
6⅔ tbsp. white wine
5 tbsp. butter
¼ lb. mushrooms, chopped

¾ cup stock (recipe 69)
juice of 1 lemon
1 shallot
chopped parsley and scallion

Place fish in baking dish; cover with wine. Bake 10 min. in moderate oven. Combine chopped mushrooms, scallion, parsley, shallot, butter; stuff fish with mixture. Replace stuffed fish in baking dish; cover with stock. Bake 10 min. in very slow oven. Sprinkle with lemon juice before serving.

155. SOLE À LA NORMANDE
PREPARATION TIME: 1½ HOURS. COOKING TIME: 25 MIN.

3 med. sole, cleaned, dressed
¼ lb. mushrooms, cooked, with their cooking liquid
¾ cup white wine
½ cup flour
¼ lb. butter

1 qt. Mussels, cooked, with their cooking liquid (recipe 168)
6 oysters
6 Crawfish, cooked (recipe 162)
2 egg yolks

Cover sole with wine and ¾ cup combined mushroom and mussel liquid; dot with 3½ tbsp. butter. Bring to boil; lower heat and cook 20 min. Arrange fish on warm serving dish. Make a White Sauce (recipe 8 or 9) with flour, 4 tbsp. butter, 2 cups strained cooking liquid. Bind with egg yolks and remaining butter. Garnish sole with oysters, mussels, mushrooms; nap with sauce. Surround with crawfish.

156. FILETS OF SOLE À LA ORLY
PREPARATION TIME: 45 MIN. COOKING TIME: 7 MIN.

3 med. sole, cleaned and dressed
1 carrot
1 onion, sliced
2 tbsp. oil
1 egg, beaten
1 lb. peas, cooked

1 lemon, sliced
fine bread crumbs
shortening for frying
2 cups Tomato Sauce (recipe 31)

Separate fish into fillets. Marinate for 30 min. in mixture of oil, carrot, onion, lemon slices. Roll up fillets, secure with toothpicks or string. Roll in beaten egg, then in bread crumbs. Cook 5 min. in hot shortening; turn and brown thoroughly. Heap cooked peas in center of serving dish; surround with fish rolls. Cover with Tomato Sauce.

157. TUNA À LA CASSEROLE
PREPARATION TIME: 10 MIN.   COOKING TIME: 1 HOUR.

1¼ lbs. fresh tuna	1 clove garlic, minced
¾ cup oil	1 shallot, minced
¾ cup white wine	juice of 1 lemon
¼ lb. salt pork, diced	salt, pepper
2 tbsp. Butter	fine bread crumbs
Marinade (recipe 858)	several strips fresh pork fat or blanched bacon

Marinate tuna for 2 hours in marinade. Drain. Wrap in pork fat or bacon. Brown fish and salt pork in hot oil; add marinade and wine, salt, pepper, garlic, shallot. Sprinkle with bread crumbs; dot with butter. Cover and simmer for 1 hour.

158. TUNA CUTLETS
PREPARATION TIME: 10 MIN.   COOKING TIME: 10 MIN.

1½ lbs. tuna, cut in ½-in. slices	8-10 thin slices bread fried in butter
1 egg, beaten with 3 tbsp. milk	1 lemon, sliced
1 cup flour	salt, pepper, parsley
	shortening for frying

Soak tuna slices in egg-and-milk mixture, then dredge in flour. Brown 5 min. each side in very hot shortening. Drain; season to taste. Serve very hot, garnished with parsley, bread cut in fancy shapes, lemon slices.

159. TURBOT AU GRATIN
PREPARATION TIME: 20 MIN.   COOKING TIME: 40 MIN.

1 turbot, 2 lbs., cleaned and dressed	6⅔ tbsp. water
¼ lb. mushrooms, chopped	6⅔ tbsp. white wine
1 large onion, chopped	salt, pepper, chopped parsley
1 shallot, chopped	fine bread crumbs

Spread layer of chopped onion, shallot and parsley in well-buttered baking dish. Place in fish, dark side down. Dot with butter; add wine, water, seasonings, mushrooms. Sprinkle with bread crumbs. Cook 5 min. over high heat; then bake 30 min. in slow oven.

160. WHITINGS À LA DUGLÉRÉ
PREPARATION TIME: 20 MIN. COOKING TIME: 30 MIN.

6 whitings, cleaned and dressed	½ lb. tomatoes, washed, seeded,
1 shallot, finely chopped	crushed
3½ tbsp. butter	1¾ cups white wine
6 tbsp. flour	1 slice lemon
1 small onion, finely chopped	salt, pepper, chopped parsley
2¼ tsp. cream	

Combine shallot, onion, parsley, tomatoes; spread mixture in lightly buttered baking dish, season with salt and pepper. Top with whitings; add wine. Bring to boil over high heat, then cover with waxed paper and bake 15 min. in hot oven. Remove fish, keep warm. Reduce cooking liquid by half; bind with butter and flour, add cream and slice of lemon. Place fish on serving dish; nap with sauce. Garnish with parsley.

BOUILLABAISSE: See recipe 918.

BOURRIDE (Provençal Fish Stew): See recipe 915.

MEURETTE (Fish Stew with red wine): See recipe 900.

PAUCHOUSE (Fish Stew with white wine): See recipe 900A.

POUPETON (Fish Pudding): See recipe 916.

SHELLFISH

161. CRABS À L'INDIENNE
PREPARATION TIME: 30 MIN. COOKING TIME: 20 MIN.

6 crabs	court-bouillon (recipe 866 or 867)
½ cup tomato purée (recipe 876)	curry powder
3½ tbsp. butter	Cayenne pepper

Cook crabs 10 min. in court-bouillon. Chop meat finely; add crushed liver from crabs, tomato purée, pepper and curry powder to taste. Fill crab shells with mixture; dot with butter. Bake 10 min. in very hot oven.

162. CRAWFISH

Remove intestine by pulling on fin in center of tail with a sharp jerk. Cook 10 min. in court-bouillon (recipes 866 through 870).

163. CRAWFISH À LA NANTUA

PREPARATION TIME: 1½ HOURS. COOKING TIME: 1¼ HOURS.

40 crawfish, cooked, with Court-bouillon	⅓ lb. mushrooms
¾ cup butter	¾ cup cream
	4 egg yolks

Remove meat from shells. Crush shells; cook with 3½ tbsp. butter and 1 qt. court-bouillon for 1 hour over low flame. Rub through sieve or food mill (resulting purée should be about half the original volume). Cook crawfish tails 10 min. in 4 tbsp. butter. Add purée, cream, mushrooms cooked for 10 min. in 3½ tbsp. butter. Bind with egg yolks just before serving.

164. LOBSTER

Attach live lobster to a plank and plunge into boiling court-bouillon (recipe 866 or 867). Cooking time:

1-lb. lobster—12 min.

1¾ lbs.—20 min.

2 lbs.—25 min.

4 lbs.—30 min.

Chill lobster in the court-bouillon. Remove it from plank; dry thoroughly. Rub shell with a little oil. Turn lobster on its back; slash abdominal wall down entire length. Remove intestine and coral. Cut tail in ½-in. slices. Place empty shell on serving dish; arrange slices of meat on top. Garnish with sliced hard-boiled eggs, tomatoes, lettuce, parsley, Mayonnaise, etc. If desired, serve hot with Hollandaise Sauce (recipe 64) or Maître d'hôtel Butter (recipe 4).

165. LOBSTER COTENTIN
PREPARATION TIME: 30 MIN.   COOKING TIME: 1¼ HOURS.

1 lobster, about 2½ lbs., cooked	2 cups Tomato Sauce (recipe 31)
4 tbsp. butter	1 truffle
1¼ cups flour	1 qt. mussels
3 tbsp. brandy	12 oysters
6 tbsp. white wine	¼ lb. mushrooms, cut in pieces
½ lb. shrimp, shelled	salt, black and Cayenne
3 tbsp. Madeira wine	pepper

Make a Light Brown Sauce (recipe 30) with butter, flour, brandy, Madeira and white wines and Tomato Sauce. Chop half the truffle; add to sauce together with lobster meat, seasonings. Cook over low heat 40 min. Add sliced lobster tail, mushrooms, remaining truffle in slices, shrimp and oysters. Continue cooking 20 min. Serve in a hot patty or pie shell.

166. LOBSTER THERMIDOR
PREPARATION TIME: 1 HOUR.   COOKING TIME: 40 MIN.

1 lb. lobster meat, cooked, diced	6⅔ tbsp. Madeira wine
¼ lb. butter	6⅔ tbsp. Cognac
¾ cup cream	6 tbsp. flour
	salt, Cayenne pepper

Cook diced lobster in butter for 5 min. Sprinkle with flour; add cream, Madeira, Cognac, season with salt and Cayenne pepper. Pour mixture into earthenware dish; heat in hot oven for 5 min.

167. LOBSTER SOUFFLÉ
PREPARATION TIME: 1 HOUR.   COOKING TIME: 20 MIN.

1 Lobster, about 1 lb., cooked (recipe 164)	3 tbsp. milk
5 tbsp. butter	3 tbsp. white wine
6 tbsp. flour	1½ tsp. brandy
4 egg whites, stiffly beaten	salt, Cayenne pepper
3 egg yolks	3 tbsp. cream

Remove lobster from shell; finely chop and crush meat. Make a Béchamel Sauce (recipe 10) with flour, 2 tbsp. butter, milk, wine. Add lobster meat, remaining butter, cream, egg yolks and whites, brandy, salt and pepper. Turn mixture into mold; bake 20 min. in hot oven.

168. MUSSELS AU NATUREL
PREPARATION TIME: 40 MIN. COOKING TIME: 6 MIN.

3 qts. mussels	2 tbsp. butter
1 small onion	parsley, thyme, bay leaf
1 small carrot	

Use only tightly closed mussels. Scrape and wash them in several changes of water. Drain. Place in pot with remaining ingredients; cook about 6 min. over high heat. As soon as mussels begin to open, toss several times to cook them evenly. Serve in soup bowl, with cooking liquid.

169. MUSSELS MARINIÈRE
PREPARATION TIME: 40 MIN. COOKING TIME: 9 MIN.

3 qts. Mussels, cooked (recipe 168) with their cooking liquid	1 shallot, chopped
	1 clove garlic
3½ tbsp. butter	4 tbsp. bread crumbs
¾ cup white wine	chopped parsley

Add remaining ingredients to cooking liquid; toss mussels in liquid for 3 min. Serve hot.

170. MUSSELS À LA POULETTE
PREPARATION TIME: 40 MIN. COOKING TIME: 20 MIN.

2 qts. Mussels Marinière (recipe 169)	1 egg yolk
	juice of 1 lemon
1 cup Light Brown Sauce (recipe 30), made with cooking liquid from mussels	chopped parsley

Bind sauce with egg yolk; add lemon juice. Pour sauce over cooked mussels; sprinkle with chopped parsley.

171. *MUSSELS BÉCHAMEL AU GRATIN*
PREPARATION TIME: 20 MIN. COOKING TIME: 20 MIN.

2 qts. Mussels, cooked   2 tbsp. flour
   (recipe 168)   2 cups milk
4 tbsp. butter   fine bread crumbs

Remove mussels from shells. Make a Béchamel Sauce (recipe 10) with 2 tbsp. butter, flour, milk; simmer mussels in it for 5 min. Pour into baking dish; sprinkle with bread crumbs and dot with remaining butter. Brown 10 min. in hot oven.

172. *MUSSELS IN SHELLS*
PREPARATION TIME: 1½ HOURS. COOKING TIME: 15 MIN.

2 qts. Mussels, cooked   ¾ cup fine dry bread crumbs
   (recipe 168)   salt, pepper
4 tbsp. butter   6 large shells or individual
2 tbsp. chopped scallion   baking dishes
2 tbsp. chopped parsley

Remove mussels from shells. Combine bread crumbs, butter, chopped parsley and scallion, seasonings. Spread layer of mixture in bottom of each shell; cover with mussels, then top with layer of bread crumb mixture. Brown 8 min. in hot oven.

173. *FRIED OYSTERS*
PREPARATION TIME: 10 MIN. COOKING TIME: 5 MIN.

5 doz. oysters, opened, removed   fine bread crumbs
   from shells   salt, pepper
6⅔ tbsp. butter   Tomato Sauce (recipe 31)
1 egg, beaten

Sprinkle oysters with salt and pepper. Roll in beaten egg, then in bread crumbs; brown in hot butter. Arrange on serving dish; nap with Tomato Sauce.

174. *STUFFED OYSTERS IN SHELLS*
PREPARATION TIME: 15 MIN. COOKING TIME: 15 MIN.

18 oysters   small quantity of bread
¾ cup chopped cooked   crumbs, soaked in
   mushrooms   6⅔ tbsp. warm milk
2 tbsp. butter   juice of ½ lemon
yolk of 1 hard-boiled egg

Remove oysters from shells; sprinkle with lemon juice. Wash shells; replace oysters, two to each shell. Combine bread crumbs, crushed egg yolk, mushrooms, seasonings; spread mixture over oysters. Sprinkle with bread crumbs, dot with butter. Brown for 10 min. in very hot oven.

175. SCALLOPS AU GRATIN (COQUILLES SAINT-JACQUES AU GRATIN)

PREPARATION TIME: 50 MIN. COOKING TIME: 15 MIN.

9 scallops	1 egg yolk
6⅔ tbsp. butter	¼ lb. mushrooms, chopped
6 tbsp. flour	1 shallot, chopped
6⅔ tbsp. white wine	fine bread crumbs
2 cups Stock (recipe 69)	chopped parsley

Remove scallops from shells; wash thoroughly, cook 3 min. in boiling salted water. Brown parsley, shallot and chopped mushrooms in 2 tbsp. butter. Make a Light Brown Sauce with flour, 2⅔ tbsp. butter, white wine and stock; boil 2 min. Bind sauce with egg yolk; add scallops. Fill 6 shells, baking dishes or ramekins with mixture. Sprinkle with bread crumbs, dot with butter. Brown 10 min. in hot oven.

176. SHRIMP

Cook 3-5 min. in small quantity of well-salted boiling water.

177. SHRIMP CROQUETTES

PREPARATION TIME: 30 MIN. + TIME REQUIRED TO SHELL SHRIMP. COOKING TIME: 40 MIN.

1 lb. shrimp, cooked	1¼ cups flour
3 cups milk	salt, pepper, nutmeg
6⅔ tbsp. butter	oil or butter for frying

Shell cooked shrimp. Scald milk; throw in shells, boil 5 min., then reduce heat and cook gently for 15 min. Strain, reserving liquid. Mash shells; strain again. Make a White Sauce (recipe 8 or 9) with flour, butter, cooking liquid; add crushed shrimp shells. Add shrimp and seasonings; cook 5 min. Chill. Form mixture into croquettes. Brown in hot butter or oil.

178. *FROGS' LEGS, SAUCE POULETTE*
PREPARATION TIME: 10 MIN. COOKING TIME: 15 MIN.

Fry frogs' legs for 5 min. in small quantity of butter. Add Poulette Sauce (recipe 15); simmer 10 min.

179. *FRIED FROGS' LEGS*
PREPARATION TIME: 20 MIN. COOKING TIME: 8 MIN.

Marinate frogs' legs 30 min. in marinade (recipe 855). Dip in batter for frying (recipe 884); brown in very hot shortening.

180. *FROGS' LEGS À LA CRÈME*
PREPARATION TIME: 10 MIN. COOKING TIME: 15 MIN.

3½ tbsp. butter
1 doz. frogs' legs per person
2 tbsp. flour
6⅔ tbsp. white Burgundy wine
1 onion, minced

3 tbsp. cream
dash of lemon juice
salt, pepper, chopped parsley

Cook onion gently in butter. Add flour (do not brown); then wine. Add frogs' legs and seasonings; simmer 15 min. Bind sauce with cream; add a little chopped parsley and dash of lemon juice.

181. *SNAILS*

Starve snails for one week. Soak for 12 hours in mixture of 1 tbsp. salt and 6⅔ tbsp. vinegar for 2 doz. snails. Cook gently for 30 min. in salted water. Remove snails from shells; cut off black portion of tail, then cook animals for 2 hours in court-bouillon (recipe 866). Chill in court-bouillon.

Wash shells thoroughly; drain. Place a bit of stuffing (see below) in each shell. Place in snail, then finish with bit of stuffing. Arrange snails in special snail dish. Heat 8 min. in oven.

Stuffing:

For 1 doz. snails:
4 tbsp. butter

½ tsp. chopped shallot
chopped garlic and parsley
salt, pepper

Work chopped shallot, garlic and parsley into butter. Season with salt and pepper.

Suggestions for Leftovers

182. SHELLS DEBELLEYME
PREPARATION TIME: 30 MIN. COOKING TIME: 30 MIN.

½ lb. cooked fish, cut in pieces
¼ lb. mushrooms, cut in pieces
1 med. onion, finely chopped
3½ tbsp. butter

1 cup bread crumbs, soaked in
¾ cup warm milk
6 tbsp. white wine
salt, pepper

Cook onion for 30 min. in 2 tbsp. butter. Add mushrooms; cook 8 min. Add bread crumbs, wine, salt and pepper; simmer 10 min. Divide fish evenly among 6 shells or individual baking dishes; cover with bread crumb mixture. Sprinkle with bread crumbs; dot with butter. Heat for 10 min. in hot oven.

183. FISH CROQUETTES
PREPARATION TIME: 15 MIN. COOKING TIME: 5 MIN.

½ lb. cooked fish, finely crushed
1 or 2 eggs
1 cup thick White Sauce
(recipe 8 or 9)

bread crumbs
Tomato Sauce (recipe 31)
shortening for frying

Combine fish, sauce, 1 or 2 eggs, depending on consistency of mixture. Cook for 3 min., stirring constantly. Chill. Form mixture into small balls. Roll in bread crumbs; brown in very hot shortening. Serve with Tomato Sauce.

RICE JAMBALAYA: See recipe 587.

184. FISH RISSOLES

PREPARATION TIME: 1 HOUR. COOKING TIME: 20 MIN.

Pastry Dough (recipe 796 or 800)
½ lb. cooked fish, cut in small pieces

¾ cup White Sauce (recipe 8 or 9)
¼ lb. chopped, cooked mushrooms (optional)
1 egg, beaten

Cut pastry into circles. Mix fish with sauce, season to taste; add mushrooms if desired. Place spoonful of fish mixture on one half of each pastry circle; fold over other half and seal edges with a little water. Brush with beaten egg. Bake 20 min. in hot oven, or fry in very hot shortening if preferred.

185. SHELLS À LA MORNAY

PREPARATION TIME: 15 MIN. COOKING TIME: 10 MIN.

1 lb. any shellfish, cooked   2 cups Mornay Sauce (recipe 14)

Fill 6 shells or individual baking dishes with fish; cover with sauce. Heat 10 min. in oven.

SHELLS À LA MAYONNAISE: See recipe 621.

186. FISH SOUFFLÉ

PREPARATION TIME: 20 MIN. COOKING TIME: 45 MIN.

½ lb. cooked fish
3½ tbsp. butter
1 cup flour

1⅓ cups milk
₃ ₃gs, separated

Make a thick Béchamel Sauce (recipe 10) with flour, butter and milk; mix in fish, egg yolks. Fold in stiffly beaten egg whites. Pour mixture into baking dish; bake 45 min. in very slow oven. Serve with any desired sauce.

187. TIMBALE PARMENTIER

PREPARATION TIME: 1 HOUR. COOKING TIME: 30 MIN.

1 lb. potatoes, cooked, mashed
1 lb. cooked fish
2 cups White Sauce (recipe 8 or 9)

3 eggs
¼ lb. mushrooms, chopped
6⅔ tbsp. butter
salt, pepper

Combine potatoes and eggs; season to taste. Spread mixture in baking dish, leaving opening in center; dot with 2⅔ tbsp. butter, brown 20 min. in hot oven. Cook chopped mushrooms in 2 tbsp. butter; combine with sauce, fish, remaining butter, and heat for 10 min. Pour mixture into center of potato ring. Serve immediately.

VOL-AU-VENT: See recipe 354.

Eggs

Is it fresh?

Eggs should be consumed as soon as possible after laying, as air and germs quickly penetrate the porous shell. Here's a simple test for freshness:

Place egg in salted water (2½ tsp. salt to 1 qt. water). A fresh egg will go straight to the bottom of the pot; the large end of a 1- or 2-day-old egg will rise slightly. A 5-day-old egg will remain just below the surface of the water; older eggs will rise above the surface (a 10- or 12-day-old egg will rise halfway out of the water).

188. SOFT-BOILED EGGS IN THE SHELL (OEUFS COQUE)

1st method: Plunge eggs carefully into boiling water. Cook 2 min. (3 at most). Remove from water immediately.

2nd method: Plunge eggs carefully into boiling salted water. Cover and remove from heat. Let stand 4-5 min.

3rd method: Place eggs in pot of cold water (use 1 part water to 1 egg). Place over heat; bring water to boil. Eggs are cooked when water begins to boil.

189. POACHED EGGS

Bring mixture of 3 qts. water and 4 tbsp. vinegar to "shivering" point. Break eggs and gently slide them into water; gather whites around yolks if necessary. Simmer 3½ min. over low flame. Remove and drain; arrange on serving dish. If desired, nap with one of the following sauces: White (recipe 8 or 9), Béchamel (10), Robert (50), Tomato (31), Piquant (41),

Brown Butter (6), Mornay (14). Sprinkle with grated cheese; brown 10 min. in very hot oven.

Poached eggs may be kept warm until serving time by keeping them in a pan of salted warm water (1 tsp. salt per quart of water).

190. SOFT-BOILED EGGS (OEUFS MOLLETS)

Carefully plunge eggs into boiling salted water. Cook 5 min. Plunge into cold water. Remove shells.

Serve whole with vegetables or with one of the following sauces: White (recipe 8 or 9), Béchamel (10), Mornay (14), Tomato (31), Robert (50).

191. HARD-BOILED EGGS (OEUFS DURS)

Carefully plunge eggs into well-salted boiling water. Cook 10 min.

Halve lengthwise and serve on bed of spinach or with one of following sauces: White, Béchamel, Mornay, Tomato, Robert.

Hard-boiled eggs may also be served as a salad (see recipe 613), or as a garnish for salads, cold fish dishes and vegetables, cooked spinach or other greens.

192. SCRAMBLED EGGS (OEUFS BROUILLÉS)
PREPARATION TIME: 5 MIN. COOKING TIME: 12 MIN.

6 eggs
4 tbsp. butter (in small pieces)

3 tbsp. milk
salt, pepper

Beat together eggs, milk, salt, pepper until well blended but not foamy. Gradually add butter while beating (reserve one piece for cooking). Melt butter in pan. Pour in egg mixture; cook over low heat, stirring constantly, for 12 min.

If desired, add one or more of following before cooking: cheese, cooked asparagus tips, cooked mushrooms, shrimp, etc.

193. FRIED EGGS

Break an egg into ladle or spoon; slide into very hot shortening, gathering white around yolk. Turn once during cooking (about ½ min.). Garnish with fried parsley (recipe 874) or croutons. If desired, nap with Brown Butter (6), Tomato (31) or Chasseur (55) Sauce. Or serve with puréed celery or spinach, or mashed potatoes.

194. SHIRRED EGGS (OEUFS MIROIR, OEUFS SUR LE PLAT)

Use 2 eggs per person. Melt 2 tsp. butter in pan; quickly break in 2 eggs. Cook 2-3 min. over low flame. Cover yolk with 2 or 3 drops of melted butter. Place in slow oven for a few seconds, until desired firmness is attained. Sprinkle salt over whites before serving.

194A. SHIRRED EGGS À LA CRÈME: Place ½ cup cream in pan; heat gently to as high a temperature as possible without causing it to curdle. Break eggs carefully into pan and continue as for Shirred Eggs.

194B. SHIRRED EGGS IN CHEESE: Cook eggs in mixture of 1½ tsp. butter, 1 tbsp. grated Gruyère, and a little chopped parsley for each egg.

195. BAKED EGGS I (OEUFS EN CAISSE)
PREPARATION TIME: 10 MIN. COOKING TIME: 10 MIN.

6 eggs	salt, pepper
¼ cup grated Parmesan	fine bread crumbs
12 tsp. butter	chopped *fines herbes*
	6 ramekins

Place 2 tsp. butter and a little salt, pepper and *fines herbes* in each ramekin; heat for a few minutes in oven. Break an egg into each ramekin; sprinkle with cheese and bread crumbs. Brown 10 min. in hot oven.

196. BAKED EGGS II (OEUFS COCOTTE)
PREPARATION TIME: 5 MIN. COOKING TIME: 8 MIN.

6 eggs	salt, pepper
½ cup cream	6 small porcelain cocottes or baking dishes

Place 1 tbsp. cream in each cocotte; place cocottes in pan of boiling water and heat for 2 min. Break an egg into each cocotte; cover with a little cream, season to taste. Place pan in oven; bake 6 min. at very high temperature.

197. OMELET

PREPARATION TIME: 5 MIN. COOKING TIME: 5 MIN.

Beat 6 eggs with a little salt and pepper until foamy. Melt 2 tbsp. butter in skillet. When butter is sizzling hot and begins to turn brown, pour in eggs. Cook until small balloons form around edge and omelet is well set. Shaking skillet with left hand, draw edge of omelet toward center with fork held in right hand. Fold; slide omelet onto warm serving dish.

A good omelet should be slightly moist.

If desired, add one or more of following just before folding omelet: grated cheese, mushrooms, cooked asparagus tips, potatoes, rice, macaroni, pieces of cooked meat and vegetables, etc.

197A. OMELET AUX FINES HERBES: Add chopped *fines herbes* to eggs before cooking.

EGGS À LA RUSSE: See recipe 616.

EGGS MIMOSA: See recipe 615.

198. STUFFED EGGS

PREPARATION TIME: 20 MIN. COOKING TIME: 20 MIN.

6 hard-boiled eggs	1 tbsp. butter
½ cup coarse fresh bread crumbs, soaked in 6⅔ tbsp. milk	salt, pepper, *fines herbes*

Halve eggs lengthwise; carefully remove yolks. Cook chopped *fines herbes* in butter for 10 min.; mash with egg yolks, soaked bread crumbs, salt, pepper. Fill egg whites with stuffing, rounding off tops. Arrange on serving dish and nap with White (recipe 8 or 9) or Béchamel (recipe 10) Sauce. Heat in hot oven 10 min.

If desired, truffles, shrimp, anchovies or mushrooms may be added to stuffing.

199. EGGS BRUXELLOIS

PREPARATION TIME: 40 MIN. COOKING TIME: 35 MIN.

1 lb. Brussels Sprouts, cooked (recipe 449)	6 tbsp. flour
	¾ cup grated Gruyère
3 hard-boiled eggs, coarsely chopped	2 cups milk
3½ tbsp. butter	salt, pepper, nutmeg

Rub drained cooked sprouts through sieve or food mill; add half the Gruyère. Spread mixture in buttered baking dish. Prepare a thick Béchamel Sauce (recipe 10) with butter, flour, milk; season to taste. Mix chopped eggs with sauce; pour over puréed sprouts. Sprinkle with remaining grated cheese. Bake 10 min. in very hot oven.

200. EGGS À LA ROYALE

PREPARATION TIME: 15 MIN. COOKING TIME: 30 MIN.

6 hard-boiled eggs	⅓ cup flour
3 tbsp. thick Tomato Sauce (recipe 31)	3½ tbsp. butter
¾ cup milk	salt, pepper
	Béchamel Sauce (recipe 10)

Halve eggs lengthwise. Remove yolks; rub through sieve or food mill. Heap yolks in center of serving dish; surround with whites. Garnish whites with Tomato Sauce; nap yolks with Béchamel Sauce. Serve very hot.

201. EGGS À LA TRIPE or À LA BÉCHAMEL SOUBISÉE

PREPARATION TIME: 15 MIN. COOKING TIME: 30 MIN.

6 hard-boiled eggs	1 cup Stock (recipe 69)
2 tbsp. butter	2 med. onions
4 tbsp. flour	salt, pepper

Prepare a Light Brown Sauce with butter, onions, flour and stock. Slice eggs crosswise; add to sauce. Simmer 10 min.

202. EGGS CHIMAY

PREPARATION TIME: 25 MIN. COOKING TIME: 15 MIN.

6 hard-boiled eggs
  Duxelle (recipe 865)
2 cups Mornay Sauce
  (recipe 14)

⅓ cup grated Gruyère
salt, pepper
chopped parsley

Halve eggs lengthwise; remove yolks, crush, combine with Duxelle, parsley, 1 tbsp. sauce, seasonings. Stuff whites with mixture. Arrange eggs in buttered baking dish, nap with remaining sauce and sprinkle with grated Gruyère. Bake 15 min. in hot oven.

203. EGGS BASQUE STYLE

PREPARATION TIME: 25 MIN. COOKING TIME: 40 MIN.

6 hard-boiled eggs
3½ tbsp. butter
⅓ cup flour
  juice of 1 lemon

¼ lb. mushrooms, cut in pieces
¼ lb. cooked shrimp with their
  shells
salt, pepper, *fines herbes*

Cook mushrooms 10 min. in mixture of lemon juice, 1 tbsp. butter, small quantity of water; drain. Into same liquid throw shrimp shells; boil 10 min. Strain. Make a thin White Sauce (recipe 8 or 9) with cooking liquid, flour, butter. Halve eggs lengthwise. Mash together shrimp, egg yolks, mushrooms, *fines herbes*, salt and pepper. Stuff whites with mixture. Arrange stuffed eggs in baking dish; nap with sauce. Heat for 5 min. in hot oven.

204. TARTINES STRASBOURGEOISES

PREPARATION TIME: 15 MIN. COOKING TIME: 5 MIN.

6 slices white bread
¼ lb. butter
6 Poached Eggs (recipe 189)

2 cups Périgueux Sauce
  (recipe 45)
1 can goose liver paste
  truffles (optional)

Fry slices of bread on both sides in butter; arrange on serving dish. Spread with goose liver paste; top with poached egg. Nap with sauce and garnish with truffles. Serve immediately.

205. EGGS-IN-A-NEST

PREPARATION TIME: 1 HOUR. COOKING TIME: 45 MIN.

6 eggs, poached (recipe 189)
6 Artichoke Hearts, cooked
   (recipe 444)

2 cups Bordelaise Sauce
   (recipe 34)
salt, pepper

Arrange artichoke hearts on serving dish. Top each with a poached egg. Season to taste. Nap with sauce.

206. POACHED EGGS WITH ASPARAGUS TIPS

PREPARATION TIME: 15 MIN. COOKING TIME: 20 MIN.

6 eggs, poached (recipe 189)
18 asparagus (tips only)
3 tbsp. cream

1⅓ tbsp. butter
2 tbsp. flour

Cook asparagus tips in boiling salted water for 10 min.; drain. Combine cream, butter, asparagus tips; place over heat. Sprinkle with flour; thicken, season to taste. Place poached eggs on serving dish; nap with sauce.

206A. POACHED EGGS WITH MUSHROOMS: Replace asparagus tips with mushrooms sautéed in a little butter.

207. EGGS IN WINE SAUCE (OEUFS EN MATELOTE)

PREPARATION TIME: 15 MIN. COOKING TIME: ⁄ MIN.

6 eggs
2 cups water
2 cups red wine
1 large onion
1 clove garlic

3½ tbsp. butter
3 tbsp. flour
salt, pepper, *bouquet garni*
6 slices white bread

Boil together wine, water, onion, garlic and seasonings 20 min. Remove onion and seasonings; poach eggs in boiling liquid. Remove and keep warm. Blend butter and flour; add to liquid, beating with wire whisk. Fry slices of bread on both sides in additional butter; rub with garlic. Arrange on serving dish; top with eggs and nap with sauce.

208. DUCHESS EGGS

PREPARATION TIME: 10 MIN. COOKING TIME: 15 MIN.

1 cup Rice, Cooked (recipe 582)
   leftover chopped chicken or
   other poultry

6 Eggs, Poached (recipe 189)
3½ tbsp. butter, melted
⅓ lb. asparagus tips

Heat chopped meat in a little butter. Cook asparagus tips 15 min. in boiling water; drain, toss in melted butter. Heap chicken in center of serving dish; surround with asparagus tips. Garnish with rice. Finish with ring of poached eggs.

209. EGGS VERT-PRÉ
PREPARATION TIME: 35-40 MIN. COOKING TIME: 40 MIN.

6 Eggs, Poached (recipe 186)	3 tbsp. flour
6 med. potatoes	⅓ cup grated Gruyère
¼ lb. spinach	3½ tbsp. butter
6⅔ tbsp. cream	salt, pepper, nutmeg
¾ cup milk	

Bake potatoes in their jackets about 30 min. in hot oven, turning them frequently. Carefully scoop out interior of potatoes, without breaking skins. Mash; add 1⅓ tbsp. butter, season with salt and pepper. Wash, drain and dry spinach; chop coarsely. Cook until tender in 1⅓ tbsp. butter, over high flame, stirring constantly. Prepare a Béchamel Sauce (recipe 10) with remaining butter, flour, milk; add salt, pepper, nutmeg, half the Gruyère. Fill skins with mixture; top with poached eggs. Surround with spinach, and nap with sauce. Sprinkle with remaining Gruyère; dot with additional butter. Brown 5-10 min. in very hot oven.

210. EGGS BENEDICTINE
PREPARATION TIME: 30 MIN. COOKING TIME: 20 MIN.

6 Baked Tart Shells (recipe 796)	Hollandaise Sauce (recipe 64)
6 Eggs, Poached (recipe 189)	salt, pepper
6 slices ham	sliced truffles

Place 1 slice of ham in each tart shell; top with poached egg. Season to taste. Nap with sauce; garnish with truffles. Serve very hot.

211. EGGS À LA CHANOINESSE
PREPARATION TIME: 45 MIN. COOKING TIME: 20 MIN.

6 eggs	¼ cup grated Gruyère
2 medium onions, minced	4 tbsp. butter
chestnut purée (recipe 470)	salt, pepper

Cook onion 15 min. in butter. Spread in bottom of baking dish; top with layer of chestnut purée. Break eggs in middle of mixture; sprinkle with grated Gruyère. Bake 20 min. in very hot oven. Season to taste.

212. EGGS À L'ARDENNAISE
PREPARATION TIME: 10 MIN. COOKING TIME: 10 MIN.

6 eggs	2 tbsp. butter
⅔ cup cream	salt, pepper

Separate eggs, being careful not to break yolks. Beat egg whites until stiff; turn into well-buttered pie plate. Nap with cream. Arrange egg yolks in circle on top. Bake 10 min. in slow oven.

212A. EGGS À LA ROSSINI: Sprinkle egg whites with ⅓ cup grated Gruyère instead of cream. Arrange yolks on top of whites; sprinkle with ⅓ cup grated Gruyère, dot with butter. Bake 6 min. in slow oven. Sprinkle with 6 tbsp. cream; season to taste.

213. EGGS À LA MEYERBEER
PREPARATION TIME: 10 MIN. COOKING TIME: 10 MIN.

3 lamb kidneys, split lengthwise	4 tbsp. butter
6 eggs	salt, pepper

Sauté kidneys 4 min. in butter; place in well-buttered baking dish. Break eggs over kidneys; season. Bake 5 min. in hot oven.

214. EGGS PARMENTIER
PREPARATION TIME: 20 MIN. COOKING TIME: 35 MIN.

1¾ lbs. Mashed Potatoes (recipe 529)	6 eggs
	3½ tbsp. butter
2 cups milk	6 tbsp. cream

Spread mashed potatoes in shallow, buttered baking dish. Make 6 depressions in top; break an egg into each. Nap with cream, season with salt and pepper. Bake 15 min. in hot oven.

215. BAKED EGGS IN TOMATOES

PREPARATION TIME: 10 MIN.   COOKING TIME: 25 MIN.

6 large tomatoes
6 eggs
½ clove garlic, finely chopped

2 tbsp. olive oil
salt, pepper, *fines herbes*

Cut slice from tops of tomatoes; scoop out seeds and pulp. Break an egg into each tomato; season. Place in baking dish which has been greased with mixture of olive oil and chopped garlic. Bake 25 min. in slow oven.

216. EGGS BELGIAN STYLE

PREPARATION TIME: 25 MIN.   COOKING TIME: 5 MIN.

6 slices white bread
½ cup grated Gruyère
3 eggs, separated

6 slices ham
3 tbsp. oil

Mix egg yolks and Gruyère; spread on one side of bread. Top each slice of bread with ham; spread with stiffly beaten egg whites. Heat oil in skillet; fry slices on one side only. Season to taste. Serve very hot.

217. EGGS PAPRIKA

PREPARATION TIME: 45 MIN.   COOKING TIME: 20 MIN.

6 Eggs, Fried (recipe 193)
2 tomatoes
1 eggplant
1 onion
2 red peppers
1 zucchini

½ cup Rice, Cooked (recipe 579)
1⅓ cups Cream Sauce (recipe 11),
    seasoned with 1 tbsp. paprika
salt, pepper, garlic, *fines
herbes*
½ cup oil

Dice vegetables and sprinkle with salt; set aside for 20 min. Drain and fry in hot oil about 10 min.; season to taste. Spread rice in serving dish; top with layer of vegetables. Top with fried eggs; nap with sauce.

218. EGG TURBAN

PREPARATION TIME: 10 MIN.   COOKING TIME: 45 MIN.

6 eggs
1 qt. milk, scalded, seasoned with
    salt, pepper

2 cups Tomato Sauce (recipe 31)

Beat eggs until foamy. Gradually add milk. Pour into buttered ring mold; set mold in pan of water and bake 45 min. in moderate oven. Unmold; fill center of ring with Tomato Sauce. Serve hot.

219. EGG CROQUETTES
PREPARATION TIME: 25 MIN. COOKING TIME: 15 MIN.

7 hard-boiled eggs, diced
2 fresh eggs, separated
1 cup milk
4 tbsp. flour
3½ tbsp. butter
salt, pepper
fine bread crumbs

Prepare a very thick White Sauce (recipe 8 or 9) with flour, butter, milk; add 2 egg yolks; season to taste. Chill. Add diced eggs. Form mixture into croquettes about thickness of thumb. Roll first in stiffly beaten egg white, then in bread crumbs. Fry in very hot shortening.

220. GNOCCHI RAMEKINS
PREPARATION TIME: 30 MIN. COOKING TIME: 35 MIN.

6 egg yolks
3 egg whites
¾ cup grated Parmesan
6 tbsp. cream
pie pastry (recipe 796)
salt, pepper

Line 6 small tart molds with pastry. Beat egg whites until stiff; add egg yolks, cheese, cream; season to taste. Pour mixture into tart shells. Bake 35 min. in very slow oven.

221. ANGEVINE OMELET
PREPARATION TIME: 10 MIN. COOKING TIME: 10 MIN.

6 eggs
⅓ cup blanched diced bacon
1 large potato, peeled, cubed
2 tbsp. butter
white part of 1 leek, chopped
½ cup grated Gruyère
salt, pepper, chopped parsley
2 tsp. lard

Brown bacon and potato in combined butter and lard; cook leek in a little butter. Beat eggs until foamy; add remaining ingredients. Cook as for ordinary omelet (recipe 197), but do not fold. Place in very hot oven; bake 5 min. or until top of omelet is firm.

PROVENÇAL OMELET: See recipe 919.

222. POTATO OMELET (CRIQUE À L'ANCIENNE)
PREPARATION TIME: 10 MIN.   COOKING TIME: 15 MIN.

6 eggs	3 tbsp. milk
4 med. potatoes, grated	salt
2 tbsp. butter	

Beat eggs until foamy; add milk and grated potatoes. Season to taste. Melt butter in skillet; pour in egg mixture. Cover and cook over moderate heat for 10 min. Turn; cover and brown 5 min.

Cheese

N.B.: All recipes serve 6, unless otherwise indicated.

223. CHEESE BALLS
PREPARATION TIME: 10 MIN.   COOKING TIME: 5 MIN.

1½ cups cottage cheese
3 eggs
1¼ cups flour
6 tbsp. sugar

1 tsp. bicarbonate of soda
shortening for frying
flour or bread crumbs

Mix all ingredients; beat into smooth batter. Form mixture into balls; roll in flour or bread crumbs. Drop into very hot shortening; cook until cake tester thrust into ball comes out clean. Sprinkle with sugar and serve very hot.

224. COTTAGE CHEESE FRITTERS
PREPARATION TIME: 10 MIN.   COOKING TIME: 5 MIN.

1 lb. potatoes, cooked and
   mashed
1 cup cottage cheese
1½ cups flour
6 tbsp. sugar

1 egg
pinch of salt
1 tbsp. grated lemon rind
shortening for frying

Mix all ingredients. Form mixture into small balls; brown on all sides in hot shortening.

225. CHEESE DELIGHTS
PREPARATION TIME: 10 MIN.   COOKING TIME: 3 MIN.

4 egg whites
2 cups grated Gruyère
   shortening for frying

bread crumbs
pepper
Fried Parsley (recipe 874)

Beat egg whites until stiff. Fold in grated Gruyère; season with pepper. Form mixture into loose balls about the size of

83

an egg; roll in bread crumbs, and brown in hot shortening.
Garnish with fried parsley.

226. CHEESE FRITTERS

PREPARATION TIME: 15 MIN. COOKING TIME: 6 MIN.

1½ cups water	2 eggs
2½ cups flour	salt, pepper
3½ tbsp. butter	shortening for frying
2 cups grated Gruyère	

Bring water and butter to boil. Add flour and stir to form
a smooth batter. Add grated cheese. Chill. Add eggs; season
to taste. Drop mixture by spoonfuls into hot shortening; cook
5-6 min.

227. GRILLED CHEESE SANDWICHES (CROQUE-MESSIEURS)

PREPARATION TIME: 15 MIN. COOKING TIME: 8 MIN.

½ lb. slightly stale bread, thinly sliced	½ cup grated Gruyère
	¼ lb. butter

Butter bread slices lightly. Sprinkle with grated cheese.
Place two slices of bread together to form a sandwich. Heat
butter; brown sandwiches 4 min. on each side.

227A. GRILLED HAM-AND-CHEESE SANDWICHES: Place
slice of ham between slices of bread. Fry sandwiches in 6
tbsp. butter.

228. CHEESE CROQUETTES

PREPARATION TIME: 25 MIN. COOKING TIME: 5 MIN.

1 cup flour	1¼ cups grated Gruyère
5 tbsp. butter	2 egg yolks
2 cups milk	bread crumbs
	shortening for frying

Make a very thick Béchamel Sauce (recipe 10) with butter,
flour, milk. Add grated Gruyère and egg yolks. Form mixture
into croquettes about size of thumb. Roll in bread crumbs,
then brown in hot shortening.

229. BURGUNDIAN CHEESE LOAF
PREPARATION TIME: 15 MIN.   COOKING TIME: 1¾ HOURS.

3 cups milk
6 tbsp. butter
¼ lb. Gruyère, grated
¾ cup flour

6 eggs
Tomato (recipe 31) or
   Mushroom (recipe 43) Sauce

Make a Béchamel Sauce (recipe 10) with butter, flour, milk. Add eggs one by one, then Gruyère; season to taste. Pour mixture into buttered ring mold; place mold in pan of water, and bake 1¾ hours in moderate oven. Unmold and serve with desired sauce.

230. CHEESE RAMEKINS
PREPARATION TIME: 10 MIN.   COOKING TIME: 25 MIN.

1 cup milk, scalded
2 eggs
½ cup diced cooked ham

⅔ cup grated Gruyère
1⅔ tbsp. butter
salt, pepper, nutmeg

Beat eggs until foamy. Add diced ham. Gradually add milk, stirring constantly. Season to taste. Butter individual ramekins and pour in mixture; sprinkle with grated cheese. Bake 25 min. in very slow oven.

231. CHEESE SOUFFLÉ
PREPARATION TIME: 25 MIN.   COOKING TIME: 45 MIN.

6⅔ tbsp. butter
1¼ cups flour
2 cups milk

1 cup grated Gruyère
5 eggs, separated
salt, pepper

Make a very thick Béchamel Sauce (recipe 10) with butter, flour, milk; add grated Gruyère. Chill mixture. Add egg yolks, then stiffly beaten whites; season to taste. Pour mixture into greased baking dish. Bake 45 min. in slow oven.

232. CHEESE PIE
PREPARATION TIME: 20 MIN.   COOKING TIME: 30 MIN.

pie pastry (recipe 796)
1 cup milk
½ cup cream

1 cup grated Gruyère
3 eggs
salt, pepper

Line greased pie plate with pastry. Beat eggs; add milk, cream, grated cheese. Season to taste. Pour mixture into pie shell, and bake 30 min. in hot oven.

FONDUE FRANC-COMTOISE—See recipe 905.

233. CHEESE GALETTES
PREPARATION TIME: 1 HOUR. COOKING TIME: 25 MIN.

Puff Paste (recipe 800)
1 egg, beaten

½ lb. Gruyère, grated
pinch of salt

Roll out Puff Paste 3 times (see recipe), sprinkling each time with Gruyère. Roll pastry out to thickness of about ½ in. Cut in circles about 1½ in. in diameter. Brush with beaten egg. Bake 25 min. in very hot oven.

Meat

Meat in moderate quantities is an essential part of a balanced diet. A normal serving for an adult is 3-4 oz.

From the viewpoint of digestion, there is little difference between white meats (e.g., chicken and veal) and dark meats (e.g., beef). (Pork, however, is more difficult to digest than veal or beef, because of its high fat content.) What is important is the method of cooking. Meat simmered in a rich sauce is more difficult to digest than roasted or broiled meat.

How to cook meat

Most of the following recipes call for browning meat in butter. However, lard, margarine, oil, etc., may be substituted, especially in the case of braised meats and stews.

Broiling: Both grill and piece of meat should be brushed with oil before cooking. Garnish cooked meat with watercress, lettuce, etc.

Roasting: Bard meat before roasting, if this has not already been done by the butcher. This involves wrapping the meat in a thin sheet of fresh pork fat or in blanched bacon strips, and securing with string. Surround cooked roast with small stuffed tomatoes, mushrooms, vegetable macedoine; serve gravy separately.

Braising: Lard meat—i.e., insert small bits of fatback, bacon, fresh pork fat etc., under surface of meat with larding needle. Surround cooked meat with vegetables with which it was cooked.

If meat was cooked in a sauce, nap meat, and serve remaining sauce separately.

Sauces suitable for meat

Hot sauces for white meats:

Béarnaise (recipe 66)
Béchamel (10)
Bordelaise (34)
Butter (13)
Capers (28)
Chivry (22)
Chaud-froid (39)
Financière (32)
Hollandaise (64)

Marrow (recipe 35)
Poulette (15)
Rich (18)
Richelieu (33)
Soubise (19)
Supreme (16)
Tomato (31)
Velvet (37)
Ivory Velvet (38)

Cold sauces for white meats:

Mayonnaise (60)
Green (62)

Tartare (63)
Rémoulade (58)

Hot sauces for red meats:

Béarnaise (66)
Chasseur (55)
Chateaubriand (46)
Crapaudine (67)
Horseradish (20 or 21)
Italian (47)
Madeira (42)
Mushroom (43)

Mustard (57)
Olive (44)
Pepper (49)
Périgueux (45)
Poor Man's (3)
Portuguese (48)
Robert (50)
Tomato (31)

Cold sauces for red meats:

Mayonnaise (60)
Ravigote (56)

Deviled (68)

BEEF

Recommended methods of cooking beef

Boil	Stew	Broil	Pan-broil	Braise	Roast
neck	chuck	steak (T-bone club porter-house loin sirloin)	steak (chuck rib rump top round club T-bone cubed)	short ribs	rib
shank	round			chuck	tender-loin
plate	neck			rib	
heel of round	shank	London Broil		rump	
beef brisket	brisket			top round	
	flank	ground beef	ground beef	flank	
	plate			bottom round	
				London Broil	
				sirloin tip	

234. *BOILED BEEF (POT-AU-FEU)*

PREPARATION TIME: 25 MIN.   COOKING TIME: 3½ HOURS.

Proceed as for Meat Stock (recipe 69), but use a good cut of beef (e.g., bottom round). Cover meat with *boiling* water. Serve meat surrounded with vegetables and garnished with gherkins. Season with salt and mustard.

235. *ROAST BEEF*

Place barded cut of meat on a rack in roasting pan. Roast in moderate oven, 15 min. per lb. Sprinkle with salt when well browned.

Serve roast beef with gravy (recipe 1) or with one of following sauces: Madeira (recipe 42), soubise (recipe 19), mushroom (recipe 43), olive (recipe 44). Good vegetable accompaniments are mashed potatoes (recipe 529), puréed carrots, onions, or spinach, etc.

Meat may also be roasted uncovered in heavy pot. Brown meat on all sides in 3 tbsp. butter. Cook uncovered about 20 min. per lb., turning meat every 5 min. Season with salt when cooking is finished.

236. BROILED STEAKS

Brush steaks with oil. Broil in pre-heated broiler, 5 min. on each side for a 1-in. steak, longer for thicker steaks. Season with salt. Serve with Maître d'hôtel Butter (recipe 4), Bordelaise (34) or Béarnaise (66) Sauce.

237. PAN-BROILED STEAKS

Brown steaks in skillet in 2⅔ tbsp. butter, about 2 min. each side. Season with salt.

237A. PAN-BROILED STEAKS À L'ALSACIENNE: Brown
1 med. onion, sliced, in 4 tbsp. butter. Cook steaks in same butter. Break one egg onto each steak, season with salt and pepper. Continue cooking 3 min. Serve immediately.

238. STEAKS À LA PROVENÇALE
PREPARATION TIME: 25 MIN. COOKING TIME: 5 MIN.

1 lb. chopped beef	1 egg
¼ lb. mushrooms, finely chopped	flour
½ tsp. crushed garlic	chopped parsley
¾ cup olive oil	salt, pepper

Combine chopped beef, mushrooms, garlic, egg and seasonings. Shape mixture into individual steaks; dredge in flour. Heat olive oil; brown steaks. Garnish with chopped parsley.

239. STEAK WITH MUSHROOMS
PREPARATION TIME: 10 MIN. COOKING TIME: 10 MIN.

6 small steaks
½ lb. mushrooms, peeled, thinly sliced
3 tbsp. butter

6 slices white bread, fried in 3 tbsp. butter
¾ cup Madeira wine
salt

Pan-broil steaks in butter; remove from pan. Add sliced mushrooms and Madeira to pan; cook 5 min. Season with salt. Top slices of bread with steaks and mushrooms; nap with cooking liquid left in pan.

240. FILETS MIGNONS CHÂTELAINE
PREPARATION TIME: 25 MIN. COOKING TIME: 1½ HOURS.

6 small steaks, about 1 in. thick
6⅔ tbsp. butter
1 med. carrot, sliced
2 cups Stock (recipe 69)
6⅔ tbsp. Veal Extract (recipe 880)
3 tbsp. Madeira wine

6 small heads lettuce, thoroughly washed
2 strips blanched bacon, cut in pieces
1 small onion, sliced
salt, pepper, *bouquet garni*

Blanch lettuce 10 min. in boiling water. Line bottom of heavy pot with pieces of bacon, carrot and onion slices; place in lettuce heads. Add veal extract, seasonings; simmer for 1 hour. Pan-broil steaks in half the butter. Place steaks and lettuce on serving dish. Deglaze frying pan with Madeira; reduce liquid by boiling. Remove pan from heat; add remaining butter in small pieces. Nap steaks and lettuce with sauce.

241. BRAISED BEEF (BOEUF À LA MODE)
PREPARATION TIME: 30 MIN. COOKING TIME: 4 HOURS.

¼ lb. fresh pork fat, fatback or blanched bacon
1 calf's foot or beef or pig's knuckle
1 med. onion

2 lbs. carrots, sliced
1¾ lbs. beef, larded
¾ cup white wine
¾ cup warm Stock (recipe 69)
salt, pepper, *bouquet garni*

Line bottom of heavy pot with strips of pork fat or blanched bacon. Place in onions and carrots, beef, foot or knuckle. Add stock, wine, seasonings; cover tightly. Bring to boil, then place pot in pre-heated oven and cook for 4 hours in slow oven. During last hour of cooking, baste meat every 10 min. Uncover during last 25 min. of cooking.

242. BEEF À LA CASSEROLE
PREPARATION TIME: 30 MIN.   COOKING TIME: 3½ HOURS.

Ingredients as for Braised Beef.

Brown onion in 2⅔ tbsp. butter; then brown meat over high heat. Add fat or bacon, foot or knuckle, stock, wine and seasonings. Simmer, covered, over very low flame for 1½ hours. Add sliced carrots; continue cooking 2 hours.

243. MARINATED BEEF (BOEUF EN CHEVREUIL)
PREPARATION TIME: 10 MIN.   COOKING TIME: 3 hours

1½ lbs. beef, larded and barded	6 tbsp. white wine
¾ cup Stock (recipe 69)	Marinade (recipe 856)
3½ tbsp. butter	salt, pepper

Marinate meat for 24 hours. Brown in butter, season to taste; cook 3 hours over low heat. Prepare a Chasseur Sauce (recipe 55) with marinade; add cooking liquid from meat. Serve sauce separately.

244. DAUBE OF BEEF
PREPARATION TIME: 20 MIN.   COOKING TIME: 3¼ HOURS.

1¾ lbs. beef, cut in 1½-in. slices	marinade (recipe 856 or 858)
4 tbsp. butter	1 onion
¾ cup stock (recipe 69)	salt, pepper, bouquet garni

Marinate meat for 12 hours. Remove from marinade; dry thoroughly. Brown in butter; cook gently for 15 min. Add half the marinade, stock, seasonings; cover and cook gently 3 hours.

245. BEEF WITH RICE
PREPARATION TIME: 15 MIN.   COOKING TIME: 3½ HOURS.

1½ lbs. beef	2 small onions
3½ tbsp. butter	1 cup rice
3 cups Stock (recipe 69)	salt, pepper, bouquet garni

Brown meat in butter. Add onions, seasonings, stock; cover and cook gently for 3 hours. Add rice; continue cooking over low heat for 30 min.

246. *BEEF ESTOUFFADE*
PREPARATION TIME: 10 MIN. COOKING TIME: 5 HOURS.

1¾ lbs. beef, larded
¼ lb. fresh pork fat or blanched
    bacon
¾ cup Stock (recipe 69)
2 cups red wine

3 med. onions, sliced
½ tsp. chopped shallot
    salt, pepper, parsley, chervil
    thyme, bay leaf

Cut meat in 1½-in. slices. Place in earthenware terrine alternating with onion slices. Pour in red wine. Marinate for 6 hours. Add stock and seasonings; cover tightly and bake 5 hours in slow oven. May be served hot or cold.

247. *BEEF BIRDS* (POULETS SANS TÊTE)
PREPARATION TIME: 40 MIN. COOKING TIME: 1½ HOURS.

1 lb. beef, cut in 6 thin slices
½ lb. bacon
¾ cup Stock (recipe 69)
4 tbsp. butter

6 tbsp. flour
1 tbsp. Madeira wine
    chopped shallot and parsley
    salt, pepper

Top each slice of beef with strip of bacon, a bit of chopped shallot and parsley. Roll up tightly and secure with string. Melt butter in heavy pot; brown beef rolls. Add stock and seasonings; simmer 1½ hours. Blend flour and Madeira; bind sauce. Serve sauce separately.

248. *BEEF BURGUNDY* (BOEUF BOURGUIGNON)
PREPARATION TIME: 20 MIN. COOKING TIME: 2½ HOURS.

1½ lbs. beef, cut in pieces
¼ lb. fat salt pork, diced
4 tbsp. butter
1 med. onion, chopped
¼ lb. mushrooms, peeled, cut in
    pieces

6 tbsp. flour
1⅓ cups red wine
1⅓ cups hot Stock (recipe 69)
    salt, pepper, *bouquet garni*

Brown diced pork and onions in butter; remove from pan. Brown meat. Sprinkle in flour; brown. Add stock, pork, onion, wine and seasonings. Cook gently 2 hours. Add mushroom pieces; continue cooking 30 min.

249. CARBONADE OF BEEF AUX HERBES
PREPARATION TIME: 15 MIN. COOKING TIME: 1½ HOURS.

1½ lbs. beef (rib cut)
1 small onion
¾ cup flour
¾ cup warm Stock (recipe 69)
¾ cup vinegar

3 tbsp. butter
1 slice Spice Cake (recipe 752)
2 gherkins, sliced
salt, pepper, chopped parsley
chopped tarragon and chervil

Dredge meat in flour; brown in butter. Add onions and seasonings, stock; cook gently 45 min. Crumble slice of cake into vinegar; add to sauce together with gherkins. Simmer 45 min. longer.

VEAL

Recommended methods of cooking veal

Boil (Blanquette)	Stew	Roast	Braise
shank	shoulder	rib	chops
neck	shank	loin	shoulder
heel of round	rump	leg	rump
rump	breast	rump	rolled roast
shoulder		shoulder	
breast			

250. BLANQUETTE OF VEAL
PREPARATION TIME: 15 MIN. COOKING TIME: 2½ HOURS.

2 lbs. veal
¾ cup white wine
1 small carrot, sliced
1 small onion, sliced

2⅔ tbsp. butter
½ cup flour
1 egg yolk
salt, pepper, *bouquet garni*

Soak veal 30 min. in cold water; drain, cut in pieces. Place in heavy pot; cover with cold water. Add carrot, onion, seasonings. Bring to boil; skim. Lower heat and cook gently 1½-2 hours. Drain. Make a Light Brown Sauce (recipe 30) with butter, flour, strained cooking liquid from meat. Simmer sauce 10 min. Bind with egg yolk just before serving.

250A. BLANQUETTE OF VEAL WITH MUSHROOMS:
Add to sauce 3 or 4 small onions, cooked for 25 min. in 3 tbsp. butter, and ¼ lb. peeled, sliced mushrooms.

251. BREAST OF VEAL MÉNAGÈRE
PREPARATION TIME: 25 MIN. COOKING TIME: 2½ HOURS.

2 lbs. breast of veal	½ lb. turnip, peeled, cut in
½ lb. salt pork, cut in pieces	pieces
1 small cabbage, cut in pieces	¾ cup water
3 med. carrots, sliced	salt

Soak veal 30 min. in cold water; drain, cut in pieces. Place veal and salt pork in heavy pot; cover with water. Add vegetables, salt; cook gently 2½ hours. Serve meat surrounded with vegetables and garnished with pieces of salt pork.

252. ROAST VEAL
Bard meat and secure with string; place on rack in roasting pan. Roast in moderate oven, 30 min. per lb. When meat is browned, season with salt, baste. Test for doneness by pricking roast; juice which runs out should be colorless. Deglaze pan; serve gravy separately.

Veal may also be roasted in heavy pot on top of stove. Brown meat on all sides in 3 tbsp. butter. Cook uncovered, 30 min. per lb., turning meat every 5 min. Sprinkle with salt when well browned.

Accompany roast with mashed potatoes or puréed carrots, onion or spinach. The following sauces go well with veal: Tomato (recipe 31), Mushroom (43) or Périgueux (45).

253. ROAST STUFFED BREAST OF VEAL
PREPARATION TIME: 30 MIN. COOKING TIME: 30 MIN. PER LB.

2½ lbs. breast of veal, boned
½ lb. fresh pork fat or
    blanched bacon
½ lb. pork
3 tbsp. brandy

1 egg
salt, pepper, chopped parsley
several strips blanched bacon
    or fresh pork fat

Prepare a stuffing with pork fat or bacon, pork, brandy, seasonings. Stuff meat with mixture; roll up and secure with string after barding with strips of blanched bacon or fat. Cook as for Roast Veal.

254. VEAL CUTLETS
PREPARATION TIME: 6 MIN. COOKING TIME: 10 MIN.

6 veal cutlets
3 tbsp. butter
    juice of one lemon

chopped parsley
salt

Heat butter in skillet; brown cutlets over high flame, 5 min. on each side. Deglaze skillet with 1 tbsp. water; heat. Add lemon juice, season with salt. Pour over meat. Sprinkle with chopped parsley.

254A. VEAL CUTLETS WITH MUSHROOMS: Garnish cutlets with sauce made by cooking 1 lb. finely chopped mushrooms for 5-6 min. in ¼ lb. butter and juice of 1 lemon, then adding 2 cups Light Brown Sauce (recipe 30) and 6 tbsp. Meat Extract (recipe 880) and cooking for 5 min.

254B. VEAL CUTLETS SOUBISE: Serve cutlets with Onion Purée (recipe 513).

254C. VEAL CUTLETS ZEPHYR: Arrange cooked cutlets on serving dish; keep warm. Blend 6 tbsp. flour with 1⅓ cups cream; pour into skillet and heat, stirring constantly. Pour sauce over cutlets; garnish with slice of lemon.

255. VEAL CUTLETS À LA VIENNOISE
PREPARATION TIME: 20 MIN. COOKING TIME: 20 MIN.

6 veal cutlets, pounded very thin	1¾ cups fine bread crumbs
1 egg, well beaten	6 anchovy fillets
1 lemon, sliced	6 pitted olives
6 tbsp. flour	salt, pepper
	shortening for frying

Dredge cutlets in flour, then in beaten egg; season. Roll cutlets in bread crumbs, making sure that crumbs stick to meat. Heat shortening to smoking; carefully place in cutlets, two at a time if pan is large enough. Cook 3-4 min. each side. Arrange cutlets on serving dish; garnish with slices of lemon topped with olive wrapped in anchovy fillet.

256. BREADED VEAL CUTLETS (ESCALOPES PANÉES)
PREPARATION TIME: 10 MIN. COOKING TIME: 10 MIN.

6 veal cutlets	salt, pepper, chopped parsley
2 eggs, beaten	fine bread crumbs
4 tbsp. butter	

Roll cutlets first in beaten egg, then in crumbs. Heat butter, brown cutlets 5 min. each side. Season. Nap with cooking liquid in pan; sprinkle with chopped parsley.

256A. BREADED VEAL CUTLETS À LA MILANAISE:
Add ¾ cup grated Gruyère to bread crumbs. Add dash of lemon juice to sauce.

256B. VEAL CUTLETS À L'ITALIENNE:
Serve Breaded Veal Cutlets with a Tomato Sauce.

257. VEAL CUTLETS GRATINÉES
PREPARATION TIME: 10 MIN. COOKING TIME: 30 MIN.

6 veal cutlets, pounded very thin	¼ lb. mushrooms, washed, peeled
4 tbsp. butter	⅔ cup flour
6⅔ tbsp. cream	¾ cup milk
	⅓ cup grated Gruyère

Dredge cutlets in flour; brown over high heat in 3 tbsp.

butter. Make a White Sauce (recipe 8 or 9) with remaining butter, flour, milk. Cook mushrooms in sauce 10 min.; add cream. Place cutlets in baking dish; cover with sauce, sprinkle with cheese. Brown 10 min. in hot oven.

258. VEAL CHOPS

Cook as for veal cutlets, using 4 tbsp. butter and cooking 7-8 min. if chops are thick. If desired, serve with Tomato (recipe 31) or Madeira (recipe 42) Sauce, or on mashed potatoes, puréed spinach or onions. All recipes for breaded veal cutlets may be applied to veal chops.

259. VEAL CHOPS IN JACKETS (CÔTELETTES EN PAPILLOTES)

PREPARATION TIME: 45 MIN. COOKING TIME: 1½ HOURS.

6 veal chops	½ tsp. minced shallot
¼ lb. mushrooms, chopped	salt, pepper, chopped parsley
¼ cup diced fresh pork fat	juice of 2 lemons
or blanched bacon	strips of blanched bacon or
¼ cup finely chopped ham	fresh pork fat
5⅓ tbsp. butter	waxed paper for jackets
1 tbsp. minced onion	

Cook onion and shallot 30 min. in 2 tbsp. butter. Add mushrooms; cook 5 min., stirring constantly. Add ham, chopped bacon or pork fat, parsley and seasonings; mix well. Brown chops in remaining butter, 2 min. each side. Top each chop with spoonful of mixture; wrap in thin sheet of fat or strips of blanched bacon, then in waxed paper. Place chops in baking dish. Bake 1½ hours in very slow oven. Just before serving, sprinkle chops with lemon juice.

260. VEAL À LA BOURGEOISE

PREPARATION TIME: 25 MIN. COOKING TIME: 2½ HOURS.

1¾ lbs. veal, larded with	2 cups warm Stock (recipe 69)
¼ lb. bacon, diced	salt, pepper, *bouquet garni*
2 lbs. carrots, sliced	2⅔ tbsp. butter
¼ lb. small onions	

Melt butter in heavy pot; brown meat. Add onions, seasonings, stock. Cook gently for 1 hour. Add sliced carrots; continue cooking for 1 hour.

261. VEAL JARDINIÈRE
PREPARATION TIME: 45 MIN.   COOKING TIME: 3 HOURS.

1¾ lbs. veal	½ lb. string beans
¼ lb. fresh pork fat or blanched bacon, diced	1 small onion, sliced
½ lb. new carrots	1 head lettuce
¾ lb. new potatoes, peeled	2⅔ tbsp. butter
¾ lb. peas, shelled	6⅔ tbsp. warm Stock (recipe 69)

Cook string beans 10 min. in boiling salted water. Brown onion and fat or bacon, then meat, in butter. Add stock and seasonings; cover and cook gently 1½ hours, turning occasionally. Place vegetables (except string beans) around meat; continue cooking 1¼ hours. Add string beans; cook 15 min. longer. Serve meat surrounded with vegetables and napped with sauce.

262. STEWED VEAL
PREPARATION TIME: 5 MIN.   COOKING TIME: 2 HOURS.

1¾ lbs. veal, barded	¾ cup white wine
1 small onion, chopped	¾ cup Stock (recipe 69)
3 tbsp. butter	salt, pepper

Brown meat in butter; sprinkle with chopped onion and seasonings. Add wine and stock. Cover and simmer for 2 hours over very low heat.

263. VEAL WITH CREAM
PREPARATION TIME: 10 MIN.   COOKING TIME: 2 HOURS.

1¾ lbs. veal, barded	6⅔ tbsp. warm Stock (recipe 69)
2⅔ tbsp. butter	2 egg yolks
1 med. onion, chopped	6⅔ tbsp. cream
6 tbsp. flour	salt, pepper
6⅔ tbsp. white wine	

Brown meat in butter; sprinkle with onion and flour, add wine and stock, seasonings. Cook for 2 hours over very low heat. Strain cooking liquid; bind with cream and egg yolks. Nap meat with sauce.

264. *VEAL FRANCHARD*

PREPARATION TIME: 10 MIN.   COOKING TIME: 1½ HOURS.

2 lbs. veal, barded with
¼ lb. fresh pork fat or
    blanched bacon
6⅔ tbsp. Stock (recipe 69)
2 or 3 small onions

¼ lb. small mushrooms
3 tbsp. butter
salt, pepper, tarragon
    (1 bunch)

Brown meat in butter; add onions, seasonings, stock. Simmer 2 hours over very low heat. Add mushrooms; continue cooking 30 min. Remove tarragon before serving.

265. *ROAST OF VEAL BÛCHERONNE*

PREPARATION TIME: 20 MIN. COOKING TIME: 2½ HOURS.

2 lbs. veal roast, barded
12-15 small onions
¼ lb. mushrooms, left whole
2 cups red Bordeaux wine

1½ tbsp. sugar
1 egg yolk or 1 tbsp. cornstarch
3½ tbsp. butter
salt, pepper, *bouquet garni*

Brown meat on all sides in butter. Remove meat; brown onions in same butter, adding sugar. Replace meat; add wine, seasonings. Cover and simmer for 2 hours. Add mushrooms; continue cooking for 30 min. Bind sauce either with cornstarch (10 min. before serving) or egg yolk (after pot has been removed from heat).

266. *VEAL BIRDS* (PAUPIETTES DE VEAU)

PREPARATION TIME: 35 MIN. COOKING TIME: 1¾ HOURS.

6 large veal cutlets, pounded thin
¼ lb. mushrooms, chopped
¼ cup chopped fresh pork fat or
    blanched bacon
1 small onion, chopped

½ cup fresh bread crumbs,
    soaked in 1 tbsp. warm milk
4½ tbsp. butter
6⅔ tbsp. warm Stock (recipe 69)
salt, pepper, chopped parsley

Cook onion in 2 tbsp. butter. Make a stuffing with onion, mushrooms, parsley, fat or bacon, bread crumbs, seasonings. Place spoonful of stuffing on each cutlet; roll up and secure with string. Brown rolls in remaining butter. Add stock; cover and cook gently 1¾ hours. Remove string. Deglaze pan; strain sauce over meat.

267. VEAL SANDWICHES
PREPARATION TIME: 20 MIN.   COOKING TIME: 1¾ HOURS.

12 veal cutlets, pounded very thin   4½ tbsp. butter or lard
6 strips bacon   ¾ cup warm stock (recipe 69)
6 slices ham

Place strips of bacon and sliced ham between two cutlets; secure with string. Brown sandwiches in butter. Add stock, cook gently 1¾ hours.

268. VEAL CUTLETS WITH CHOPPED MUSHROOMS
PREPARATION TIME: 30 MIN.   COOKING TIME: 40 MIN.

6 thick, small cutlets   3½ tbsp. butter
½ lb. mushrooms, chopped   juice of 1 lemon
¾ cup Stock (recipe 69)   salt, pepper, chopped
¾ cup fresh bread crumbs   tarragon and parsley
6 slices white bread, fried in
4½ tbsp. butter

Prepare a stuffing with mushrooms, bread crumbs, chopped herbs and seasonings. Brown cutlets in butter. Top each cutlet with spoonful of stuffing. Add stock; cover and simmer 30 min. Place each cutlet on slice of bread; sprinkle with lemon juice.

269. VEAL IN ASPIC
PREPARATION TIME: 30 MIN.   COOKING TIME: 4 HOURS.

1 lb. veal, thinly sliced   chopped shallot and parsley
1 lb. pork loin, thinly sliced   2 cups white wine
1 calf's foot, boned, cut in pieces   Meat Jelly (recipe 881)
(or beef or pig's knuckle)

Spread some chopped shallot in bottom of an earthenware tureen; top with layer of sliced meat. Repeat once; add wine. Place in calf's foot. Cover and bake 4 hours in very slow oven. Remove calf's foot. Place weight on top of tureen. Chill overnight. Unmold; garnish with chopped jelly.

270. *VEAL LOAF*
PREPARATION TIME: 30 MIN. COOKING TIME: 1 HOUR.

¾ lb. chopped veal
¼ cup chopped pork
¼ lb. mushrooms, chopped,
    cooked in butter
2 eggs

nutmeg, salt, pepper
¾ cup fresh bread crumbs
3½ tbsp. butter
Tomato (recipe 31) or Poor
    Man's (recipe 3) Sauce

Combine bread crumbs, eggs, mushrooms; add chopped meat, seasonings. Form mixture into loaf; place in baking dish, dot with butter. Bake 1 hour in slow oven. Serve with desired sauce.

271. *VEAL MEAT BALLS À LA BÉCHAMEL*
PREPARATION TIME: 30 MIN. COOKING TIME: 25 MIN.

¾ lb. chopped veal
½ lb. chopped pork
2 cups stale bread crumbs,
    soaked in 2¼ cups milk
1 whole egg
2 egg yolks

1 tsp. chopped shallot, cooked
    in butter
2 cups White Sauce (recipe 8 or
    9)
salt, pepper

Combine bread crumbs, chopped meat, whole egg, shallots and seasoning. Form mixture into small balls. Poach 25 min. in salted "shivering" water. Arrange in serving dish; nap with White Sauce bound with egg yolks. Serve hot or cold.

272. *STUFFED ESCAROLE*
PREPARATION TIME: 30 MIN. COOKING TIME: 1½ HOURS.

¾ lb. chopped veal
½ lb. chopped pork
3 tbsp. rice
1 egg

1 head escarole
6⅔ tbsp. oil
2¼ cups warm Stock (recipe 69)
salt, pepper

Combine chopped meat, rice, egg, seasonings. Scald escarole in boiling water; separate leaves. Place spoonful of meat mixture on each leaf; roll up. Heat oil in heavy pot; brown rolls. Add stock; cover and cook 1½ hours.

273. VEAL STEW (RAGOÛT DE VEAU)

PREPARATION TIME: 10 MIN. COOKING TIME: 2 HOURS.

2 lbs. veal, cut in pieces
1¾ cups warm stock (recipe 69)
1 med. onion or several small ones, sliced

3½ tbsp. butter
⅔ cup flour
6⅔ tbsp. white wine (optional)
salt, pepper, *bouquet garni*

Heat butter in heavy pot; brown onions and meat thoroughly. Sprinkle with flour; brown. Add stock, seasonings, wine if desired. Cook gently 2 hours. If desired, vegetables may be added after first hour of cooking.

274. VEAL MARENGO

PREPARATION TIME: 25 MIN. COOKING TIME: 2 HOURS.

2 lbs. veal, cut in pieces
3 tbsp. oil
2 tbsp. butter
several small onions
½ tsp. chopped shallot
¼ lb. mushrooms, peeled, cut in pieces

6 tbsp. flour
1½ tbsp. tomato paste or very thick tomato sauce
6⅔ tbsp. white wine
⅔ tbsp. warm Stock (recipe 69)
salt, pepper, chopped parsley

Heat oil and butter together in heavy pot. Brown one onion and meat; sprinkle with chopped shallot and parsley. Add remaining onions, chopped, stock, wine and seasonings. Cook gently 1½ hours. Add tomato paste and mushrooms; continue to simmer for 30 min.

275. VEAL IN RED WINE SAUCE (VEAU EN MATELOTE)

PREPARATION TIME: 15 MIN. COOKING TIME: 2 HOURS.

2 lbs. veal
2⅔ tbsp. butter or other fat
6 tbsp. flour
1 small onion, chopped
¾ cup red wine

6⅔ tbsp. warm Stock (recipe 69)
¾ cup vinegar
juice of 1 lemon
salt, pepper, *bouquet garni*

Heat butter to high temperature; brown meat and onions. Remove from pan. Add flour; brown. Add stock, wine, seasonings; replace meat and onions. Simmer 2 hours. Add vinegar just before serving.

LAMB

Recommended methods of cooking lamb

Boil	Stew	Braise	Roast	Broil	Pan-broil
leg of mutton	breast	shoulder	leg	chops	chops
	shoulder	leg	crown		
shoulder of mutton	neck	breast	sirloin		
	shank	shoulder chops	leg of mutton		
		mutton chops	shoulder of mutton		
		shoulder steaks			

276. LEG OF LAMB À L'ANGLAISE
PREPARATION TIME: 25 MIN. COOKING TIME: 3½ HOURS.

3 lb. leg of lamb
½ lb. carrots
¼ lb. turnips, peeled
¼ lb. onions

salt, pepper, *bouquet garni*
3 qts. water
Capers Sauce (recipe 28)

Cook vegetables for 2 hours in boiling salted water. Add leg of lamb; continue to simmer, 15 min. per lb. Drain meat; serve surrounded with vegetables. Serve sauce separately. If desired, serve with mashed potatoes or string beans.

277. BREAST OF LAMB MÉNAGÈRE

PREPARATION TIME: 20 MIN. COOKING TIME: 2¾ HOURS.

2 lbs. breast of lamb, cut in pieces	6⅔ tbsp. butter
1 cabbage, cut in pieces	1 lb. fat salt pork, cut in pieces
½ lb. turnip, peeled, cut in pieces	½ lb. carrots, cut in pieces
2 eggs, beaten	2 qts. water
	fine bread crumbs
	salt

Place pieces of lamb and salt pork in heavy pot; cover with water. Add vegetables and salt. Cook gently 2½ hours. Remove meat; chill, placing pieces of meat under heavy weight to flatten them. Roll in beaten egg, then in bread crumbs; brown in butter. Serve surrounded with vegetables and pieces of salt pork.

278. ROAST LEG OF LAMB

Remove layer of fat covering (fell) if it is too thick. Insert a clove of garlic next to bone. Roast in hot oven 10-15 min. per lb., depending on degree of doneness desired.

278A. LEG OF LAMB FERMIÈRE: To gravy from roast, add 3½ tbsp. butter, 3 egg yolks, juice of 2 lemons. Mix well. Serve sauce separately.

279. LEG OF LAMB CHEVREUIL

PREPARATION TIME: 15 MIN. COOKING TIME: 1 HOUR.

4 lb. leg of lamb	6⅔ tbsp. heavy cream
1¾ cups water	1 tbsp. cornstarch
1¾ cups red wine	salt, pepper, bouquet garni
1 med. onion	

Marinate lamb 3-6 days (depending on season—3 days in summer, 6 in winter) in mixture of water, wine, onion, thyme, bay leaf, salt, pepper. Drain, dry. Place in roasting pan and roast according to recipe 278. Use marinade to prepare a Chasseur Sauce (recipe 55). Add gravy from roast, cream and cornstarch to sauce just before serving.

280. SHOULDER OF LAMB À LA BOULANGÈRE
PREPARATION TIME: 15 MIN. COOKING TIME: 1½ HOURS.

2 lbs. shoulder of lamb, boned   ½ lb. onions
1 lb. potatoes, peeled   4 tbsp. butter

Roast meat according to recipe 278. Cook vegetables in butter 15 min. Place around meat during last 30 min. of roasting.

281. BROILED LAMB CHOPS
PREPARATION TIME: 5 MIN. COOKING TIME: 10 MIN.

Brush chops with a little oil. Place in pre-heated broiler; broil 4-5 min. each side. Season with salt. Garnish with chopped parsley and dash of lemon juice, or serve with one of following sauces: Piquant (recipe 41), Financière (recipe 32), Mushroom (recipe 43), Tomato (recipe 31), Italian (recipe 47).

282. PAN-BROILED LAMB CHOPS

Heat small quantity of oil in frying pan until very hot. Add small quantity of butter; heat. Brown chops 2-4 min. each side, according to thickness. Serve with mashed or Duchess Potatoes (recipe 525), Stuffed Tomatoes (recipe 554), Stewed Lettuce (recipe 504), Onion Purée (recipe 513), etc.

283. BREADED LAMB CHOPS
PREPARATION TIME: 5 MIN. COOKING TIME: 5 MIN.

6 lamb chops   2 eggs, beaten with
4 tbsp. butter   ¾ tsp. oil
    fine bread crumbs

Roll chops first in beaten egg, then in bread crumbs. Heat butter in skillet; brown chops 5 min.

BRAISED LAMB

284. BRAISED LEG OF LAMB
PREPARATION TIME: 15 MIN.   COOKING TIME: 2½ HOURS.

3 lb. leg of lamb
½ lb. fresh pork fat or blanched
    bacon, cut in pieces
2 med. carrots, cut in pieces
1 med. onion, sliced

¾ cup white wine
¾ cup stock (recipe 69)
6⅔ tbsp. butter
1½ tbsp. cornstarch
    salt, pepper

Brown lamb in butter; remove. Blend flour with butter re-
of fat or bacon; place in meat and vegetables. Add stock, wine,
seasonings. Cover tightly and bring to boil; then bake 50 min.
per lb. in slow oven. Strain liquid and bind with cornstarch
just before serving.

285. BRAISED SHOULDER OF LAMB
COOKING TIME: 1½ HOURS.

2½ lbs. shoulder of lamb
2 cups stock (recipe 69)
3½ tbsp. butter

6 tbsp. flour
salt, pepper

Brown lamb in butter; remove. Blend flour with butter remaining in pan; moisten with stock. Replace meat. Simmer
gently for 1½ hours.

286. STUFFED SHOULDER
PREPARATION TIME: 45 MIN.   COOKING TIME: 2½ HOURS.

2½ lbs. lamb shoulder, boned
Stuffing (recipe 863)
3½ tbsp. butter

6 tbsp. flour
1¾ cups Stock (recipe 69)

Stuff shoulder with stuffing; roll up, secure tightly with
string. Brown in butter; remove. Make a Light Brown Sauce
(recipe 30) with flour, stock, butter remaining in pan. Replace meat; simmer gently 2½ hours. If desired, add potatoes
or turnips after first 1½ hours of cooking.

287. SHOULDER OF LAMB À LA PROVENÇALE
PREPARATION TIME: 35 MIN.   COOKING TIME: 3 HOURS.

2½ lbs. lamb shoulder, boned
  2 cups warm Stock (recipe 69)
¼ cup Tomato Purée
  (recipe 876)
3½ tbsp. butter
  Stuffing (recipe 863)

¼ lb. fresh pork fat or blanched
  bacon, diced
1 med. onion, sliced
1 med. carrot, sliced
  salt, pepper, *bouquet garni*

Stuff shoulder with stuffing; roll up, secure tightly with string. Brown bacon or fat and onion in butter; place in lamb. Add carrot, *bouquet garni*, seasonings, stock and tomato purée. Cook 3 hours, turning from time to time.

288. LAMB CHOPS À LA CHAMPALLON
PREPARATION TIME: 25 MIN.   COOKING TIME: 1 HOUR.

6 lamb chops
1¾ lbs. potatoes, peeled,
  thinly sliced
1 med. onion, chopped
3½ tbsp. butter

6⅔ tbsp. white wine
6⅔ tbsp. Stock (recipe 69)
⅓ cup tomato paste
  salt, pepper, chopped parsley

Sprinkle sliced potatoes with salt, pepper, chopped onion and parsley; set aside. Brown chops in butter, 3 min. each side. Place chops and butter from skillet in heavy pot; surround with potatoes. Add wine, stock, tomato paste. Bring to boil; cover and cook gently 1 hour.

289. LAMB STEW WITH POTATOES
PREPARATION TIME: 25 MIN.   COOKING TIME: 2½ HOURS.

2 lbs. lamb, cut in pieces
4 tbsp. butter
½ cup flour
2 cups warm Stock (recipe 69)
2 med. carrots, cut in pieces
¼ lb. turnip, peeled, cut in
  pieces

1¾ lbs. potatoes, peeled and
  quartered
¼ lb. onions
  salt, pepper, *bouquet garni*

Brown meat and vegetables in butter. Sprinkle in flour, brown; add stock and seasonings. Cook gently 1 hour. Add potatoes; continue cooking 1½ hours.

289A. *NAVARIN:* Substitute 2½ lbs. turnip, cut in pieces, for potatoes.

289B. *HARICOT OF LAMB:* Substitute 1 qt. dried haricot or fava beans for vegetables. Soak beans for several hours; cook for 30 min. before adding to stew. Simmer for a total of 2 hours.

289C. *LAMB WITH SALSIFY:* Substitute salsify (oyster plant) for vegetables. Pre-cook 30 min. in white sauce (see p. 13-14) before adding to meat.

289D. *LAMB WITH CHESTNUTS:* Substitute 2 lbs. cooked chestnuts (recipe 468) for vegetables.

290. *LAMB WITH RICE*
PREPARATION TIME: 10 MIN. COOKING TIME: 2 HOURS.

2 lbs. lamb, cut in pieces	1 clove garlic
¼ lb. small onions	2⅔ tbsp. butter or shortening
¾ cup Tomato Purée (recipe 876)	4 cups Stock (recipe 69)
1 cup rice	salt, pepper

Brown onions and meat in butter or shortening. Add 2 cups stock, garlic, tomato purée, salt and pepper. Cover and cook gently 1 hour. Add rice; cover, cook 15 min. Add remaining stock. Continue cooking 45 min.

PORK

Recommended methods of cooking pork

Boil	Bake	Roast	Braise	Broil	Pan-broil
fresh pork shoulder	chops	loin	chops	ham slice	bacon
cured pic-nic shoul-der	spareribs	crown roast	steaks	picnic slice	
boneless shoulder butt	bacon	ham picnic	cutlets	bacon	
pork hocks			tender-loin patties		
feet			spare-ribs		
fresh spare-ribs					
ham					

291. ROAST PORK

Place meat on rack in roasting pan. Brown in oven at very high temperature. Season with salt and pepper, then continue roasting in slow oven, about 30 min. per lb. Baste often.

If desired, place small new potatoes around meat during last 25 min. of cooking. Baste often.

292. PORK LOIN À LA PROVENÇALE

PREPARATION TIME: 30 MIN. COOKING TIME: 50 MIN.

1¾ lbs. pork loin, boned and tied	¼ lb. mushrooms, chopped
⅓ lb. sausage meat	6 large mushrooms
6⅔ tbsp. oil	2 cloves garlic, minced
6 small tomatoes	salt, pepper, *fines herbes*

Make incisions in fat covering of meat, and insert bits of garlic and most of chopped mushrooms. Roast according to recipe 291. To sausage meat add remaining chopped mushrooms and stems of large mushrooms, *fines herbes;* chop together finely, season with salt and pepper. Cut small slice from stem end of each tomato; scoop out pulp. Stuff tomatoes and large mushrooms with sausage mixture; brown in oil for 5 min. over high heat. Cover and cook 20 min. over low heat. Serve pork surrounded by tomatoes and mushrooms, sprinkled with gravy.

293. BROILED PORK CHOPS

Slash fat around chops. Place in greased, pre-heated broiler; broil under moderate flame, 7-8 min. each side. Season with salt and pepper.

294. PAN-BROILED PORK CHOPS

Heat 2 tsp. butter per chop in skillet. Brown chops 7-8 min. each side. Season with salt and pepper. Cover and cook 10 min. over very low heat. If desired, simmer chops 10-12 min. in one of following sauces: Tomato (recipe 31), Robert (recipe 50), Piquant (recipe 41), Mustard (recipe 57).

295. BREADED PORK CHOPS

Slash fat around chops. Roll in beaten egg; sprinkle with fine bread crumbs. Broil under moderate flame, 7-8 min. each side. Season with salt and pepper.

296. PORK CHOPS À LA DRUE
PREPARATION TIME: 20 MIN.   COOKING TIME: 1½ HOURS.

6 large pork chops, fat removed	3½ tbsp. butter
¼ lb. sliced ham	1 onion, stuck with
¼ lb. fresh pork fat or blanched	several cloves
bacon, cut in strips	salt, pepper, *bouquet garni*
⅓ lb. leftover roast veal, sliced	Onion Purée (recipe 513)
1⅓ cups Stock (recipe 69)	

Lard chops with fat removed from edges. Season with salt and pepper; brown in butter 5-6 min., over high heat. Line bottom of heavy pot with strips of bacon or fat, slices of ham and veal; place in browned chops. Add onion, seasonings, stock; simmer 1½ hours over low flame. Arrange chops on Onion Purée. Reduce cooking liquid by boiling; serve separately as sauce.

297. BRAISED PORK WITH CABBAGE
PREPARATION TIME: 20 MIN.   COOKING TIME: 1¾ HOURS.

1 lb. pork (loin or tenderloin)	1 small cabbage
¼ lb. blanched bacon, diced	1 lb. potatoes, peeled
3½ tbsp. lard	salt, pepper, parsley

Melt lard in heavy pot; brown diced bacon and pork. Season; cover and place over low heat. Wash cabbage and remove outer leaves; blanch 15 min. in boiling salted water. Drain and add to pork, together with several sprigs parsley; cook covered over low heat for 45 min. Add potatoes; continue cooking 45 min. Serve meat on bed of cabbage, surrounded by potatoes and sprinkled with cooking liquid.

298. PORK LOIN BORDELAISE
PREPARATION TIME: 10 MIN.   COOKING TIME: 2½ HOURS.

1¾ lbs. pork loin	1 cup Stock (recipe 69)
3½ tbsp. butter or lard	2 cups white wine
1 onion, stuck with	salt, peppercorns, *bouquet garni*
several cloves	

Heat butter or lard in heavy pot; brown pork. Add stock, wine, onions and seasonings. Cover and cook 2½ hours over low heat, turning frequently. Place meat on serving dish; keep warm. Reduce sauce by boiling 12-15 min. over high heat. Serve separately. Accompany meat with Chestnut (recipe 470) or Lentil (recipe 502) Purée.

CASSOULET: See recipe 924.

299. BOILED HAM (POT-AU-FEU DE JAMBON)
COOKING TIME: 1½ HOURS.

1 fresh ham, 3-4 lbs.
2 cups white wine
2 carrots, sliced

1 onion
peppercorns, *bouquet garni*
water or stock

Cover ham with water or stock and wine; add remaining ingredients. Simmer 1½ hours over low flame. Chill in liquid. Drain; cut in thin slices. If preferred, serve hot with braised cabbage, endive or lettuce.

300. HAM IN MADEIRA
COOKING TIME: 1¾ HOURS.

1 ham
2 cups Mirepoix (recipe 878)
several slices blanched bacon
1 cup Madeira wine

¼ lb. mushrooms, peeled
1 onion, sliced
bouquet garni

Cook ham for 1 hour according to recipe 299. Line heavy pot with strips of bacon and onion slices; place in ham, add Mirepoix and *bouquet garni*. Cover and simmer 30 min. Add Madeira, whole mushrooms; cook 10 min. longer. Serve sauce separately.

301. HAM MARIE-ROSE
PREPARATION TIME: 5 MIN. COOKING TIME: 1 HOUR.

6 slices cooked ham
⅔ cup cream
¾ cup white wine
6⅔ tbsp. Meat Extract
(recipe 880)

3 tsp. tomato paste
1 tsp. chopped shallot
6⅔ tbsp. butter
Dark Brown Sauce (recipe 40)

Warm ham slices in top of double boiler. Add wine and chopped shallot, tomato paste, meat extract to sauce; cook 30 min. over low heat. Add cream; cook 5 min. Strain sauce; add 3 tbsp. butter. Nap meat.

RENAISSANCE TIMBALE: See recipe 534.

302. HAM SOUFFLÉ
PREPARATION TIME: 20 MIN.   COOKING TIME: 25 MIN.

¼ lb. cooked ham, chopped
3 eggs, separated
4 tsp. butter

3 cups thick Béchamel Sauce
   (recipe 10) (with Gruyère, if
   desired)
salt, pepper

Add 3 egg yolks to sauce; fold in ham and stiffly beaten whites, seasonings. Turn mixture into buttered baking dish. Bake 25-30 min. in hot oven. Serve immediately.

303. HAM ROLLS DE LA CHANDELEUR
PREPARATION TIME: 20 MIN.   COOKING TIME: 10 MIN.

6 slices cooked ham
6 small Pancakes (recipe 733)
1 cup grated Gruyère

1 cup Tomato Sauce (recipe 31)
pepper

Place slice of ham on each pancake. Sprinkle with grated Gruyère; roll up tightly. Arrange rolls in flat baking dish; cover with Tomato Sauce to which has been added ½ cup Gruyère. Sprinkle lightly with pepper. Heat 10 min. in oven. Serve piping hot.

VARIETY MEATS

304. BRAINS
Beef, calf's, pork—Soak in cold water for 2 hours. Remove covering membrane; continue soaking, changing water until it is no longer colored. Cook 20 min. in barely "shivering" court-bouillon (recipe 866). Serve with Brown Butter (recipe 6), Mornay (recipe 14), Rich (recipe 18), Madeira (recipe 42), Tomato (recipe 31) or Piquant (recipe 41) Sauce.

Lamb's—Use 1 brain for each person. Soak in cold water; remove membrane and blood vessels. Cook 15 min. in court-bouillon (recipe 866), substituting vinegar for lemon juice.

Serve with Brown Butter (recipe 6), Maître d'hôtel Butter (recipe 4), or Mornay Sauce (recipe 14).

305. BRAINS À LA CHIVRY
PREPARATION TIME: 30 MIN.   COOKING TIME: 45 MIN.

1 lb. brains, cooked	¾ cup milk
3 whole eggs	2⅓ tbsp. butter
3 egg yolks	salt, pepper
6 tbsp. flour	Chivry Sauce (recipe 22)

Crush brains. Make a Béchamel Sauce (recipe 10) with flour, milk, butter; gradually add to crushed brains. Add whole eggs, then egg yolks; season to taste. Pour mixture into buttered mold or pan. Set mold in pan of hot water; bake in slow oven 45 min. Let stand 10 min. before serving. Serve Chivry Sauce separately.

306. FRIED BRAINS
PREPARATION TIME: 20 MIN.   COOKING TIME: 30 MIN.

1½ brains, cooked	3 tbsp. Meat Extract (recipe 881)
6 tbsp. flour	1 tbsp. cream of rice, blended
6⅔ tbsp. Madeira wine	with a little cold water
6⅔ tbsp. Stock (recipe 69)	1 tbsp. chopped parsley
5 tbsp. butter	

Cut brain in 1-in. thick slices; dredge in flour, brown in butter on both sides (about 5 min.). Remove; keep hot. Add meat extract, Madeira and stock to pan; cook 1 min. Add parsley. Bind sauce with cream of rice; nap sliced brains.

307. BRAIN FRITTERS
PREPARATION TIME: 25 MIN.   COOKING TIME: 8 MIN.

2 small calf's or pork brains, cooked, diced	1 lemon, sliced
1½ cups grated Gruyère	½ cup flour
2 eggs, beaten	4 tbsp. butter
	salt, pepper

Combine brains, cheese, flour, beaten eggs; season to taste. Drop mixture by spoonfuls into hot butter; brown. Drain; garnish with lemon slices and serve immediately.

308. BRAIN LOAF

PREPARATION TIME: 25 MIN. COOKING TIME: 3 HOURS.

3 calf's or pork brains, cooked
4 eggs
2 tsp. butter
¾ cup cream

salt, pepper, chopped parsley
fine bread crumbs
Tomato Sauce (recipe 31)

Rub cooked brains through sieve. Combine with eggs, cream, chopped parsley, seasonings. Butter a mold or pan; sprinkle with bread crumbs. Turn brain mixture into pan. Set pan in container of water; bake for 3 hours in very slow oven. Serve with Tomato Sauce.

309. BRAIN SHELLS

PREPARATION TIME: 45 MIN. COOKING TIME: 10 MIN.

3 brains, cooked, diced
¼ lb. mushrooms, diced
2⅔ tbsp. butter

1⅓ cups milk
⅔ cup flour
salt

Make a Béchamel Sauce (recipe 10) with flour, milk, 2 tbsp. butter. Cook mushrooms in a little butter; add to sauce. Season with salt; cook 5 min. Add diced brains; cook 5 min. Distribute mixture evenly in 6 shells or individual baking dishes. Cover with spoonful of Béchamel Sauce, dot with butter. Brown for 10 min. in hot oven.

310. BOILED CALF'S HEAD

COOKING TIME: 6 HOURS.

1 calf's head
¾ cup vinegar
⅔ cup flour
1 med. carrot, sliced

1 med. onion, sliced
2 qts. water
salt, pepper, *bouquet garni*

Soak calf's head for 18 hours in cold water. Bone; secure with string. Cover with cold water; bring to boil, cook 10 min. Plunge immediately into cold water. Blend flour with a little water; combine all ingredients plus 2 qts. water. Cook head 6 hours if whole, 1½-2 hours if in pieces. If desired, serve with a Vinaigrette or Ravigote (recipe 56) Sauce.

311. CALF'S HEAD FRITTERS
PREPARATION TIME: 25 MIN. COOKING TIME: 10 MIN.

Cut cooked head in pieces 1½-2 in. long. Roll in batter for frying (recipe 884), and fry in boiling shortening.

312. CALF'S HEAD EN TORTUE
PREPARATION TIME: 20 MIN. COOKING TIME: 2¼ HOURS.

1 calf's head, cooked	1 tbsp. Tomato Purée
3½ tbsp. butter	(recipe 876)
6⅔ tbsp. Madeira wine	3 gherkins, sliced
⅔ cup flour	basil, thyme, sage, marjoram,
2 cups Stock (recipe 69)	Cayenne pepper

Make a Light Brown Sauce (recipe 30) with butter, flour, stock; cook 30 min. Add tomato purée, seasonings and gherkins. Sprinkle calf's head with Madeira; place in sauce and simmer 20 min.

313. HEART

Turn heart on side to drain any remaining clotted blood. Lard and bard; secure with string. Cook as for Beef à la mode (recipe 241) or Beef à la casserole (recipe 242).

314. BRAISED HEART
PREPARATION TIME: 5 MIN. COOKING TIME: 2 HOURS.

2 calf's hearts	1 small onion, sliced
2½ tbsp. butter	1 med. carrot, cut in strips
6⅔ tbsp. warm Stock (recipe 69)	salt, pepper

Brown onion and hearts in butter. Add carrots, stock, seasonings. Cover and cook gently for 2 hours.

315. HEART IN SAUCE
PREPARATION TIME: 15 MIN. COOKING TIME: 2 HOURS.

2 calf's hearts, cut in small pieces	¾ cup white wine
¼ lb. fresh pork fat or blanched bacon, diced	6⅔ tbsp. tomato paste
2 med. onions	6 mushrooms, peeled, cut in pieces
6 tbsp. flour	4 tbsp. butter or shortening
	salt, pepper

Melt butter or shortening in heavy pot; brown diced fat or

bacon and onions. Add pieces of heart; sprinkle with flour, brown for several min. Add wine, seasoning, a little water; cook gently 1½ hours. Add tomato paste and mushroom pieces; continue cooking 30 min.

316. SAUTÉED HEART
PREPARATION TIME: 5 MIN. COOKING TIME: 15 MIN.

2 calf's hearts, cut in 1½-in. slices	3½ tbsp. butter
	6 tbsp. flour
3 tbsp. brandy	salt, pepper, chopped parsley

Brown heart slices in butter. Sprinkle with flour, chopped parsley, seasonings; continue cooking 10 min. Sprinkle with brandy; ignite. Cook 5 min. longer.

317. STUFFED HEART
PREPARATION TIME: 5 MIN. COOKING TIME: 2 HOURS.

2 calf's hearts	1 small onion
Stuffing (recipe 863)	1 med. carrot
¼ cup diced fresh pork fat or blanched bacon	3½ tbsp. butter
6⅔ tbsp. Madeira wine	bouquet garni

Stuff hearts with stuffing; secure with string. Heat butter in heavy pot; brown diced fat or bacon and onion. Cook gently for 2 hours. If desired, add cooked dried beans after first 1½ hours of cooking.

318. KIDNEYS
Preparation: Halve beef kidneys; split lamb's and veal kidneys, but do not separate completely. Remove white tubes, fat, membranes. Dry thoroughly. Cut in slices; scald 5 min. in boiling water.

319. BREADED KIDNEYS

1¾ lbs. lamb's or veal kidneys	6⅔ tbsp. butter
2 eggs, beaten	fine bread crumbs

Roll kidneys in beaten egg, then in bread crumbs. Fry in very hot butter, 4 min. each side. Serve with any desired sauce.

320. BROILED KIDNEYS
PREPARATION TIME: 15 MIN. COOKING TIME: 6 MIN.

Brush 1¾ lbs. lamb's or veal kidneys with oil; skewer. Broil under high flame, 3 min. each side. Serve with Maître d'hôtel butter (recipe 4).

321. KIDNEYS IN MADEIRA
PREPARATION TIME: 25 MIN. COOKING TIME: 20 MIN.

6 kidneys, sliced	¼ lb. mushrooms, quartered
¾ cup butter	juice of 1 lemon
6 tbsp. flour	¾ cup Stock (recipe 69)
1 small onion	salt, pepper, *fines herbes*
6⅔ tbsp. Madeira wine	

Sauté kidneys 2-4 min. in butter. Remove, keep warm. Brown flour in pan; add stock, then mushrooms, *fines herbes*, onion and seasonings. Cook 15 min. over low heat. Replace kidney slices; add Madeira and lemon juice. Heat for 5 min., being careful not to let sauce boil.

322. KIDNEYS WITH MUSHROOMS
PREPARATION TIME: 25 MIN. COOKING TIME: 1¾ HOURS.

1½ lbs. kidneys, cut in ½-in. slices	½ lb. mushrooms, peeled, cut in pieces
¾ cup Madeira wine	6 slices white bread, fried in butter
6⅔ tbsp. Tomato Purée (recipe 786)	salt, pepper, chopped parsley
6⅔ tbsp. butter	

Cook mushrooms 10 min. in 3½ tbsp. butter. Set aside, reserving cooking liquor. Melt remaining butter; sauté kidney slices 4 min. Remove from pan. Pour Madeira and tomato purée into pan; add flour blended with cooking liquor from mushrooms. Thicken sauce; add kidneys, simmer 1½ hours. Add mushrooms; season to taste, sprinkle with parsley. Serve on slices of bread.

323. SAUTÉED KIDNEYS
COOKING TIME: 2¼ HOURS.

1 lb. beef or veal kidneys, sliced	1 tbsp. chopped shallot
½ cup flour	salt
6⅔ tbsp. butter	Stock (recipe 69)

Brown kidney slices in butter. Sprinkle in flour and chopped shallots; add sufficient stock to make a smooth sauce. Simmer 2 hours.

EGGS WITH LAMB KIDNEYS (EGGS À LA MEYERBEER): See recipe 213.

324. SAUTÉED KIDNEYS IN WHITE WINE
PREPARATION TIME: 20 MIN.   COOKING TIME: 15 MIN.

6 kidneys, sliced	6⅔ tbsp. Stock (recipe 69)
¾ cup white wine	1 small onion, minced
¾ cup butter	chopped parsley

Brown onion in ⅓ cup butter over very low heat. Increase heat to high; add kidneys, sauté 3 min. each side. Remove and keep warm. Pour wine and stock into pan; cover and simmer 15 min. Add remaining butter in small pieces, chopped parsley. Pour sauce over kidneys.

325. LIVER BURGUNDY
PREPARATION TIME: 20 MIN.   COOKING TIME: 1 HOUR.

1¼ lbs. calf's or pork liver	1 cup Burgundy wine
¼ lb. bacon, diced	6⅔ tbsp. butter
¼ lb. small onions	1 tbsp. cornstarch
½ lb. mushrooms	salt, pepper, *bouquet garni*

Lard liver with half the diced bacon. Brown remaining bacon and onions in butter; remove from pan. Brown liver. Add Burgundy, replace bacon and onions; season to taste. Cook over low heat for 45 min. Add mushrooms, continue cooking 15 min. Bind sauce with cornstarch just before serving.

326. BROILED LIVER
PREPARATION TIME: 5 MIN.   COOKING TIME: 10 MIN.

Cut liver in thin slices; brush with oil. Place in pre-heated broiler; broil 5 min. each side. Serve with Maître d'hôtel Butter (recipe 4), Brown Butter (6), or Ravigote Sauce (29).

327. *LIVER À LA CASSEROLE*
PREPARATION TIME: 25 MIN. COOKING TIME: 3 HOURS.

1 lb. beef or calf's liver, larded	1⅓ cups white wine
5 tbsp. butter	1 small onion, chopped
6 tbsp. flour	salt, pepper, thyme, bay leaf

Brown onion in butter; remove from pan. Brown liver; remove. Blend flour into butter remaining in pan; moisten with wine. Replace liver, add seasonings; cook gently 3 hours, basting occasionally. Strain cooking liquid and nap meat just before serving.

328. *LIVER LOAF*
PREPARATION TIME: 30 MIN. COOKING TIME: 2 HOURS.

1 lb. calf's or pork liver, ground	¾ cup cream
¼ lb. butter	4 egg yolks

Combine all ingredients. Butter a mold; sprinkle with bread crumbs; fill with liver mixture. Set mold into pan of water. Bake 2 hours in very slow oven.

329. *PORK LIVER PASTE* (PÂTÉ DE FOIE)
PREPARATION TIME: 30 MIN. COOKING TIME: 2 HOURS.

¾ lb. pork liver, ground	2 eggs
¾ lb. blanched fat salt pork	salt, pepper, nutmeg
or blanched bacon, ground	chopped shallot

Combine all ingredients. Pour mixture into mold; cover tightly. Bake 2 hours in slow oven.

330. *LIVER SOUBISE*
PREPARATION TIME: 30 MIN. COOKING TIME: 2 HOURS.

1¼ lbs. calf's or pork liver, sliced	6⅔ tbsp. butter
¼ lb. bacon, diced	salt, pepper, garlic, thyme,
1¾ lbs. onions, thinly sliced	bay leaf

Brown diced bacon in butter; remove from pan. Brown liver slices over high heat; remove. Place sliced onions and seasonings in pan; cook 1 hour over low flame, or until onions are reduced to a purée. Cover with liver slices; continue cooking 30 min.

331. OX-TAILS

Soak in cold water for 30 min. Remove skin, cut in pieces. Cook 3 hours, according to recipe 69.

332. OX-TAIL STEW (QUEUES DE HOCHEPOT)
PREPARATION TIME: 45 MIN. COOKING TIME: 4 HOURS.

2 lbs. ox-tails, cut in pieces
4 stalks celery
2 small carrots
½ lb. turnip, peeled
1 large onion
2 leeks

3½ tbsp. butter
2 cups white wine
6⅔ tbsp. Stock (recipe 69)
salt, pepper
Horseradish Sauce
(recipe 20 or 21)

Melt butter in heavy pot; brown ox-tails. Add stock, wine, seasonings. Cover and simmer for 3 hours. Add vegetables cut in pieces; continue cooking 1 hour. Arrange ox-tails on serving dish and surround with vegetables; serve Horseradish Sauce separately.

333. PIG'S EARS À LA SAINTE-MENEHOULD
PREPARATION TIME: 15 MIN. COOKING TIME: 2 HOURS.

6 pig's ears
1 qt. Court-bouillon (recipe 868)
4½ tbsp. butter, melted

salt, pepper
fine bread crumbs

Singe ears, clean out thoroughly and wash in several changes of water. Simmer for 2 hours in court-bouillon; chill in liquid. Remove from court-bouillon; roll in bread crumbs. Broil for several minutes under moderate flame, basting with melted butter. Season. Serve hot.

334. BROILED SAUSAGES

Pierce sausages in several places; place on broiling rack. Broil 10 min. under moderate flame, turning frequently.

335. PAN-BROILED SAUSAGES

Pierce sausages; place in skillet with 2⅔ tbsp. butter. Cook 8 min. over high flame. Serve on mashed potatoes, with peas, chestnuts, or Braised Cabbage (recipe 454), or with Rich Rice (recipe 582).

336. SAUSAGES IN WHITE WINE
PREPARATION TIME: 10 MIN.   COOKING TIME: 30 MIN.

pan-broiled sausages, cooked in 4 tbsp. butter
⅓ cup flour

1 onion, minced
6⅔ tbsp. white wine
salt, pepper

Arrange cooked sausages on serving dish; keep warm. Brown onion in remaining butter; slowly pour in flour. Add white wine; season to taste. Cook 30 min. Pour sauce over sausages.

337. SWEETBREADS
Preparation: Soak in cold water for 5 hours. Place in cold Court-bouillon (867), substituting lemon juice for vinegar. Bring to boil; cover and cook gently for 5 min. Remove membrane and cartilage. Wrap sweetbread in clean cloth; cover with board, top with a 4-5 lb. weight. Set aside for at least 1 hour. Proceed with desired recipe.

338. BRAISED SWEETBREADS
PREPARATION TIME: 45 MIN.   COOKING TIME: 1 HOUR.

1½ sweetbreads, cooked and larded
1 med. carrot, sliced
1 med. onion, sliced
¾ cup white wine

3½ tbsp. butter
several strips fresh pork fat or blanched bacon
salt, pepper, *bouquet garni*

Brown onion and carrot slices in butter. Add fat or bacon, seasonings, sweetbreads, wine. Cover and bring to boil; lower heat and cook gently about 50 min. Uncover and brown 5 min. in oven. Nap sweetbreads with strained, thickened cooking liquid.

339. SWEETBREAD CROQUETTES
PREPARATION TIME: 1 HOUR.   COOKING TIME: 5 MIN.

1 sweetbread, cooked, diced
1 whole egg
3 eggs, separated
½ lb. mushrooms
2⅔ tbsp. butter

½ cup flour
juice of 1 lemon
¾ cup milk
shortening for frying

Make White Sauce (recipe 8 or 9) with butter, flour, milk. Add whole egg, 3 egg yolks, lemon juice. Cook mushrooms 20 min. in boiling salted water; add to sauce. Season to taste. Add diced sweetbread. Chill. Form mixture into croquettes; roll in egg white, then in flour. Brown in very hot shortening.

340. SWEETBREADS NIÇOISE
PREPARATION TIME: 30 MIN. COOKING TIME: 1½ HOURS.

1½ sweetbreads, cooked, larded	1 med. onion
4 tbsp. butter	1 cup Tomato Sauce (recipe 31)
8 oz. black olives, pitted	salt, pepper, *bouquet garni*

Brown sweetbreads in butter. Add onions and seasonings; cook over low heat 1 hour. Add olives and tomato sauce; simmer 30 min.

341. SAUTÉED SWEETBREADS
PREPARATION TIME: 30 MIN. COOKING TIME: 15 MIN.

1 sweetbread, sliced, cooked	chopped parsley
4 tbsp. butter	

Brown sweetbread slices in butter, 5 min. each side. Cover and cook 5 min. Sprinkle with chopped parsley and butter remaining in pan. If preferred, serve with any desired sauce.

342. SWEETBREADS VALOIS
PREPARATION TIME: 20 MIN. COOKING TIME: 20 MIN.

1½ sweetbreads, cooked, sliced	1 small truffle, sliced
½ lb. mushrooms, sliced	juice of 1 lemon
¼ lb. butter	Mousseline Sauce (recipe 65)

Cook mushrooms in lemon juice. Add mushrooms, butter and truffle slices to Mousseline Sauce; serve with sweetbread slices.

343. BEEF OR CALF'S TONGUE
Soak tongue for 24 hours in cold water. Scrub vigorously with brush. Cook for 20 min. in boiling water; plunge immediately into cold water. Remove skin, bones and gristle.

344. SHEEP'S TONGUE

Soak tongue for 2 hours in cold water. Cook in hot water 10 min. Remove skin, bones and gristle.

345. BOILED TONGUE

Place prepared tongue in cold court-bouillon (recipe 867 or 868). Cook 3 hours over low flame. Slice tongue, either lengthwise or crosswise on the bias, into ½-in. slices. Serve with Capers (recipe 28), Soubise (19), Piquant (41) or Tomato (31) Sauce. Accompany with Chestnut (470) or Lentil (502) Purée.

346. BRAISED SHEEP'S TONGUES

PREPARATION TIME: 30 MIN. COOKING TIME: 2 HOURS.

4 sheep's tongues	¼ lb. onions, sliced
¼ lb. fresh pork fat or	2 cups Stock (recipe 69)
blanched bacon, diced	salt, pepper
2 carrots, sliced	

Line bottom of heavy pot with diced fat or bacon, sliced carrots and onions; place prepared tongues in pot. Add stock and seasonings. Bring to boil; lower heat, cook 2 hours. Halve tongues lengthwise; arrange on serving dish and baste with cooking liquid. May be served with Capers (recipe 28), Piquant (41) or Tomato (31) Sauce. If desired, serve with kidney beans, lentils, chestnuts, sorrel or spinach.

347. TONGUE À LA CASSEROLE

PREPARATION TIME: 40 MIN. COOKING TIME: 3 HOURS.

1 beef or calf's tongue	2 small onions
4 tbsp. shortening	1 heaping tbsp. cornstarch
¾ cup white wine	salt, pepper

Cook tongue for 2 hours, following recipe 345. Drain and dry. Brown onions and tongue on all sides in hot shortening. Add wine and seasoning; simmer gently 1 hour. Strain cooking liquid and bind with cornstarch; nap meat.

348. TONGUE À L'ITALIENNE
PREPARATION TIME: 1 HOUR. COOKING TIME: 4½ HOURS.

1 beef or calf's tongue	½ lb. macaroni, cooked
¾ cup white wine	2 cups grated Gruyère
¾ cup Stock (recipe 69)	6 small Stuffed Tomatoes
1 onion, sliced	(recipe 554)
1 carrot, sliced	salt, pepper
¼ lb. blanched bacon strips	

Cook tongue 1½ hours, following recipe 345. Line heavy pot with strips of bacon, onions, carrots; place tongue in pot. Add wine, stock, seasonings. Cover tightly; bake in slow oven for 2½ hours. Arrange slices of cooked tongue on serving dish; surround with cooked macaroni mixed with grated Gruyère, stuffed tomatoes. Strain and skim grease off cooking liquid; serve separately.

349. TRIPE

Wash, scrub and scrape tripe. Soak for 4 hours in cold water. Drain. Cover with large quantity of cold salted water; cook gently for at least 5 hours. If desired, add carrots, onion, white wine, pepper and cloves to water.

Cooked tripe may be sliced and simmered for 20 min. in Béchamel (recipe 10), Poulette (recipe 15), Piquant (recipe 14) or Tomato (recipe 31) Sauce. Or chill, slice thinly and serve as a salad, with Vinaigrette (recipe 56), Ravigote (recipe 56) or Deviled (recipe 68) Sauce.

350. TRIPE À LA LYONNAISE
PREPARATION TIME: 20 MIN. COOKING TIME: 15 MIN.

1 lb. cooked tripe, thinly sliced	6⅔ tbsp. vinegar
¼ lb. onions, finely chopped	chopped parsley
6⅔ tbsp. oil	

Brown chopped onions in hot oil. Add tripe; continue cooking 15 min. Just before serving, moisten with vinegar, sprinkle with chopped parsley.

351. *TRIPE À LA MODE*
PREPARATION TIME: 35 MIN. COOKING TIME: 8 HOURS.

2 lbs. cooked tripe	⅔ cup butter
1½ cups bread crumbs	chopped scallion, parsley and
4 med. onions, minced	*fines herbes*
2 tsp. minced shallot	salt, pepper
1¾ cups white wine	

Line an earthenware terrine with alternating layers of tripe and stuffing made with onion, shallot, scallion, bread crumbs, *fines herbes;* season with salt and pepper. Finish with wine; dot with bits of butter. Cover and bake 6-8 hours in very slow oven.

352. *SHEEP'S TROTTERS*
Soak trotter in cold water for 12 hours. Cook 10 min. in boiling water. Remove bone.

353. *BOILED TROTTERS*
PREPARATION TIME: 10 MIN. COOKING TIME: 4 HOURS.

12 sheep's trotters	1 med. onion
3 qts. water	salt, pepper, cloves, thyme,
¾ cup flour	bay leaf
¾ cup vinegar	

Blend flour with a little water; combine with remaining ingredients except trotters. Bring liquid to boil. Add trotters; lower heat and simmer gently 4 hours. Serve with Poulette (recipe 15), Pepper (recipe 49) or Tomato (recipe 31) Sauce.

MEAT PASTRIES, PATTY SHELLS, ETC.

354. *VOL-AU-VENT (FILLED PATTY SHELLS)*
PREPARATION TIME: 10 MIN. COOKING TIME: 35 MIN.

Puff Paste (recipe 800)	1 tsp. butter
1 egg yolk, beaten with a little water	

Roll out pastry to thickness of about 1 in. Cut out circles 5-7 in. in diameter; brush tops with beaten egg yolk. With tip of knife, trace circle inside of pastry rounds, about 1 in. from edge (do not cut too deeply). Score top with a few criss-cross lines. This will be the cover of the patty. Place pastry rounds on buttered cooky sheet; bake in very hot oven 35 min. or until brown. Detach cover; remove any flakes of pastry from inside. Fill shell with desired filling (creamed meat, fish, etc.); replace cover, serve immediately.

355. BOUCHÉE À LA REINE

Proceed as for Vol-au-vent, but circle should be 2-2½ in. in diameter. Fill with Financière Sauce (recipe 32).

356. MEAT PIE (TOURTE À LA VIANDE)
PREPARATION TIME: 10 MIN. COOKING TIME: 35 MIN.

Puff Paste (recipe 800)
½ cup leftover meat, chopped
¼ cup chopped ham
¼ cup chopped fresh pork fat
or blanched bacon
½ cup fresh bread crumbs,
soaked in 1½ tsp. milk

2 eggs
salt, pepper, *fines herbes*
truffles and cooked
mushrooms, if desired

Line pie tin with half the pastry. Fill with mixture of remaining ingredients. Roll out remaining pastry dough for use as top crust. Bake pie for 35 min. in hot oven. If preferred, this mixture can be used to fill Vol-au-vent.

357. FRIANDS (SAUSAGE ROLLS)
PREPARATION TIME: 10 MIN. COOKING TIME: 30 MIN.

Roll out Puff Paste (recipe 800) to thickness of ¼ in.; cut into rectangles about 1½ in. x 3 in. Place a sausage on rectangle; cover with another rectangle. Press edges together with a little water to seal. Bake 30 min. in very hot oven.

357A. ANCHOVY FEUILLANTINES: Substitute anchovy fillets for sausages.

358. PÂTÉ EN CROÛTE (FILLED PASTRY SHELL)
PREPARATION TIME: 1½ HOURS.   COOKING TIME: 2 HOURS.

6 cups flour
¾ cup butter, in small pieces
¾ cup water
2 tsp. salt
Stuffing (recipe 863)

½ lb. fresh pork fat or
    blanched bacon
½ lb. ham
½ lb. veal, thinly sliced
1 egg yolk, beaten with a little
    water

Heap up flour; make a depression in top, fill with salt and butter. Moisten with water. Using hands, work dough into a ball; knead with palm of hand. Repeat kneading operation three times. Set dough aside for 12 hours. Roll out half the pastry; line a pie plate, letting pastry protrude 1 in. above edge. Fill with alternating layers of fat, stuffing, ham, veal; repeat in reverse order. Roll out remaining pastry; cover pie, pinching edges together. Brush with beaten egg yolk. Bake 1½-2 hours in hot oven.

RISSOLES (PETITS PÂTÉS): See recipe 803.

SOUFFLÉED RISSOLES (PETITS PÂTÉS SOUFFLÉS): See recipe 804.

LEFTOVERS

Sliced Meat in Sauce

Roast Beef—Heat thin slices gently (do not boil) in a Mushroom (recipe 43), Piquant (41) or Tomato (31) Sauce.
    Serve cold slices with Tartare Sauce (recipe 63) or Mayonnaise (60).
Boiled Beef—Heat slices in one of above sauces. Or pan-broil in 2½ tbsp. butter, 2 min. each side.
Lamb—Heat slices gently in Piquant (recipe 41), Tomato (31) or Poor Man's (3) Sauce.
    Serve cold slices with Tartare Sauce (recipe 63) or Mayonnaise.

Veal—Simmer slices for 10 min. in Tomato (recipe 31), Richelieu (33), Poulette (15) or Soubise (19) Sauce.
Serve cold slices with Mayonnaise (recipe 60), garnished with parsley and gherkins.

Pork—Heat slices for 10 min. in Piquant (recipe 41), Mustard (57) or Tomato (31) Sauce.
Serve cold slices with Mayonnaise (recipe 60), garnished with parsley and gherkins.

359. BEEF MIROTON
PREPARATION TIME: 10 MIN. COOKING TIME: 15 MIN.

Prepare a Dark Brown Sauce (recipe 40). Pour half the sauce into a flat baking dish; arrange slices of cold beef on top. Nap with remaining sauce. Heat 15 min. in hot oven.

360. BEEF À LA PERSILLADE
PREPARATION TIME: 20 MIN. COOKING TIME: 30 MIN.

12 slices cooked beef	6⅔ tbsp. vinegar
¼ cup flour	2⅔ tbsp. butter
1 tbsp. mustard	2 tbsp. chopped parsley
¾ cup warm Stock (recipe 69)	salt, pepper

Marinate slices of beef for 30 min. in mixture of vinegar, salt, pepper. Melt butter; sprinkle with flour, cook until brown. Add hot stock and vinegar marinade, then parsley and mustard. Nap sliced meat with sauce.

361. FRIED BEEF
PREPARATION TIME: 10 MIN. COOKING TIME: 5 MIN.

12 slices cooked beef	Batter for Frying (recipe 884)
6⅔ tbsp. oil	shortening for frying
6⅔ tbsp. vinegar	

Marinate meat for 30 min. in mixture of oil and vinegar. Roll in batter. Brown in boiling shortening.

362. *STUFFED PANCAKES*
PREPARATION TIME: 35 MIN. COOKING TIME: 8 MIN.

12 small Pancakes (recipe 733)	3½ tbsp. butter
½ lb. veal	¾ cup fresh bread crumbs,
¼ lb. ham	soaked in 6⅔ tbsp. milk
¼ lb. mushrooms	salt, pepper, *fines herbes*

Chop together veal, ham, mushrooms, bread crumbs; season to taste. Place spoonful of mixture in center of each pancake; roll up. Place rolls in baking dish; dot with butter. Heat 8 min. in hot oven. If desired, nap with a White Sauce (recipe 8 or 9) seasoned with a little grated Gruyère; heat for 10 min.

363. *LAMB ÉMINCÉ*
PREPARATION TIME: 10 MIN. COOKING TIME: 20 MIN.

1 lb. cooked lamb, thinly sliced	6 tbsp. flour
1⅓ cups warm Stock (recipe 69)	1 tsp. chopped shallot
3½ tbsp. butter	sliced gherkins

Heat lamb in top of double boiler. Prepare a Dark Brown Sauce (recipe 40) with flour, butter, stock; add shallots and sliced gherkins. Nap meat with sauce.

364. *LAMB STEW* (MOUTON EN HOCHEPOT)
PREPARATION TIME: 45 MIN. COOKING TIME: 1¾ HOURS.

1¾ lbs. cooked lamb, cut in pieces	¼ lb. potatoes, peeled
2 stalks celery	¾ cup Stock (recipe 69)
4 med. carrots	4 tbsp. butter
¼ lb. turnip, peeled	6 tbsp. flour
	salt, pepper, *bouquet garni*

Cut vegetables in pieces. Brown lamb in butter; remove from pan. Make a Dark Brown Sauce (recipe 40) with flour, butter remaining in pan, stock; season to taste. Replace meat; cook gently for 30 min. Add vegetables; simmer 1½ hours.

365. MEAT BALLS

PREPARATION TIME: 30 MIN.   COOKING TIME: 5 MIN.

1½ cups finely chopped, cooked veal or pork	1¾ cups Stock (recipe 69) fine bread crumbs
3 eggs	salt
2 tbsp. butter	shortening for frying
½ cup flour	

Make a White Sauce (recipe 8 or 9) with butter, flour, stock; season with salt. Add meat and 2 eggs; heat but do not boil, stirring constantly. Chill. Form mixture into small balls; roll in remaining beaten egg, then in bread crumbs. Brown in boiling oil. Serve with Fried Parsley (recipe 874) or with Tomato Sauce (recipe 31).

366. CROQUETTES

PREPARATION TIME: 45 MIN.   COOKING TIME: 5 MIN.

1½ cups chopped cooked meat	2 tbsp. butter
1¾ cups fresh bread crumbs, soaked in 6⅔ tbsp. warm milk	⅔ cup flour
	1 egg
¼ lb. bacon, chopped	chopped parsley
1 med. onion, chopped	shortening for frying

Cook onion in butter. Combine chopped meat, bacon, onion, bread crumbs, chopped parsley; bind with egg. Form mixture into small balls; dredge in flour. Brown in very hot shortening. Serve with Fried Parsley (recipe 874).

367. HASH PARMENTIER

PREPARATION TIME: 1 HOUR.   COOKING TIME: 35 MIN.

Line a buttered baking dish with layer of mashed potatoes. Top with layer of croquette mixture (recipe 366); finish with another layer of mashed potatoes. Sprinkle with grated Gruyère or fine bread crumbs; dot with butter. Brown 20 min. in hot oven.

368. MEAT LOAF

PREPARATION TIME: 30 MIN.   COOKING TIME: 40 MIN.

1 cup chopped cooked meat	2⅔ tbsp. butter
1⅓ cups milk	3 eggs, separated
½ cup flour	salt, pepper

Make a White Sauce (recipe 8 or 9) with milk, butter, flour; season. Add chopped meat and egg yolks; fold in stiffly beaten egg whites. Pour mixture into well-buttered pan or mold. Bake 40 min. in moderate oven.

369. POTTED MEAT
PREPARATION TIME: 20 MIN.

1 cup ground cooked meat	salt, pepper, nutmeg
½ lb. butter	lard or goose fat
1½ tsp. Anchovy Sauce	
(recipe 23)	

Cream butter with ground meat; add sauce and seasoning. Place mixture in earthenware terrine. Cover with layer of lard or goose fat. Will keep for 5-6 days.

Leftover Ham: See the following recipes:
Cheese Ramekins (230)   Stewed Macaroni (570)
Lentils à la Dijonnaise (500) Stuffed Macaroni (569)
Macaroni Loaf (567)   Neapolitan Croquettes (568)
Macaroni Niçois (565)

Leftover Tongue: See recipe for Stewed Macaroni (570).

Other recipes for leftovers:
Canneloni (574)   Meat Pie (356)
Mother Mary's Lettuce (592)   Ravioli (575)
Gratin of Egg Plant (479)   Rice Jambalaya (587)
Poor Man's Meat Pie (896)   Rissoles (803)

Poultry and Rabbit

N.B.: All recipes serve 6, unless otherwise indicated.

How to prepare bird for roasting

Be sure carcass has been completely emptied and cleaned. Singe off any remaining down and hairs by holding over flame.

Truss bird. Fold wings back and press tips against back. Press thighs close to the body. Tie the ends of the legs together; bring string down around tail of bird. Turn bird over on breast; bring each end of string forward over breast and tip of one wing, then across back. Tie ends in middle of back Bird may be skewered, if preferred.

If bird is young, or not very fat, cover chest with thin sheet of fat; secure with string.

How to cut up bird

Insert fork in thigh and lift away from body. Cut skin between thigh and body; remove leg. Insert fork under wing, lift away from body and cut skin joining wing to body. Slice breast meat downward from ridge of breastbone.

DUCK AND DUCKLING

Duckling is a bird aged from 6 weeks to 3 months; the duck ranges from 4 months to one year old. The meat is difficult to digest, and should be thoroughly cooked.

370. ROAST DUCK

Brush cleaned and dressed duck with melted butter. Roast in hot oven (or on a spit), 20 min. per lb. for duck, 12 min. for duckling.

371. DUCK À L'ORANGE
COOKING TIME FOR SAUCE: 20 MIN.

1 duck, roasted	⅓ cup flour
⅓ cup Curaçao	1½ tsp. Meat Extract
6⅔ tbsp. veal Stock (recipe 69)	(recipe 880)
2 oranges	salt, pepper
3½ tbsp. butter	

Peel one orange, reserving rind. Cut orange sections in pieces and place inside duck while roasting.

Chop rind finely; scald 10 min. in boiling water. Drain; mash together with duck's liver. Moisten with Curaçao. Combine stock, meat extract, butter blended with flour, orange rind. Bring to boil, then strain through fine strainer.

Place cooked duck on serving dish; remove orange stuffing. Garnish with fresh orange quarters; serve sauce separately.

372. BRAISED DUCK
PREPARATION TIME: 10 MIN. COOKING TIME: 2 HOURS.

1 duck, cleaned and dressed	2⅔ tbsp. butter
¾ cup Stock (recipe 69)	1⅓ tbsp. cornstarch
juice of 1 lemon	salt, pepper

Melt butter in heavy pot. Brown trussed bird on all sides. Add stock and seasonings. Cover tightly and bake in slow oven or cook over low heat for 2 hours. Strain cooking liquid; bind with cornstarch, add lemon juice. Serve sauce separately.

372A. BRAISED DUCK WITH OLIVES: Ten min. before serving, add ½ lb. olives to sauce. Nap bird with sauce, surround with olives.

372B. BRAISED DUCK WITH ONIONS: Cook ¾ lb. small onions for 20 min. in boiling salted water. Brown for 10 min. in 4 tbsp. butter. Sprinkle with sugar; brown 5 min. in oven. Use to garnish duck.

372C. BRAISED DUCK WITH PEAS: Cook 2 lbs. peas (see recipe 516) for 40 min. Add to duck during last 15 min. of cooking.

372D. BRAISED DUCK WITH TURNIP: Peel 1¾ lbs. turnip, cut in small balls or slices. Cook 10 min. in boiling salted water; drain. Brown in 4 tbsp. butter; cover and cook 1½ hours. Add turnip to sauce after binding; heat for 10 min.

373. DUCKLING WITH TARRAGON
PREPARATION TIME: 25 MIN. COOKING TIME: 1¼ HOURS.

2 ducklings, cleaned and prepared
3½ tbsp. butter
¾ cup Stock (recipe 69)
1⅓ tbsp. cornstarch
1 sprig tarragon
1 tbsp. chopped tarragon
salt, pepper

Brown ducklings in butter. Add stock, sprig of tarragon, salt and pepper; cover and simmer 1¼ hours. Strain cooking liquid, bind with cornstarch; add chopped tarragon.

TURKEY

374. ROAST TURKEY
PREPARATION TIME: 15 MIN. COOKING TIME: 2 HOURS.

Roast in hot oven, 20 min. per lb. If desired, wrap in foil to slow down browning process. Serve with gravy made by deglazing roasting pan with a little hot water. Garnish with watercress.

375. ROAST TURKEY WITH CHESTNUT STUFFING

PREPARATION TIME: 45 MIN. COOKING TIME: 3 HOURS.

1 turkey, about 6 lbs.	1 turkey liver
¼ lb. veal	¼ lb. pork
¼ lb. fresh pork fat or	1¾ lbs. chestnuts, shelled
blanched bacon	1 tsp. minced shallot, cooked
3 cups Stock (recipe 69)	in butter

Chop together veal, pork fat, turkey liver. Cook chestnuts 25 min. in stock; rub through fine sieve. Combine all ingredients. Stuff turkey; roast.

376. BRAISED TURKEY

PREPARATION TIME: 45 MIN. COOKING TIME: 3 HOURS.

1 turkey, about 6 lbs.	6⅔ tbsp. butter
several small carrots	6⅔ tbsp. brandy
2 cups Stock (recipe 69)	salt, pepper
1 or 2 small onions	

Heat butter in heavy pot; brown trussed bird on all sides. Add carrots, onions, stock and seasonings. Cover and cook slowly for 1 hour. Add brandy; ignite. Continue cooking 1½-2 hours.

377. BRAISED TURKEY À LA FLAMANDE

PREPARATION TIME: 1 HOUR. COOKING TIME: 3 HOURS.

1 turkey, braised	1⅓ cups Stock (recipe 69)
6 heads lettuce, halved	6⅔ tbsp. cooking liquid
½ cup flour	from turkey
2 tbsp. butter	salt, pepper

Cook lettuce 20 min. in boiling salted water; drain. Prepare a White Sauce (recipe 8 or 9) with flour, butter, stock and cooking liquid from turkey, seasonings. Cook lettuce in sauce 30 min. over low heat. Cut braised turkey in pieces; add to lettuce, and arrange on serving dish.

378. TURKEY WITH SAUSAGE

PREPARATION TIME: 15 MIN. COOKING TIME: 2 HOURS.

1 small turkey, cut in pieces	6⅔ tbsp. butter
¼ lb. bacon, sliced	½ lb. sausages
½ cup flour	2 cups warm Stock (recipe 69)
1 lb. chestnuts, shelled	salt, pepper

Brown pieces of turkey in half the butter. Sprinkle with flour; add stock. Add diced bacon, seasonings; cook 45 min. Add chestnuts; continue cooking 1¼ hours. Brown sausages in remaining butter; add to turkey. Continue cooking 10 min.

GOOSE

A tasty bird, but difficult to digest due to its high proportion of fat. May be roasted as for turkey (see recipe 374), stuffed with chestnut stuffing (see recipe 375) or with 2 lbs. potatoes peeled and quartered. Do not lard bird.

379. GOOSE STEW
PREPARATION TIME: 25 MIN. COOKING TIME: 2½ HOURS.

2 lbs. goose, cut in pieces
⅔ cup flour
1¾ cups warm Stock (recipe 69)
½ lb. turnip, peeled, cut in pieces
3½ tbsp. butter

6⅔ tbsp. white wine
¾ lb. carrots, cut in pieces
¾ lb. potatoes, peeled and quartered
salt, pepper, *bouquet garni*

Heat butter; brown pieces of goose, carrots, turnips. Sprinkle in flour; brown. Add stock and seasonings; cook gently for 1 hour. Add potatoes; continue cooking 1½ hours. Remove *bouquet garni* before serving.

GOOSE LIVER (FOIE GRAS D'OIE)
PREPARATION:
First method: Separate liver into two halves; carefully remove gall. Soak 30 min. in cold water; then scald 5 min. in boiling water.
Second method: Remove gall; soak liver for 6 hours in salted water (2 tsp. salt per quart of water). Melt small quantity of butter or goose fat over low heat; add liver, salt, pepper, bay leaf, clove. Cook gently 30 min. Liver prepared in this way can be kept for about 2 weeks.

380. *GOOSE LIVER IN ASPIC*

Prepare a Meat Jelly according to recipe 881. Rinse an earthenware terrine in cold water. Pour in a layer of jelly. When it begins to set, add prepared goose liver. Cover with jelly. Chill overnight.

381. *GOOSE LIVER POACHED IN MADEIRA*
PREPARATION TIME: 5 MIN. COOKING TIME: 30 MIN.

1¾ lbs. goose liver,
   prepared, sliced
1⅓ cups warm Madeira wine

1⅓ cups warm stock (recipe 69)
salt, pepper
truffles, if desired

Arrange goose liver slices in baking dish; sprinkle with salt and pepper, add truffles. Cover with stock and Madeira. Bake 30 min. in moderate oven, basting frequently. If desired, serve on slices of bread fried in butter. May also be used in the preparation of Goose Liver in Aspic.

382. *GOOSE LIVER MOUSSE*
PREPARATION TIME: 20 MIN.

½ lb. goose liver
6⅔ tbsp. butter
¾ cup cream, whipped

3 oz. truffles
salt, pepper
baked Tart Shells (recipe 796)

Pound and crush together liver, butter, truffles. Add whipped cream, salt, pepper. Pour mixture into baked tart shells.

SQUAB

383. *ROAST SQUAB*
PREPARATION TIME: 15 MIN. COOKING TIME: 30 MIN.

Clean, dress and truss squab; salt interior. Wrap in sheet of fat, or cover with strips of fat or blanched bacon. Roast 25-30 min. at 375°F. Cut in half or in quarters. If desired, serve with Mushroom Sauce (recipe 43).

May be stuffed with stuffing 860, or with mixture of chopped liver and gizzard and bread crumbs soaked in milk, the whole bound with an egg.

384. SQUAB À LA CRAPAUDINE
PREPARATION TIME: 20 MIN.   COOKING TIME: 20 MIN. + 20 MIN.

3 squab	salt, pepper
4 tbsp. butter	melted butter
bread crumbs	Crapaudine Sauce (recipe 67)

Split squab down the back; flatten slightly. (Liver and lungs may be left in.) Cook slowly in butter without browning, 10 min. each side. Remove from pan; cool. When cold, roll in melted butter, then in bread crumbs; broil 20 min. under low flame. Serve with Crapaudine Sauce made with same butter used for cooking squab.

385. SQUAB WITH PEAS
PREPARATION TIME: 1 HOUR.   COOKING TIME: 50 MIN.

3 squab, cleaned and dressed	3½ tbsp. butter
2 lbs. peas, shelled	salt, pepper
¼ lb. fresh pork fat or blanched bacon, diced	

Brown diced fat and squab in butter; add a little water. Add peas, seasonings. Cover tightly and cook gently 50 min.

CHICKEN

386. COQ AU VIN (CHICKEN IN WINE SAUCE)
PREPARATION TIME: 25 MIN.   COOKING TIME: 1 HOUR.

1 young chicken, about 3 lbs., cut in pieces	6⅔ tbsp. brandy
3 tbsp. oil	2 cloves garlic, minced
3½ tbsp. butter	2 cups red Burgundy wine
1 small onion	¼ lb. bacon, diced
⅔ cup flour	⅓ lb. mushrooms, cooked
2 small onions cooked in butter	salt, pepper

Heat together butter and oil; brown chicken pieces and

small onion. Sprinkle with flour and brandy; ignite. Add wine and seasonings; cook 1 hour. Chill overnight. To serve, heat over low flame, adding diced bacon, 2 small onions, mushrooms. Garnish with Potato Straws (recipe 526B).

387. *CHICKEN IN WHITE SAUCE*
PREPARATION TIME: 20 MIN. COOKING TIME: 1¼ HOURS.

1 chicken, 2½-3 lbs.	juice of 1 lemon
4 tbsp. butter	6⅔ tbsp. white wine
2 or 3 small onions	1½ qts. water
⅔ cup flour	salt, *bouquet garni*
2 egg yolks	

Soak chicken in cold water for 2 hours. Prepare a court-bouillon (recipe 868) with water, onions, wine, *bouquet garni;* chill. Place chicken in court-bouillon, season with salt; cook gently 1 hour. Strain court-bouillon. Blend flour and butter, add sufficient court-bouillon to make a smooth sauce. Bind with egg yolks; finish with lemon juice. Arrange chicken on serving dish; nap with sauce.

387A. *CHICKEN IN OYSTER SAUCE:* Add ¼ lb. mushrooms, cut in pieces and cooked in butter for 5 min., to sauce. Open 2 doz. oysters; place with their liquid in casserole and heat until liquid begins to boil. Season to taste. Add oysters to sauce together with 2-3 tbsp. of their liquid.

388. *CHICKEN BLANQUETTE*
Cut chicken in pieces. Proceed as for Veal Blanquette (recipe 250).

CHICKEN À LA COMTOISE: See recipe 904.

389. *CHICKEN FRICASSEE*
PREPARATION TIME: 25 MIN. COOKING TIME: 1 HOUR.

1 chicken, cut in pieces	½ cup mushrooms, in pieces
1 med. carrot, sliced	2 egg yolks
1 med. onion, sliced	juice of 1 lemon
4 tbsp. butter	1½ qts. water
¾ cup white wine	salt, pepper, *bouquet garni*

Soak chicken pieces for 30 min. in cold water; drain. Place in cold water with carrot, onion, *bouquet garni;* bring to boil, cook 20 min. Drain and dry chicken pieces. Melt butter; cook chicken slightly, without browning. Add wine and ¾ cup of liquid in which chicken was cooked; season to taste. Bring to boil; lower heat, simmer 35 min. Remove chicken pieces; keep warm. Strain sauce and reduce it by boiling to one-third its original volume. Add mushroom pieces. Bind sauce with egg yolks; finish with lemon juice. Arrange pieces of chicken on serving dish; cover with sauce. Surround with rice and mushrooms.

390. CHICKEN "QUO VADIS?"
PREPARATION TIME: 50 MIN. COOKING TIME: 45 MIN.

1 chicken, about 2 lbs.	4 tbsp. butter
chicken liver and gizzard	2 tsp. mustard
1 large sprig tarragon, chopped	2 or 3 small onions
6⅔ tbsp. cream	3 egg yolks
¾ cup flour	Stock (recipe 69)
1½ cups bread crumbs	salt, pepper

Chop liver and gizzard finely; combine with bread crumbs, tarragon, salt and pepper. Cook mixture 5 min. in 1⅓ tbsp. butter. Stuff chicken with mixture; sew up opening and truss bird. Place bird in heavy pot together with onions; cover with stock. Cook gently 30 min. Using remaining butter, flour, ¾ of the stock, make a Dark Brown Sauce (recipe 40); chill. Blend egg yolks and cream, add to cold sauce; add 1 tbsp. chopped tarragon. Thicken sauce in top of double boiler. Add mustard just before serving. Nap chicken with sauce.

391. ROAST CHICKEN
PREPARATION TIME: 15 MIN. COOKING TIME: 20 MIN. PER LB.

Truss bird. Bard, or dot with bits of butter. Roast 20 min. per lb. in hot oven, turning and basting from time to time. Serve with a garnish of watercress. Serve with gravy made by deglazing pan with hot water.

Chicken may also be roasted on a spit. Truss bird and

brush with melted butter; impale on spit. Cook 20 min. per lb., turning every 8 min. and basting with butter.

392. CHICKEN À LA CASSEROLE
PREPARATION TIME: 5 MIN. COOKING TIME: 30 MIN. PER LB.

Brown chicken in 2⅔ tbsp. butter; season with salt. Cover and cook gently 30 min. per lb. Before serving, uncover and brown over high heat. Serve with gravy made by deglazing pot.

392A. CHICKEN CHASSEUR:
Cook ½ lb. mushrooms and 2 or 3 small onions for 25 min. in 3½ tbsp. butter. Add to chicken during last 15 min. of cooking.

392B. CHICKEN À LA CRÈME:
Add ¼ lb. mushrooms, in pieces, to chicken after first hour of cooking. Make a White Sauce (recipe 8 or 9) with 4 tbsp. butter, 6 tbsp. flour, 2 cups milk, salt and pepper; add cooking liquid from chicken. Cut chicken in pieces and arrange on serving dish; nap with sauce.

393. CHICKEN WITH CHESTNUT STUFFING
PREPARATION TIME: 30 MIN. COOKING TIME: 1¼ HOURS.

Shell ¾ lb. chestnuts and cook in boiling salted water with 2 tbsp. butter for 25 min. Crush, reserving a few; add 6⅔ tbsp. each milk and Meat Extract (recipe 881), 1⅓ tbsp. butter, whole chestnut meats. Stuff 2-lb. chicken. Truss, bard and roast.

394. CHICKEN VILLEROY
PREPARATION TIME: 20 MIN. COOKING TIME: 55 MIN.

1 chicken, about 2½ lbs., roasted	2 egg yolks
	fine bread crumbs
3½ tbsp. butter	shortening for frying
⅔ cup flour	Madeira Sauce (recipe 42)
2 cups water	salt, pepper

Cut roasted chicken into pieces. Prepare a thick White

Sauce (recipe 8 or 9) with butter, flour, water; add egg yolks, season to taste. Roll chicken pieces in sauce, then in bread crumbs, and fry in hot shortening. Serve with sauce.

395. CHICKEN EN COCOTTE
PREPARATION TIME: 10 MIN. COOKING TIME: 1 HOUR.

1 chicken, trussed	2 small onions
¼ lb. mushrooms, cut in pieces	2⅔ tbsp. butter
¼ lb. fresh pork fat or blanched bacon, diced	6⅔ tbsp. white wine
	salt, pepper

Cook diced fat and onions in butter until golden; remove. Brown chicken; replace fat and onions, add wine and seasonings. Cover tightly; cook in slow oven or over low heat for 1 hour, adding mushrooms during last 20 min. of cooking.

396. CHICKEN WITH TARRAGON
PREPARATION TIME: 45 MIN. COOKING TIME: 40 MIN.

1 chicken, about 2 lbs.	1½ tsp. brandy
1 chicken liver	4 tbsp. butter
¼ lb. veal	1⅓ tbsp. cornstarch
¼ lb. pork	2 or 3 small onions
½ lb. bacon, diced	salt, pepper, tarragon

Stuff chicken with mixture of chopped chicken liver, pork, veal, half the bacon, brandy and chopped tarragon; truss bird. Cook onions and remaining bacon in butter; remove. Brown chicken; replace bacon and onion, add seasonings and sprig of tarragon. Cover and cook over low heat for 40 min. Strain cooking liquid; bind with cornstarch, add some chopped tarragon. Serve sauce separately.

397. POULET PAPRIKA
PREPARATION TIME: 10 MIN. COOKING TIME: 1¼ HOURS.

1 chicken, about 2 lbs. cut in pieces	¾ cup stock
	¼ tsp. paprika
3½ tbsp. butter	2 cups cream

Brown chicken pieces in butter. Add stock; cover and cook in slow oven for 1 hour. Blend cream with cooking liquid; add paprika. Nap chicken with sauce.

398. *SAUTÉED CHICKEN*

PREPARATION TIME: 10 MIN. COOKING TIME: 1 HOUR.

1 chicken, about 2½ lbs., cut
   in pieces
⅔ cup flour
3½ tbsp. butter
¼ lb. mushrooms, cut in pieces

¾ cup Stock (recipe 69)
6⅔ tbsp. brandy
2 or 3 small onions, browned in
   butter
salt, pepper, *bouquet garni*

Brown chicken pieces in butter. Sprinkle in flour; add stock and brandy, ignite. Add onions and seasonings. Cover and cook gently 30 min. Add mushrooms, continue cooking 20 min. Nap chicken with sauce.

399. *CHICKEN MARENGO*

PREPARATION TIME: 20 MIN. COOKING TIME: 1¾ HOURS.

1 chicken, about 2½ lbs., cut in
   pieces
1½ tsp. oil
2 tbsp butter
½ cup flour
1 tbsp. chopped shallot

¾ cup Stock (recipe 69)
¾ cup white wine
½ lb. mushrooms, cut in pieces
3 tbsp. tomato purée (recipe
   876)
chopped parsley

Heat together oil and butter; brown chicken pieces. Sprinkle with chopped parsley and shallot, continue to brown. Add flour, brown; add stock and wine. Cook gently 1 hour. Add mushrooms; continue cooking 30 min. or longer.

400. *CHICKEN TERRINE*

PREPARATION TIME: 1¼ HOURS. COOKING TIME: 3½ HOURS.

1 chicken, about 2½ lbs., cut in
   pieces
½ lb. ham, diced
¼ lb. bacon, cut in pieces
4 tbsp. Butter
Stuffing (recipe 860)

¾ lb. strips of fresh pork fat or
   blanched bacon
goose livers, as desired
truffles (optional)
salt, pepper, brandy

Brown chicken pieces and bacon in butter. Season to taste; cook 30 min. Add ham and truffles to stuffing. Bone chicken pieces. Cover bottom of earthenware terrine with strips of fat or blanched bacon; cover with layer of stuffing, then chicken, then goose liver slices. Top with another layer of chicken, then finish with fat or blanched bacon. Moisten with brandy.

Cover terrine; seal cover with flour-and-water paste. Bake 3½ hours in very slow oven. Prepare a meat jelly (see recipe 881) with bones and liver of chicken. Remove cover from terrine; pierce several holes in contents, pour in jelly. Chill overnight. Unmold and serve.

401. CHICKEN WITH RICE
PREPARATION TIME: 5 MIN. COOKING TIME: 3 HOURS.

1 fowl, about 3 lbs.	2 small carrots, sliced
2½ qts. water	2 small onions, sliced
1½ cups rice	salt, pepper, *bouquet garni*

Place fowl in water with carrots, onions, salt, pepper and *bouquet garni*. Cook 2½ hours over low heat. Skim off grease; add rice; continue cooking 30 min.

402. CHICKEN LIVER PÂTÉ
PREPARATION TIME: 25 MIN. COOKING TIME: 1 HOUR OR LONGER.

¾ lb. each veal and chicken livers	2 eggs
¾ lb. fresh pork fat or blanched bacon	chopped parsley and shallot
¾ cup Madeira wine	salt, nutmeg

Soak livers overnight in Madeira. Chop finely, together with fat. Add eggs, shallot, parsley, seasonings. Turn mixture into buttered mold. Place mold in pan of water; bake 1 hour in moderate oven, or until knife blade inserted in mixture comes out clean.

LEFTOVER POULTRY

Hot: Simmer slices of meat for 10 min. in a Velvet (recipe 37), Tomato (31), Financière (32) or Bordelaise (34) Sauce.
Cold: Arrange slices of meat on platter; garnish with parsley and hard-boiled egg slices. Serve with Mayonnaise (recipe 60).

OMELET: Add ½ cup finely chopped cooked meat to beaten egg just before cooking.

FRITTERS: Marinate pieces of meat for 1 hour in mixture of 1 tbsp. vinegar, 1 tbsp. oil, salt and pepper. Prepare batter (884). Dip pieces of marinated meat into batter, then fry in boiling shortening. Serve with lemon quarters.

RISSOLES: See recipe 803.

QUENELLES: See recipe 871.

403. CHICKEN CROQUETTES
PREPARATION TIME: 25 MIN. COOKING TIME: 8 MIN.

1 cup finely chopped cooked chicken (or other fowl)	¼ cup chopped ham
3½ tbsp. butter	⅔ cup flour
¾ cup milk	1 egg, beaten with
¼ lb. mushrooms, finely chopped	1 tbsp. oil
fine bread crumbs	shortening for frying
	salt, pepper

Prepare a thick Béchamel Sauce (recipe 10) with flour, milk, butter; cook mushrooms in it for 5 min. Chill sauce. Fold chopped meat into sauce; season. Shape mixture into balls; roll in beaten egg, then in bread crumbs. Brown about 8 min. in hot shortening.

404. CHICKEN SOUFFLÉ
PREPARATION TIME: 15 MIN. COOKING TIME: 30 MIN.

1 cup diced, cooked chicken	⅔ cup flour
⅓ lb. mushrooms, diced	milk
3 eggs, separated	salt, pepper
2⅔ tbsp. butter	

Make a Béchamel Sauce (recipe 10) with butter, flour, milk. Sauté mushrooms in a little butter. Add chicken, mushrooms and egg yolks to sauce. Chill. Season to taste. Fold in stiffly beaten egg whites. Pour mixture into greased mold; bake 20 min. in hot oven. Serve immediately.

See also following recipes:

Duchess Eggs (208)   Rice à la reine (586)
Mother Mary's Lettuce (592)   Shells à la reine (571)

RABBIT

405. ROAST RABBIT

Entire rabbit or simply the back may be roasted. Lard fleshy parts; or, if preferred, envelop meat completely in piece of fresh pork fat and secure with string. Roast in hot oven 20 min. per lb. Serve with Pepper Sauce (recipe 49) or with cooking juice and lemon slices.

406. SAUTÉED RABBIT

PREPARATION TIME: 10 MIN. COOKING TIME: 25 MIN.

2 lbs. young rabbit, cleaned and dressed	¼ lb. chopped mushrooms
1 tbsp. chopped onion	6⅔ tbsp. hot water
1 tbsp. chopped shallot	6⅔ tbsp. white wine
3½ tbsp. butter	salt, pepper, chopped parsley

Cut rabbit in pieces; brown in butter 10 min. Sprinkle with chopped onion, shallot, parsley, mushrooms; season to taste. Add wine, cook 15 min. Arrange pieces of rabbit on serving dish. Serve with gravy made by deglazing skillet with hot water.

407. RABBIT STEW (LAPIN EN GIBELOTTE)

PREPARATION TIME: 20 MIN. COOKING TIME: 1¼ HOURS.

1 rabbit, about 3 lbs., cut in pieces	1¾ cups white wine
⅓ lb. fresh pork fat or blanched bacon, diced	¾ cup warm Stock (recipe 69)
	3½ tbsp. butter
3 small onions	1¾ lbs. small potatoes, peeled
½ cup flour	¼ lb. mushrooms, peeled
	salt, pepper, *bouquet garni*

Brown onions and diced fat in butter. Remove; brown

pieces of rabbit. When well browned, sprinkle with flour; add stock, wine, seasonings, replace fat and onions. Cook gently ¾ hour. Add potatoes, verifying seasoning. Continue cooking 30 min. Add mushrooms during last 15 min. of cooking.

408. RABBIT MARENGO: *See recipe for Chicken Marengo (399).*

409. RABBIT FRICASSEE: *See recipe for Chicken Fricassee (389).*

410. CIVET DE LAPIN (RABBIT STEW WITH WINE)
PREPARATION TIME: 25 MIN. COOKING TIME: 1½ HOURS.

3 lbs. rabbit, cut in pieces, with liver and blood	⅔ cup flour
	¾ cup warm Stock (recipe 69)
¼ lb. fresh pork fat or blanched bacon, diced	1¾ cups red wine
	2 tbsp. butter
¼ lb. onions	bouquet garni, salt, pepper

Brown onions and diced fat in butter; remove from pan. Brown pieces of rabbit thoroughly; remove from pan. Make a Dark Brown Sauce (recipe 40) in pan with flour, stock, wine. Replace onions, fat, rabbit; add seasonings. Cook gently 1½ hours. Crush liver, add with blood to sauce just before serving.

411. CURRIED RABBIT
PREPARATION TIME: 10 MIN. COOKING TIME: 1½ HOURS.

3 lbs. rabbit, cut in pieces	1⅓ cups white wine
½ lb. fresh pork fat or blanched bacon, diced	1⅓ cups Stock (recipe 69)
	2⅔ tbsp. butter
2 or 3 small onions	salt, pepper
⅔ cup flour	2 tsp. curry powder

Brown onions and diced fat in butter; add pieces of rabbit, brown on all sides. Add flour, stock, wine and seasonings. Cook gently 1¼ hours. Serve rabbit with rice; serve sauce separately.

412. RABBIT LOAF

PREPARATION TIME: 30 MIN. COOKING TIME: 2 HOURS.

2 lbs. rabbit, cut in pieces
¾ lb. fresh pork fat or blanched
   bacon
6⅔ tbsp. brandy
1½ cups fresh bread crumbs

marinade (recipe 113)
2 eggs, separated
chopped parsley
Tomato Sauce (recipe 31)

Marinate rabbit 24 hours. Bone; chop meat finely together with fat. Crush bread crumbs with egg yolks; add to chopped meat together with brandy and stiffly beaten egg whites. Pour mixture into well-buttered mold; set mold in pan of water. Bake 2 hours in slow oven. Serve with Tomato Sauce.

Game

N.B.: All recipes serve 6, unless otherwise indicated.

WILD BOAR

The best parts of the animal are the loin, chops, haunch and head. Use only fresh, clean-smelling meat, of bright red color. Boar should always be marinated before cooking.

Most recipes for pork may be applied to boar.

413. ROAST BOAR

PREPARATION TIME: 10 MIN. COOKING TIME: 45 MIN.

1¾ lbs. boar (loin)
2 cups Marinade (recipe 358)
salt, pepper

1 cup Chasseur Sauce (recipe 55)

Bard and truss meat. Marinate for 2-3 days. Drain and dry. Roast as for beef (recipe 235). Serve with Chasseur Sauce.

414. BRAISED BOAR

PREPARATION TIME: 10 MIN. COOKING TIME: 5 HOURS.

1 haunch of boar
Marinade (recipe 857)
1 or 2 sheets fresh fat
salt, pepper, *bouquet garni*

6⅔ tbsp. brandy
leftover ham, fat, etc.
(optional)

Marinate meat for 3-4 days. Drain and dry; lard deeply. Cook as for Braised Beef (recipe 241), substituting marinade for stock. Simmer 4½-5 hours. One hour before serving time, add brandy, ignite.

415. *FILETS MIGNONS*

PREPARATION TIME: 15 MIN.   COOKING TIME: 1¾ HOURS.

1 lb. loin of boar
  Marinade (recipe 858)
¼ lb. fresh pork fat or blanched
  bacon
¾ cup brandy
	shallot and garlic
	salt, pepper, large *bouquet
	  garni*
	4½ tbsp. butter
	6 tbsp. olive oil

Cut meat into ½-in. slices; marinate 1-2 days. Drain and wipe dry. Line a sauté pan with fat, garlic, shallot, *bouquet garni*. Brown meat slices in butter; add to sauté pan together with olive oil, salt, pepper, brandy, 2 tbsp. marinade. Cover and simmer for 1½ hours.

This recipe may also be used for chops.

416. *BOAR CHOPS À LA ROMAINE*

PREPARATION TIME: 15 MIN.   COOKING TIME: 20 MIN.

6 chops
6 slices white bread, fried in
  butter
¼ lb. butter
¾ cup white wine
	marinade (recipe 857)
	salt, pepper
	Chasseur Sauce (recipe 55, omit
	  currant jelly)

Score edges of chops; marinate for 2 days. Drain and dry. Cook 15 min. in 3½ tbsp. butter. Place one chop on each slice of bread; keep warm. Pour wine into pan, scraping meat juices from bottom of pan. Add 1 cup Chasseur Sauce, season to taste; boil 5 min. over high heat. Pour sauce over chops.

417. *STEWED BOAR* (SANGLIER EN HARICOT)

PREPARATION TIME: 20 MIN.   COOKING TIME: 3 HOURS.

1 lb. breast of boar, cut in pieces 2 cups white wine 1 tsp. vinegar 2 cups Stock (recipe 69)	½ lb. turnip, peeled, cut in pieces 6 tbsp. Meat Extract (recipe 880) salt, pepper, *bouquet garni*

Combine meat, stock, wine, vinegar, seasonings; simmer 2 hours over low heat. Add turnips; continue cooking, uncovered, for 1 hour. Add meat extract. Arrange meat on serving dish, surround with turnips. Nap with sauce.

418. *ROAST SADDLE OF BOAR*
PREPARATION TIME: 20 MIN.   COOKING TIME: 20 MIN. PER LB.

1¾ lbs. saddle of boar
  2 cups marinade (recipe 857)
¼ lb. fresh pork fat or blanched
    bacon

1 cup Sherry
  several juniper berries
¾ cup Pepper Sauce (recipe 49)

Marinate meat 2-3 days. Drain, wipe dry. Bard with strips of fat or bacon. Place meat in baking dish with a little water. Brown at high temperature, then roast 20-25 min. per lb. in slow oven. (May also be roasted on spit.) Strain marinade; add juniper berries, Pepper Sauce, gravy from degreased baking dish. Boil 10-15 min. over high heat; strain, season to taste. Serve sauce separately with roast.

VENISON

Venison should be cooked within 3 or 4 days after killing. It is usually marinated before cooking.

The best meat comes from animals of from 1 to 2½ years old. The best parts are the haunch, chops, loin and tenderloin.

419. *LOIN OF VENISON CHASSEUR*
PREPARATION TIME: 15 MIN.   COOKING TIME: 1 HOUR.

2 lbs. venison
  2 cups marinade (recipe 858)
¼ cup diced fresh pork fat or
    blanched bacon

1 cup white wine
1 cup Stock (recipe 69)
  salt, pepper

Marinate meat 3-4 days. Brown diced fat in small quantity butter; add venison, brown over medium heat. Add wine, stock, 1 cup marinade. Cover and simmer 1 hour. Strain sauce; serve separately.

420. *ROAST HAUNCH OF VENISON:* Proceed as for
Roast Saddle of Boar (recipe 418).

421. *ROAST LEG OF VENISON:* Proceed as for Braised Boar (recipe 414).

WILD RABBIT

All recipes for domesticated rabbit may be applied to wild rabbit.

422. *WILD RABBIT À LA NIÇOISE*
PREPARATION TIME: 15 MIN. COOKING TIME: 50 MIN.

1 young rabbit, cleaned and dressed	3½ tbsp. butter
⅔ cup flour	15-18 black olives, pitted
¾ cup white wine	1 cup Tomato Sauce
1½ tsp. olive oil	(recipe 31)
	salt, pepper, *bouquet garni*

Cut rabbit in pieces; dredge in flour. Heat oil in sauté pan; brown rabbit thoroughly. Add remaining ingredients, except butter. Simmer 25 min. over low heat. Arrange meat on serving dish; bind sauce with butter, pour over meat.

423. *RABBIT ÉMINCÉ*
PREPARATION TIME: 30 MIN. COOKING TIME: 20 MIN.

1 wild rabbit	2 cups Piquant Sauce (recipe 41)
¼ cup diced fresh pork fat or blanched bacon	

Clean and bone rabbit; cut meat in pieces. Brown rabbit and fat in sauté pan. Pour in sauce; simmer 20 min. without boiling.

This recipe may also be applied to leftover roast rabbit.

424. *POTTED HARE* (TERRINE DE LIÈVRE)
PREPARATION TIME: 40 MIN. COOKING TIME: 3 HOURS.

1 hare	1 egg
½ lb. fresh pork fat or blanched bacon	6⅔ tbsp. brandy
⅔ lb. calf's liver	7 or 8 juniper berries
2 bay leaves	salt, peppercorns, sprig of thyme
½ cup cream	

Bone rabbit; cut meat into pieces. Chop liver and half the fat; combine with cream, egg, salt, peppercorns, juniper berries. Line an earthenware terrine with a few strips of fat or blanched bacon. Place in layer of chopped meat mixture; top with layer of rabbit slices. Continue in alternating layers until terrine is full. Finish with remaining strips of fat or bacon; add thyme and bay leaf. Cover terrine; place in pan of water. Bake 2½ hours in slow oven. This dish will keep for 5 or 6 days if stored in refrigerator.

PARTRIDGE

425. ESTOUFFADE OF PARTRIDGE

PREPARATION TIME: 20 MIN.   COOKING TIME: 3 HOURS.

2 partridges, cleaned, dressed and trussed	2 carrots
⅓ lb. fresh pork fat or blanched bacon	2 onions
¼ lb. veal or ham, diced	1½ cups Stock (recipe 69)
¾ cup white wine	salt, pepper, *bouquet garni*
	Meat Extract (recipe 880), optional

Line a heavy pot with strips of fat or bacon, diced veal or ham, onions, carrots. Place in partridges; add stock, wine, seasonings. Cook uncovered for 3 hours, over very low heat. Serve sauce on the side, adding small quantity of meat extract if desired.

426. PARTRIDGE WITH CABBAGE

PREPARATION TIME: 30 MIN.   COOKING TIME: 3 HOURS.

2 partridges, cleaned and dressed	2 onions
⅓ lb. fresh pork fat or blanched bacon, diced	1 carrot
⅓ lb. ham or veal, thinly sliced	1 head cabbage
4 link sausages, cut in pieces	2 cups Stock (recipe 69)
	salt, pepper, *bouquet garni*

Bard and truss partridges. Place in heavy pot with fat or bacon, ham or veal, onions, carrot, sausage. Cook until well browned. Scald cabbage 15 min. in boiling salted water;

drain, pressing to remove all water. Add cabbage, stock and seasonings to partridges. Cover and simmer 2–3 hours, depending on age and tenderness of partridges. Arrange birds on serving dish; surround with vegetables and sausage. Reduce sauce by boiling to about 1 cup; pour over meat and vegetables.

427. ROAST PARTRIDGES
PREPARATION TIME: 30 MIN. COOKING TIME: 30 MIN.

2 or 3 young partridges, cleaned and prepared
¼ lb. fresh pork fat or blanched bacon

salt, pepper

Bard and truss birds. Roast on spit, or in very hot oven, 25-30 min., seasoning after first 10-15 min. Serve with gravy.

428. SALMIS OF PARTRIDGE
PREPARATION TIME: 1 HOUR.

2 young partridges, roasted and chilled
4½ tbsp. butter
6⅔ tbsp. white wine
6⅔ tbsp. Stock (recipe 69)
6⅔ tbsp. Dark Brown Sauce (recipe 40)

⅓ lb. mushrooms, peeled, minced
1 onion, minced
juice of 1 lemon
salt, pepper, bouquet garni
6 slices white bread, fried in butter

Cut birds into pieces and place in sauté pan with half the butter. Break up carcasses; place in casserole with wine, stock, onion, seasonings; boil 20 min. over very high heat. Strain; add mushrooms and Dark Brown Sauce, cook 30 min. Pour mixture over meat in sauté pan; heat without boiling. Add lemon juice. Arrange meat on slices of bread; nap with sauce. Serve immediately.

429. MANSELLE OF PARTRIDGE
PREPARATION TIME: 30 MIN. COOKING TIME: 1½ HOURS.

2 or 3 young partridges, cleaned and prepared
6⅔ tbsp. white wine
6⅔ tbsp. Stock (recipe 69)

1 cup Portuguese Sauce (recipe 48)
1 shallot
salt, pepper, nutmeg
bouquet garni

Truss and bard partridges; roast. Remove legs and wings; keep warm. Bone carcass; crush meat and bones in mortar together with heads and necks of birds, shallot, pepper, *bouquet garni*. Place mixture in heavy pot with sauce, wine, stock; season with salt, pepper and nutmeg. Cook 1 hour over low flame. Strain sauce, pour over legs and wings of birds.

430. PARTRIDGE SUPREME
PREPARATION TIME: 20 MIN. COOKING TIME: 1¼ HOURS.

3 young partridges, cleaned and dressed	1 cup white wine
¼ lb. fresh pork fat or blanched bacon	6⅔ tbsp. Meat Extract (recipe 880)
4½ tbsp. butter	salt, Cayenne pepper, *fines herbes*
3 shallots	goose liver paste, a few truffles (optional)
½ cup cream	

Truss and bard partridges. Prepare a stuffing by chopping together fat, *fines herbes*, salt, pepper, truffles; stuff birds with mixture. Place birds in sauté pan with butter; brown thoroughly over high heat. Cover and cook 30 min. over low heat. Cut birds apart, reserving joints and breast meat; crush remains in a mortar, then combine in a casserole with wine, meat extract and shallots. Cook 30-35 min. over moderate heat. Strain mixture; replace in casserole, together with reserved joints and breast meat. Add cream, stirring constantly; add goose liver paste and a few truffles, if desired. Simmer 5 min. Serve piping hot.

QUAIL

431. ROAST QUAIL
PREPARATION TIME: 15 MIN. COOKING TIME: 10 MIN.

4 quail, cleaned and dressed	salt, pepper
¼ lb. fresh pork fat or blanched bacon	

Roast barded quail for 10 min. in very hot oven.

432. QUAIL À L'ASTI

PREPARATION TIME: 15 MIN. COOKING TIME: 25 MIN.

4 quail, cleaned and dressed
¾ cup Asti wine
6⅔ tbsp. Meat Extract (recipe 880)

salt, pepper
white truffles, if desired

Truss and bard quail. Brown in butter 15 min. Add Asti, meat extract, surround with truffles. Season to taste. Cover and simmer for 10 min.

433. QUAIL À L'ANGLAISE

PREPARATION TIME: 30 MIN. COOKING TIME: 45 MIN.

3 young quail, cleaned and dressed
1 calf's brain
1 doz. sausages
¾ cup Madeira wine

¾ cup Stock (recipe 69)
⅓ lb. fresh pork fat or blanched bacon, sliced
salt, pepper, bouquet garni

Truss and bard quail. Soak brain 30 min. in cold water; remove membrane, slice thinly. Line a heavy pot with slices of fat, brain, sausages, bouquet garni. Place in quail; add Madeira and stock, season to taste. Cover and cook 45 min. over low heat.

434. QUAIL EN COCOTTE: Proceed as for Chicken en Cocotte (recipe 395).

PHEASANT

435. ROAST PHEASANT

PREPARATION TIME: 25 MIN. COOKING TIME: 40 MIN.

1 pheasant, cleaned and dressed
¼ lb. fresh pork fat or blanched bacon

1 slice white bread, fried in butter
salt and pepper

Proceed as for Roast Chicken (recipe 391), cooking 35-40 min. in slow oven. Place on slice of bread, baste with cooking liquid. If desired, garnish with head, wings and tail.

Vegetables

N.B.: All of the following recipes serve 6, unless otherwise indicated.

Green Vegetables—Cook uncovered in large quantity of rapidly boiling water, adding 2 tsp. salt per quart of water.

White Vegetables—Cook covered in slowly boiling water, adding 2 tsp. salt per quart of water.

Dried Vegetables—Wash, soak for several hours in lukewarm water. Drain, cover with cold water; place over high heat until water begins to "shiver." Reduce heat and cook over low flame (2½-3 hours for haricot and kidney beans, peas; 1½ hours for lentils), adding an onion and a *bouquet garni* if desired. Salt (2 tsp. per quart of water) should be added halfway through cooking.

If desired, vegetables may be cooked in a white sauce made by adding for every quart of water 1 tbsp. flour blended with 3 tbsp. water and 1 tbsp. vinegar.

If the water in your area is very calcareous, add a pinch of bicarbonate of soda to cooking water, to prevent vegetables from toughening.

The following sauces go well with vegetables:

Béchamel (10)	Madeira (42)
White (8 or 9)	Printanière (22)
Maître d'hôtel Butter (4)	Portuguese (48)
Brown Butter (6)	Rémoulade (58)
Mayonnaise Mousseline (60)	Rich (18)
Mornay (14)	Tomato (31)

442. ARTICHOKES

Break off stem; remove tough outer leaves, and cut off tips of other leaves. Cook 45 min. in boiling salted water. Drain by turning artichoke upside down, leaves pointing downward. If desired, remove heart. Serve with Vinaigrette (recipe 56), White (recipe 8 or 9) or Cream (recipe 11) sauce.

443. ARTICHOKES À LA BARIGOULE

PREPARATION TIME: 1¾ HOURS.   COOKING TIME: 1½ HOURS.

6 artichokes	2 med. carrots
½ lb. mushrooms, chopped	1 large onion
¼ lb. blanched fat salt pork, chopped	1⅓ cups white wine
4 tbsp. butter	6½ cups Stock (recipe 69)
6⅔ tbsp. oil	1⅓ tbsp. cornstarch
16 thin strips fresh pork fat or blanched bacon	chopped parsley

Cook artichokes 10 min. in boiling salted water. Remove heart, replace with stuffing of chopped mushrooms, parsley, salt, pepper, chopped salt pork. Wrap each artichoke in 2 strips pork fat or blanched bacon; secure with string. Heat butter and oil together; brown artichokes. Line a heavy pot with carrots, onions, remaining strips of fat or bacon; place in the artichokes, sprinkle with wine. Bring to a boil; add stock, cover, and bake 1 hour in slow oven. Strain cooking liquid, bind with cornstarch. Arrange artichokes on serving dish; nap with sauce.

444. ARTICHOKE HEARTS

Remove leaves from cooked artichoke, leaving edible portion at bottom of each leaf attached to heart. Cut off fibrous parts; remove choke. Rub heart with lemon. Cook 25 min. in boiling water.

445. ARTICHOKE HEARTS PRINTANIÈRE

PREPARATION TIME: 50 MIN. COOKING TIME: 1 HOUR.

6 artichokes
⅓ cup chopped ham
¼ lb. mushrooms, washed, thinly sliced
Stock (recipe 69)
4 tbsp. butter

½ cup flour
1 hard-boiled egg, chopped
½ tsp. minced shallot
chopped parsley and tarragon
bread crumbs

Cook artichokes 30 min. in boiling water. Remove leaves and choke from heart. Remove lower edible portion from each leaf; chop, blend with chopped ham and egg. Cook mushrooms and shallot together in 2 tbsp. butter. Make a thick brown sauce (recipe 40) with flour, remaining 2 tbsp. butter, sufficient stock to moisten; season well. Blend in ham mixture, parsley, tarragon. Stuff artichoke hearts with mixture. Cook in heavy pot over low flame for 20 min. Arrange hearts in baking dish; sprinkle with bread crumbs and dot with butter; brown 15 min. in hot oven.

446. ASPARAGUS

Use 8-10 asparagus per person (about 5 lbs. is sufficient for 6). Cut off tough ends; peel white portion. Cook 20 min. in rapidly boiling salted water. Drain; dry thoroughly. Serve with one of following sauces: Mayonnaise (recipe 60), Mayonnaise Mousseline (60), Vinaigrette (56), White (8 or 9), Mornay (14).

447. ASPARAGUS WITH PEAS

PREPARATION TIME: 45 MIN. COOKING TIME: 1 HOUR.

50 asparagus
3½ tbsp butter
⅔ cup flour
2 small onions

2 cups Stock (recipe 69)
1 egg yolk
bouquet garni, salt, pepper

Dice asparagus. Make a White Sauce (recipe 8 or 9) with flour, butter, stock; add onions, asparagus, seasonings. Cook gently 1 hour. Bind with egg yolk just before serving.

448. ASPARAGUS SOUFFLÉ
PREPARATION TIME: 35 MIN. COOKING TIME: 1¼ HOURS.

36 cooked asparagus	1 cup grated Gruyère
3½ tbsp. butter	4 eggs, separated
⅔ cup flour	Supreme or English Sauce
2 cups milk	(recipe 16 or 17)

Cut cooked asparagus into small pieces about 1 in. long. Prepare a Mornay Sauce (recipe 14) with butter, flour, milk and cheese; add asparagus. Chill. Add egg yolks to mixture, then fold in stiffly beaten egg whites. Pour into buttered mold or pan; set mold in pan of water. Bake 45 min. in slow oven. Serve with desired sauce.

449. BRUSSELS SPROUTS
Remove withered leaves from sprouts. Cook 15 min. in boiling salted water. Serve with Cream Sauce (recipe 11) if desired.

450. BRUSSELS SPROUTS WITH CHESTNUTS
PREPARATION TIME: 1 HOUR. COOKING TIME: 20 MIN.

1½ lbs. Brussels Sprouts, cooked	4 tbsp. butter, melted
1 lb. Chestnuts, cooked (recipe 468)	

Combine sprouts and chestnuts. Add melted butter just before serving.

451. SAUTÉED BRUSSELS SPROUTS
PREPARATION TIME: 30 MIN. COOKING TIME: 25 MIN.

2 lbs. cooked Brussels Sprouts	salt, pepper
5 tbsp. butter	

Melt 4 tbsp. butter. Add drained sprouts; sauté. As soon as they begin to brown, season with salt and pepper, add remaining butter.

452. BRUSSELS SPROUTS SOUFFLÉ
PREPARATION TIME: 25 MIN. COOKING TIME: 45 MIN.

1 lb. Brussels Sprouts	½ cup grated Gruyère
½ lb. potatoes, peeled	3 eggs, separated
3½ tbsp. butter	salt, pepper

Cook sprouts and potatoes 20 min. in boiling salted water; drain and rub through sieve or food mill. Add egg yolks and butter; season to taste. Fold in stiffly beaten egg whites. Pour mixture into baking dish; sprinkle with grated Gruyère. Bake 25 min. in slow oven.

453. CABBAGE

Cut off stump; remove withered leaves. Wash thoroughly. Cook 20 min. in boiling salted water.

454. BRAISED CABBAGE

PREPARATION TIME: 15 MIN.   COOKING TIME: 2½ HOURS.

½ lb. fresh pork fat or blanched bacon	1 large head cabbage, cooked and quartered
1 large carrot, sliced	¾ cup warm Stock (recipe 69)
1 small onion	thyme, bay leaf, salt, pepper

Line bottom of heavy pot with strips of pork fat or blanched bacon; place cabbage quarters, carrots slices, onion, seasonings in pot. Cover with thin sheet of fat or several strips of bacon. Moisten with stock. Cook 2 hours over low flame.

455. STEWED CABBAGE

PREPARATION TIME: 15 MIN.   COOKING TIME: 2 HOURS.

1 cabbage (about 3 lbs.), cooked	6 tbsp. flour
½ cup lard	¾ cup warm Stock (recipe 69)

Cut cabbage in pieces; add to melted lard. Season to taste. Sprinkle in flour; moisten with stock. Cook 2 hours over low flame.

456. STUFFED CABBAGE À LA CHÂTELAINE

PREPARATION TIME: 45 MIN.   COOKING TIME: 2½ HOURS.

1 head cabbage, cooked Stuffing (recipe 863)	3½ tbsp. butter fine bread crumbs
¼ lb. fresh pork fat or blanched bacon	Tomato Sauce (recipe 31)

Place layer of cabbage in baking dish, then layer of stuffing; top with thin sheet of fat or several strips blanched bacon. Repeat until all ingredients have been used, finishing with layer of fat or bacon. Sprinkle with bread crumbs; dot with butter. Bake 2 hours in slow oven. Serve with Tomato Sauce.

457. CARROTS

Scrape carrots if necessary. Young carrots should be cooked whole, old ones should be diced or sliced. Cook about 30 min. Serve with Maître d'hôtel Butter (recipe 4), or with a Béchamel Sauce (recipe 10) bound with an egg yolk or ¾ cup cream.

458. CARROTS WITH PORK

PREPARATION TIME: 1 HOUR. COOKING TIME: 1¼ HOURS.

1¾ lbs. carrots
½ lb. fat salt pork, diced
2¼ cups Stock (recipe 69)

2⅔ tbsp. butter
bouquet garni, salt, pepper

Brown diced salt pork in butter. Add carrots; moisten with stock, add seasonings. Cook gently 1¼ hours.

459. CAULIFLOWER

Separate head into individual flowerets. Soak 30 min. in water to which dash of vinegar has been added. Cook 25 min. in boiling salted water. If desired, serve with White (recipe 8 or 9) or Tomato (recipe 31) Sauce. Or nap with Mornay Sauce (recipe 14), sprinkle with grated Gruyère and brown 10 min. in hot oven.

460. CAULIFLOWER WITH BROWN BUTTER

Cook cauliflower 30 min. in boiling salted water. Make a Brown Butter Sauce (recipe 6); pour over cauliflower in serving dish. Garnish with crushed yolk of hard-boiled egg.

461. CAULIFLOWER CROQUETTES

PREPARATION TIME: 35 MIN. COOKING TIME: 25 MIN.

1½ lbs. cauliflower, cooked
2 cups milk
1 whole egg
1 egg, separated
2 tbsp. butter

⅔ cup flour
½ cup grated Gruyère
fine bread crumbs
shortening for frying

Cut flowerets into small pieces. Prepare a Béchamel Sauce (recipe 10) with butter, flour, milk, grated Gruyère; bind with whole egg and 1 egg yolk. Add cauliflowerets to sauce; season to taste. Chill. Form mixture into croquettes; roll in beaten egg white, then in bread crumbs. Fry in very hot shortening.

462. CAULIFLOWER FRITTERS

Marinate cooked flowerets for 2 hours in marinade (recipe 855). Dip flowerets in a batter for frying (recipe 884 or 733). Brown in very hot shortening.

CAULIFLOWER À LA MAYONNAISE: See recipe 602.

463. CAULIFLOWER TIMBALE

PREPARATION TIME: 45 MIN. COOKING TIME: 2 HOURS.

1 head cauliflower (about 2 lbs.), cooked	Stuffing (recipe 863) Mushroom Sauce (recipe 43)

Place layer of cauliflowerets in baking dish; cover with layer of stuffing. Repeat until all ingredients have been used, finishing with layer of cauliflowerets. Set dish in pan of water; bake 1½ hours in slow oven. Serve with Mushroom Sauce (recipe 43).

464. CELERIAC

Peel celeriac roots, cut in quarters or thin slices. Place in cold salted water; bring to boil, cook 30 min. If desired, serve with a White Sauce (recipe 8 or 9) to which has been added 6 tbsp. cream.

465. CELERIAC PURÉE

PREPARATION TIME: 20 MIN. COOKING TIME: 45 MIN.

1¾ lbs. celeriac, peeled, quartered	¾ cup cream
½ lb. potatoes, peeled, quartered	salt, pepper
4 tbsp. butter	

Cook celeriac 20 min. in boiling salted water. Add potatoes; continue cooking 20 min. Drain and rub through sieve or food mill. Season to taste. Beat in cream and butter.

466. CELERY

Scrape stalks, cut into pieces about 4 in. long. Cook 45 min. in white sauce for vegetables (p. 161). Serve with White (recipe 8 or 9) or Cream (recipe 11) Sauce, or with Maître d'hôtel Butter (recipe 4).

467. CELERY AU JUS

PREPARATION TIME: 30 MIN. COOKING TIME: 2 HOURS.

3 heads celery, cut in large pieces	4 tbsp. butter
1 med. carrot, sliced	1 cup Stock (recipe 69)
1 med. onion, sliced	1 cup Meat Extract (recipe 880)

Cook celery 10 min. in white sauce for vegetables (see p. 161); drain. Brown onion and carrot slices in butter. Add pieces of celery, season with salt and pepper; moisten with stock. Cook gently 1½ hours. Add meat extract; continue cooking 10 min.

468. CHESTNUTS

Slit shells; plunge chestnuts into boiling water for 5 min. Remove inner and outer shells. Cook chestnut meats 25 min. in boiling milk or water.

469. CHESTNUTS WITH ONIONS

PREPARATION TIME: 45 MIN. COOKING TIME: 30 MIN.

2 lbs. small chestnuts, shelled	1 quart Stock (recipe 69)
¼ lb. butter	salt, pepper
½ lb. onions	

Brown onions in butter; add chestnut meats, season to taste. Moisten with stock. Cook 30 min.

470. CHESTNUT PURÉE

PREPARATION TIME: 1 HOUR. COOKING TIME: 30 MIN.

2 lbs. chestnuts, shelled	1 tsp. sugar
6 tbsp. butter	salt
3 cups milk	

Cook chestnut meats 30 min. in milk; season with salt and sugar. Rub through sieve; moisten with whatever is left of cooking liquid. Gradually beat in butter.

471. CHICORY

Remove tough or wilted leaves; cut head into 4 sections and wash thoroughly. Cook 15 min. in boiling salted water.

472. CHICORY IN MEAT SAUCE
PREPARATION TIME: 25 MIN. COOKING TIME: 1½ HOURS.

4 lbs. chicory, cooked	4 tbsp. butter
½ cup flour	¾ cup warm Stock (recipe 69)
salt, pepper	¾ cup Meat Extract (recipe 880)

Make a Light Brown Sauce (recipe 30) with flour, 2 tbsp. butter, stock. Add chicory and half the meat extract; season with salt and pepper. Cover and simmer gently 45 min. Add remaining meat extract; continue cooking 45 min. Just before serving, add remaining butter.

473. CHICORY IN WHITE SAUCE
PREPARATION TIME: 25 MIN. COOKING TIME: 1¼ HOURS.

4 lbs. chicory, cooked	3 hard-boiled eggs, quartered
¾ cup milk	2 egg yolks
3½ tbsp. butter	salt, pepper

Place chicory in heavy pot, with butter and milk; season to taste. Cook gently 1 hour. Bind with egg yolks just before serving. Garnish with hard-boiled eggs.

474. CHICORY PURÉE
PREPARATION TIME: 40 MIN. COOKING TIME: 25 MIN.

4 lbs. chicory, cooked	3½ tbsp. butter
2 cups Béchamel Sauce (recipe 10)	salt, pepper, nutmeg
6 slices white bread, fried in butter	

Drain chicory, pressing to remove all water. Chop coarsely, then rub through sieve or food mill. Add Béchamel Sauce; season to taste. Garnish with slices of bread cut in fancy shapes if desired.

475. CHICORY LOAF À L'ANCIENNE
PREPARATION TIME: 30 MIN. COOKING TIME: 2½ HOURS.

4 lbs. Chicory, cooked and puréed (recipe 474)	3 eggs
2 cups Béchamel Sauce (recipe 10)	3½ tbsp. butter
	nutmeg, salt, pepper
	Cream Sauce (recipe 11)

Mix Béchamel Sauce and puréed chicory; season to taste. Cover and cook 1½ hours over low flame. Beat eggs until foamy; add to mixture together with butter. Pour into buttered ring mold. Place mold in pan of hot water; bake 45 min. in slow oven. Serve with Cream Sauce.

476. CUCUMBERS

Peel and halve cucumbers; remove seeds, cut in thin slices. Cook 20 min. in boiling salted water. If desired, serve with Poulette (recipe 15) or Béchamel (recipe 10) Sauce.

CUCUMBER À L'ANTIBOISE: See recipe 603.

477. STUFFED CUCUMBERS
PREPARATION TIME: 45 MIN. COOKING TIME: 1½ HOURS.

6 small cucumbers	1½ tbsp. cornstarch
Stuffing (recipe 863 or 865)	¾ cup stock
juice of 1 lemon	salt, pepper
3½ tbsp. butter	

Cut off stem end of cucumbers and hollow them out with spoon. Fill with stuffing; replace ends. Melt butter; place in cucumbers, moisten with stock and season. Cover and cook 1½ hours. Just before serving, bind sauce with cornstarch; add lemon juice.

478. FRIED EGGPLANT

Peel eggplants (use 1 eggplant for every 2 persons), cut into 1-in. slices. Sprinkle with salt; soak 1 hour in cold water. Dry slices. Dip in batter for frying (recipe 884); cook 5 min. in very hot oil.

479. GRATIN OF EGGPLANT
PREPARATION TIME: 25 MIN. COOKING TIME: 1 HOUR.

3 eggplants, peeled and sliced	1½ tsp. tomato paste
6⅔ tbsp. oil	3½ tbsp. butter
1 onion, minced	chopped parsley
½ tsp. minced garlic	salt, pepper
fine bread crumbs	
leftover cooked meat, chopped	

Soak eggplant slices 1 hour in salted cold water; drain and dry. Sauté in hot oil. Melt 2 tbsp. butter in skillet; cook onion and garlic 10 min. Add small quantity chopped cooked meat, tomato paste, chopped parsley; season to taste. Cook 5 min.

Place layer of eggplant in baking dish; top with layer of stuffing mixture. Repeat until all ingredients have been used. Sprinkle with bread crumbs, dot with remaining butter. Bake 45 min. in hot oven.

480. STUFFED EGGPLANT
PREPARATION TIME: 35 MIN. COOKING TIME: 1 HOUR.

3 eggplants	2⅔ tbsp. butter
Stuffing (recipe 865)	fine bread crumbs

Split eggplants in half lengthwise; do not peel. Remove part of pulp; chop finely and mix with stuffing. Fill eggplant halves with mixture. Sprinkle with bread crumbs, dot with butter. Bake 1 hour in very slow oven.

481. STUFFED EGGPLANT À LA CRÈME
PREPARATION TIME: 20 MIN. COOKING TIME: 1 HOUR.

3 eggplants	1 cup thick Béchamel Sauce
6⅔ tbsp. cream	(recipe 10)
½ cup grated Gruyère	

Split eggplants in half lengthwise; do not peel. Remove portion of pulp; chop finely, mix with Béchamel Sauce and cream. Fill eggplant halves with mixture; sprinkle with grated Gruyère. Bake 1 hour in very slow oven.

482. EGGPLANT WITH TOMATOES

PREPARATION TIME: 45 MIN. COOKING TIME: 45 MIN.

3 eggplants, peeled, cut in ½-in. slices
1¾ lbs. tomatoes
2⅔ tbsp. butter
½ tsp. minced garlic
chopped parsley
oil for frying

Cook tomatoes without water for 10 min.; rub through sieve or food mill. Fry eggplant slices in oil. Place layer of tomato purée in baking dish, then a layer of eggplant; sprinkle with chopped parsley and garlic. Repeat until all ingredients have been used. Dot with butter. Bake 45 min. in slow oven.

483. ENDIVE

Cut off ends and remove wilted leaves. Dry thoroughly. Cook in very small quantity of water—too much water causes endive to become bitter.

484. BRAISED ENDIVE

PREPARATION TIME: 10 MIN. COOKING TIME: 1 HOUR.

2 lbs. endive
juice of 1 lemon
4 tbsp. butter
Salt

Melt butter; place in endive. Season with salt, sprinkle with lemon juice. Cover tightly and cook gently for 1 hour.

ENDIVE À LA FLAMANDE: Serve Braised Endive with a Pepper Sauce (recipe 49).

485. ENDIVE WITH CHEESE

PREPARATION TIME: 20 MIN. COOKING TIME: 45 MIN.

2 lbs. endive
1 cup grated Gruyère
2 cups Béchamel Sauce (recipe 10)

Cook endive 20 min. in boiling salted water. Place in baking dish; cover with sauce, sprinkle with grated cheese. Bake 25 min. in moderate oven.

486. STUFFED ENDIVE

PREPARATION TIME: 45 MIN. COOKING TIME: 1½ HOURS.

2 lbs. endive   Stuffing (recipe 863)
2 cups White Sauce (recipe 8 or 9)   salt, pepper

Cook endive 20 min. in boiling salted water. Place alternating layers of endive and stuffing in baking dish; season to taste, cover with sauce. Bake 1 hour in slow oven.

487. FAVA BEANS

Young beans may be cut in pieces about 1 in. long. For larger beans, shell, remove skins, cut beans in half. Cook 15 min. in boiling salted water to which 1 tbsp. savory has been added. If desired, serve with Maître d'hôtel Butter (recipe 4) or Poulette Sauce (recipe 15).

Lima Beans, which resemble the Fava Bean, may be substituted for it in all of the following recipes.

488. FAVA BEANS À LA CRÈME

PREPARATION TIME: 15 MIN. COOKING TIME: 1¼ HOURS.

2 lbs. fava beans, cooked   5 tbsp. butter
¾ cup cream

Cook beans gently in butter for 1 hour. Add cream 5 min. before serving.

489. FAVA BEANS WITH PORK

PREPARATION TIME: 40 MIN. COOKING TIME: 1 HOUR.

2 lbs. fava beans, cooked   3½ tbsp. butter
¼ lb. fresh pork fat or blanched   1 tbsp. savory
    bacon, diced   salt, pepper

Brown diced fat or bacon in butter. Add beans and seasonings. Cook gently 1 hour.

490. HARICOT BEANS À LA BRETONNE

PREPARATION TIME: 20 MIN. COOKING TIME: 3 HOURS.

1 lb. dried haricot beans, cooked   ¼ tsp. crushed garlic
½ lb. onions, chopped   4 tbsp. butter
1¾ cups warm stock   6 tbsp. flour
3 tbsp. Tomato Purée (recipe   bouquet garni, salt, pepper
    876)

Heat butter; brown onions. Sprinkle in flour; stir until it turns light brown. Add stock, tomato purée, garlic, seasonings; cook gently until sauce is reduced by about one-half. Rub cooked beans through sieve or food mill. Blend sauce into bean purée. Simmer about 10 min.

491. *HARICOT BEANS AU JUS*
PREPARATION TIME: 30 MIN. COOKING TIME: 1¼ HOURS.

2 lbs. haricot beans, cooked
2 cups Meat Extract (recipe 880)

1 med. onion, minced
chopped parsley

Heat meat extract in casserole; cook onion in it 15 min. Add beans, chopped parsley; simmer 20 min.

492. *HARICOT BEANS À LA PROVENÇALE*
PREPARATION TIME: 30 MIN. COOKING TIME: 3½ HOURS.

2 lbs. haricot beans, shelled
¼ lb. butter
¼ lb. onions, stuck with cloves
1 tsp. minced garlic
1 tsp. minced shallot

1 tomato, peeled
2 cups Stock (recipe 69)
1 bay leaf
salt, pepper

Brown onions in melted butter; add stock. When liquid begins to boil, add beans, garlic, shallot, bay leaf, tomato. Simmer gently 3 hours, adding salt and pepper after 2 hours. Add additional stock as liquid is absorbed.

493. *HARICOT BEANS WITH TOMATOES*
PREPARATION TIME: 30 MIN. COOKING TIME: 1 HOUR.

2 lbs. haricot beans, shelled
3½ tbsp. butter

2 small onions
1 lb. tomatoes, sliced

Cook beans 30 min. in boiling salted water; drain. Brown onions in butter. Add tomatoes and beans; simmer 30 min. If desired, serve with tomato sauce.

494. *JERUSALEM ARTICHOKES*
Wash and peel artichokes. Cook 20 min. in boiling salted water. If desired, simmer cooked drained artichokes 10 min. in White Sauce (recipe 8 or 9), or serve with Tomato Sauce (recipe 31). Recipes for Turnip Purée (recipe 558) and Fried

Salisfy (recipe 542) may also be applied to Jerusalem Artichokes.

495. KIDNEY BEANS WITH PORK

PREPARATION TIME: 10 MIN. COOKING TIME: 3 HOURS.

¾ lb. dried kidney beans	3½ tbsp. butter
¼ lb. fresh pork fat or blanched bacon	6 tbsp. flour
1 med. onion	¾ cup red wine

Cook kidney beans with fat or bacon and wine. After first 1½ hours of cooking, remove fat; dice it, brown in butter. Drain beans at end of 3 hours; place in serving dish. Bind cooking liquid with flour; add diced pork fat. Nap beans with sauce.

496. LEEKS

Use about 24 medium leeks for 6 persons. Remove roots and broken parts; wash thoroughly. Cook 30 min. in boiling salted water. Serve with one of following sauces: Mousseline (recipe 65), White (recipe 8 or 9), Vinaigrette (recipe 56), Mayonnaise (recipe 60).

497. LEEKS À LA POULETTE

PREPARATION TIME: 20 MIN. COOKING TIME: 45 MIN.

Cut cooked leeks in pieces; simmer 15 min. in Poulette Sauce (recipe 15).

498. LEEKS AU GRATIN

PREPARATION TIME: 15 MIN. COOKING TIME: 50 MIN.

Place cooked drained leeks in baking dish; cover with White Sauce (recipe 8 or 9), sprinkle with grated Gruyère. Brown 20 min. in hot oven.

FLAMIQUE PICARDE (Picard Leek Pie): See recipe 914.

499. LEEK PURÉE

PREPARATION TIME: 20 MIN. COOKING TIME: 40 MIN.

1 lb. potatoes, peeled, cut in pieces	12 leeks, cut in pieces
	⅔ cup cream

Cook leeks 10 min. in boiling salted water. Add potatoes, continue cooking until vegetables are tender (about 30 min.). Rub through sieve or food mill. Stir in cream just before serving.

500. LENTILES À LA DIJONNAISE
PREPARATION TIME: 10 MIN. COOKING TIME: 1½ HOURS.

1 lb. lentils, cooked (see p. 161)	¼ lb. diced cooked ham
3½ tbsp. butter	1 med. onion, chopped
⅓ cup flour	1¾ cups Stock (recipe 69)
2 tbsp. mustard	salt, pepper

Brown onion and ham together in butter. Sprinkle in flour; add stock and seasonings, cook until smooth. Add sauce to drained cooked lentils.

501. LENTILS À LA MAÎTRE D'HÔTEL
PREPARATION TIME: 10 MIN. COOKING TIME: 1½ HOURS.

¾ lb. cooked lentils (see p. 161)	juice of 1 lemon or dash of
4 tbsp. butter	vinegar

Add butter and lemon juice or vinegar to cooked lentils just before serving.

502. LENTIL PURÉE
PREPARATION TIME: 20 MIN. COOKING TIME: 2 HOURS.

1 lb. lentils	1 med. onion
5 tbsp. butter	bouquet garni, salt, pepper
1 med. carrot	

Cook lentils 1½ hours with carrot, onion, *bouquet garni*. Rub through sieve or food mill. Beat in butter, season to taste.

Recipes for Haricot Beans Au Jus and Haricot Beans with Tomatoes may also be applied to lentils.

LENTIL SALAD: See Recipe 604.

503. LETTUCE
Remove stem and withered leaves. Cook 10 min. in boiling salted water.

Recipes for Chicory in Meat Sauce (recipe 472), Chicory in White Sauce (recipe 473), and Chicory Loaf à l'ancienne (recipe 475) may also be applied to lettuce.

504. *STEWED LETTUCE*
PREPARATION TIME: 25 MIN. COOKING TIME: 1¼ HOURS.

6 heads lettuce, thoroughly washed	1 med. onion, chopped
6⅔ tbsp. Stock (recipe 69)	6 slices white bread, fried in butter
5⅓ tbsp. butter	Printanière Sauce (recipe 22)

Simmer heads of lettuce 20 min. in melted butter. Add chopped onion, stock, seasoning to taste. Cover tightly and cook 1 hour. Place one head of lettuce on each slice of bread. Serve sauce separately.

505. *STUFFED LETTUCE*
PREPARATION TIME: 45 MIN. COOKING TIME: 1¼ HOURS.

6 heads lettuce, cooked	¼ lb. mushrooms, chopped and cooked in butter
3½ tbsp. butter	3 hard-boiled eggs, crushed
¼ cup Rice, cooked (recipe 579)	

Add crushed eggs and mushrooms to rice; season with salt and pepper. Stuff heads of lettuce with rice mixture; secure with string. Place in heavy pot with melted butter. Cover and cook 1 hour over low flame.

506. *MUSHROOMS*
Buy only the cultivated variety available in stores, as many species of mushrooms are poisonous. Do not peel mushrooms unless recipe requires it, as the best of their flavor is removed with the skin. To prevent them from changing color, scrub them in water to which dash of vinegar or lemon juice has been added.

507. *MUSHROOMS EN BLANQUETTE*
PREPARATION TIME: 15 MIN. COOKING TIME: 25 MIN.

1 lb. mushrooms	2 egg yolks
4 tbsp. flour	½ cup cream
6⅔ tbsp. butter	salt, pepper
juice of 1 lemon	croutons fried in butter

Cook mushrooms 2-3 min. in 4 tbsp. butter. Sprinkle in flour, moisten with a little warm water, stirring until sauce is smooth. Season to taste. Simmer 20 min. Just before serving, bind sauce with egg yolks and add lemon juice. Serve over croutons fried in remaining butter.

508. BROILED MUSHROOMS

PREPARATION TIME: 10 MIN. COOKING TIME: 12 MIN.

6 to 12 large mushrooms
3½ tbsp. butter

chopped *fines herbes*
salt and pepper

Remove mushroom stems and place caps on broiler rack, round portion facing downward. Brush with half the butter (melted). Broil 10-12 min. under moderate flame. Blend remaining butter with salt, pepper, *fines herbes*. Place mushrooms on warm serving dish; fill with butter mixture. Serve as entrée or as garnish for roast.

509. MUSHROOM CANAPÉ

PREPARATION TIME: 15 MIN. COOKING TIME: 10 MIN.

½ lb. mushrooms
juice of 1 lemon
3 tbsp. flour
4 tbsp. butter
6⅔ tbsp. dry white wine

2 egg yolks
salt, pepper
6 slices white bread, fried in 3 tbsp. butter

Sauté mushrooms 5 min. in butter. Add lemon juice. Gradually add flour in a rain, then white wine; mix well, cook 5 min. Remove from heat; bind with egg yolks and season to taste. Pour over bread cut into fancy shapes. Serve immediately.

MUSHROOMS À LA GRECQUE: See recipe 608.

MUSHROOM SALADS I and II: See recipes 606 and 607.

510. MUSHROOM RAGOÛT

PREPARATION TIME: 10 MIN. COOKING TIME: 15 MIN.

1 lb. mushrooms
3½ tbsp. butter
¾ tsp. vinegar *or* lemon juice

chopped *fines herbes*
2 egg yolks
salt, nutmeg

Combine all ingredients except egg yolks; cover and boil 12-15 min. Remove from heat and bind with egg yolks.

511. ONIONS
Peel onions. Cook 10 min. in boiling salted water.

512. GLAZED ONIONS
PREPARATION TIME: 15 MIN. COOKING TIME: 1 HOUR.

1 lb. small onions, peeled
6 tbsp. butter

stock or water
salt, pepper

Place onions in sauté pan with salt, pepper, butter, enough stock or water to cover. Cover and cook over low flame for about 1 hour, or until liquid has been almost completely absorbed. Shake pan so that onions are completely coated with remaining liquid. Use as a garnish for roasts, etc.

PISSALADIÈRE (Onion Pie): See recipe 921.

513. ONION PURÉE
PREPARATION TIME: 20 MIN. COOKING TIME: 25 MIN.

1¾ lbs. medium onions, cooked

2 cups Béchamel Sauce
(recipe 10)

Rub cooked onions through sieve or food mill. Blend into sauce; season to taste.

514. STUFFED ONIONS
PREPARATION TIME: 45 MIN. COOKING TIME: 40 MIN.

6 large onions
2⅔ tbsp. butter
Stuffing (recipe 863 or 865),
    bound with a little White
    Sauce
fine bread crumbs

Cook onions 15 min. in boiling water. Hollow out insides with spoon; fill with stuffing. Place in baking dish; sprinkle with bread crumbs, dot with butter. Bake 25 min. in hot oven.

515. PEAS À LA FLAMANDE
PREPARATION TIME: 40 MIN. COOKING TIME: 45 MIN.

3 lbs. peas, shelled
½ lb. young carrots, diced

2 cups water
2⅔ tbsp. butter

Cook diced carrots 15 min. in butter and water. Add peas, season with salt; cook gently 30 min. If desired, a few pea pods may be added to enhance flavor; remove before serving.

516. PEAS À LA FRANÇAISE
PREPARATION TIME: 40 MIN. COOKING TIME: 1¾ HOURS.

4 lbs. peas, shelled
1 small onion
1½ tbsp. sugar

3½ tbsp. butter
2 heads lettuce
salt

Add peas to melted butter; cover and simmer 20 min. over very low flame. Add remaining ingredients; cover and simmer 1-1½ hours over very low flame. Pour water on cover of pot during cooking to maintain humidity in pot.

517. PEAS PEASANT-STYLE
PREPARATION TIME: 40 MIN. COOKING TIME: 30 MIN.

4 lbs. peas, shelled
2 small onions
¼ cup flour
salt

2 tbsp. butter
1 head lettuce
1½ tbsp. sugar
3 cups water

Combine peas, water, butter, lettuce, onions and salt; cook 25 min. over moderate heat. Add sugar. Bind cooking liquid with flour. If desired, add a Cream Sauce (recipe 11).

518. PURÉE OF DRIED PEAS
PREPARATION TIME: 20 MIN. COOKING TIME: 3 HOURS.

1 lb. dried peas, cooked (see p. 161)
1 cup warm milk

2 tbsp. butter
croutons fried in butter

Mash cooked peas; add warm milk and butter. Serve topped with croutons.

519. *POTATOES À L'ANGLAISE*
PREPARATION TIME: 20 MIN. COOKING TIME: 20 MIN.

1½ lbs. small potatoes, peeled   chopped parsley
6⅔ tbsp. butter melted

Cook potatoes 20 min. in boiling salted water. Drain. Add melted butter and chopped parsley.

If desired, substitute chopped chives, mint or chervil for parsley. Or nap with one of following sauces: White (recipe 8 or 9), Tomato (31), Brown (40) or Poulette (15), and brown for a few minutes in hot oven.

520. *POTATOES ANNA*
PREPARATION TIME: 30 MIN. COOKING TIME: 1¼ HOURS.

2 lbs. potatoes, peeled   ¾ cup butter, melted
1 tbsp. shortening or oil   salt, pepper

Thinly slice enough potatoes to line a mold; soak 10 min. in salted water. Heat shortening in mold to smoking point; pour off. Arrange potato slices in overlapping fashion on bottom and up sides of mold. Cut remaining potatoes in slices about ½ in. thick and sauté them quickly in a little butter. Heap up in center of mold, seasoning with melted butter, salt and pepper. Cover and cook 15 min. on top of stove; then bake 35-40 min. in moderate oven. Unmold before serving.

521. *BOILED POTATOES IN JACKETS* (EN ROBE DES CHAMPS)
COOKING TIME: 30 MIN.

Wash potatoes; do not peel. Place in cold salted water. Bring water to boil, then reduce heat and cook 20 min. Drain, and dry for 10 min. over low flame, if possible. Serve with butter.

522. *POTATOES IN BUTTER*
PREPARATION TIME: 25 MIN. COOKING TIME: 30 MIN.

2 lbs. potatoes, peeled   4 tbsp. butter
salt   chopped parsley

Use small new potatoes, or cut large ones into small balls. Have them thoroughly dry. Melt butter in pan; place potatoes in pan, being sure that all rest in butter. Cook gently 30 min., shaking pan often so that potatoes brown evenly. Season with salt and sprinkle with chopped parsley before serving.

POTATO CAKE: See recipe 913.

523. POTATOES À LA CRÈME
PREPARATION TIME: 15 MIN. COOKING TIME: 30 MIN.

2 lbs. cooked, peeled, quartered   4 tbsp. butter
    potatoes   ¾ cup cream

Simmer ingredients together for 5 min.

524. POTATO CROQUETTES
PREPARATION TIME: 10 MIN. COOKING TIME: 10 MIN.

Form chilled mashed potatoes (recipe 529) into croquettes. Roll in beaten egg, then in bread crumbs; fry in boiling shortening.

525. DUCHESS POTATOES
PREPARATION TIME: 30 MIN. COOKING TIME: 35 MIN.

2 lbs. potatoes, cooked   3 egg yolks
4½ tbsp. butter   salt, pepper, nutmeg
2 eggs, well beaten   flour

Mash potatoes, following recipe 529, but replace milk with eggs. Spread mixture in baking dish, chill. Using cooky cutter, cut potato mixture into various shapes. Roll in flour, then in beaten egg; bake 15 min. in hot oven. Use as a garnish for roasts, etc.

526. FRENCH FRIES (POMMES FRITES, POMMES DE TERRE PONT-NEUF)

Peel and quarter potatoes, cut in slices ½ in. thick. Dry. Plunge into boiling shortening; cook until soft. Remove, reheat shortening. Return potatoes to pot and brown. Serve hot with salt.

526A. *CHIPS:* Follow recipe 526, but cut potatoes into very thin slices.

526B. *STRAWS:* Cut potatoes into thin straw-like strips.

POTATOE FRITTERS: See recipe 892.

527. POTATO GNOCCHIS
PREPARATION TIME: 30 MIN. COOKING TIME: 35 MIN.

1 lb. potatoes, peeled, quartered	1¼ cups flour
2 whole eggs	¾ cup grated Gruyère
2 egg yolks	nutmeg, salt
4½ tbsp. butter	

Cook potatoes in boiling salted water; mash. Blend in eggs, egg yolks, flour, 3½ tbsp. butter; season with salt and pinch of nutmeg. Form mixture into balls about size of a small egg; flatten slightly. Poach 3-4 min. in boiling water. Drain and arrange in baking dish. Sprinkle with grated cheese, dot with butter. Bake 15 min. in hot oven.

GRATIN DAUPHINOIS: See recipe 903.

528. POTATO HASH PARMENTIER
PREPARATION TIME: 35 MIN. COOKING TIME: 15 MIN.

Place layer of Mashed Potatoes (recipe 529) in baking dish, then a layer of Stuffing (recipe 863); finish with layer of mashed potatoes. Dot with butter; sprinkle with grated Gruyère, if desired. Brown 15 min. in hot oven.

529. MASHED POTATOES
PREPARATION TIME: 15 MIN. COOKING TIME: 30 MIN.

2 lbs. potatoes, peeled	4 tbsp. butter
2 cups milk	

Place potatoes in cold salted water: bring to a boil, cook 30 min. Drain; rub through sieve or food mill while still hot.

Add butter and milk, beating vigorously. Eggs, cream or grated cheese may be added if desired. Or top with bits of butter, sprinkle with grated Gruyère, brown for a few minutes in very hot oven.

530. POTATO RAGOÛT

PREPARATION TIME: 30 MIN. COOKING TIME: 1¾ HOURS.

1¾ lbs. potatoes, peeled,
    quartered
4 tbsp. butter
2 cups Stock (recipe 69)
2 small onions

¼ lb. fresh pork fat or blanched
    bacon, diced
½ cup flour
6⅔ tbsp. vinegar
bouquet garni, salt, pepper

Brown onions and fat or bacon in butter. Add flour, stock and vinegar to make a Dark Brown Sauce (recipe 40); season to taste. Add potatoes. Cook gently 1¼ hours.

POTATO SALAD: See recipe 609.

531. SAUTÉED POTATOES

PREPARATION TIME: 20 MIN. COOKING TIME: 50 MIN.

1¾ lbs. potatoes, cooked
4 tbsp. butter

salt
chopped parsley

Slice potatoes; chill. Melt butter in skillet, brown potato slices. Season and sprinkle with chopped parsley.

532. SOUFFLÉED POTATOES

Peel and slice 1¾ lbs. potatoes; dry slices in cloth. Heat large quantity of shortening or oil in 2 frying utensils; shortening in first utensil should be hot, in second one it should be boiling. Plunge potato slices into first utensil; cook 7 min. Remove and drain. Plunge into second utensil; stir carefully as potatoes swell. When slices are firm and well-browned, remove and drain. Sprinkle with salt.

533. STUFFED POTATOES

PREPARATION TIME: 15 MIN. COOKING TIME: 35 MIN.

2 lbs. potatoes
Stuffing (recipe 863 or 865)

6 tbsp. Meat Extract (recipe
    880), mixed with 6 tbsp.
    boiling water

Halve potatoes lengthwise; hollow out. Cook 10 min. in boiling salted water. Fill with stuffing. Place in buttered baking dish; baste with mixture of water and meat extract. Bake 25 min. in hot oven.

534. RENAISSANCE TIMBALE
PREPARATION TIME: 20 MIN. COOKING TIME: 1¼ HOURS.

2 lbs. potatoes, boiled in jackets	3 eggs, beaten
¼ lb. ham, diced	4 tbsp. butter, slightly softened
6⅔ tbsp. cream	salt, pepper

Peel and mash potatoes; mix with ham and beaten eggs. Add cream and butter; season to taste. Mix well. Turn mixture into buttered round mold. Bake 45 min. in moderate oven. Serve piping hot.

535. PUMPKIN
Peel one-quarter of pumpkin; remove seeds. Dice. Cook 20 min. in boiling salted water.

536. PUMPKIN AU GRATIN
PREPARATION TIME: 15 MIN. COOKING TIME: 40 MIN.

1½ lbs. pumpkin, cooked	2 eggs, beaten
3½ tbsp. butter	¾ cup grated Gruyère
½ lb. potatoes, cooked	salt, pepper

Mash together pumpkin and potatoes. Blend in eggs, butter, salt and pepper. Place mixture in baking dish; sprinkle with grated cheese. Brown 20 min. in hot oven.

537. RED CABBAGE
Remove wilted leaves. Cook 15 min. in boiling salted water.

538. RED CABBAGE WITH BACON
PREPARATION TIME: 20 MIN. COOKING TIME: 2½ HOURS.

1½ lbs. red cabbage, finely chopped	½ cup lard
1 small onion	1 lb. bacon
1 cup water	6⅔ tbsp. Meat Extract (recipe 880)

Brown onion in melted lard. Add cabbage, water and meat extract; season to taste. Cook gently 1 hour. Add bacon; continue cooking 1½ hours.

RED CABBAGE WITH CHESTNUTS: Omit bacon; add 1 lb. shelled chestnuts, cut in pieces.

539. RED CABBAGE IN WINE

PREPARATION TIME: 20 MIN.   COOKING TIME: 2½ HOURS.

½ lb. red cabbage, finely chopped	6 tbsp. flour
5 tbsp. butter	¾ cup red wine
	salt, pepper

Cook cabbage gently in butter 30 min. Season to taste. Add flour; moisten with wine. Cover and simmer for 2 hours.

540. SALSIFY (OYSTER PLANT)

Cut off ends; scrape stalks. Wash in water seasoned with dash of vinegar. Cook 1½ hours in white sauce for vegetables (see p. 161).

541. SALSIFY WITH CHEESE

PREPARATION TIME: 40 MIN.   COOKING TIME: 2 HOURS.

30 salsify, cooked	1¼ cups grated Gruyère
2⅔ tbsp. butter	fine bread crumbs
¾ cup milk	

Arrange salsify in buttered baking dish; cover with milk and cheese. Sprinkle with bread crumbs. Bake 20 min. in hot oven.

542. FRIED SALSIFY

Macerate salsify stalks for several hours in Marinade (recipe 885). Dry thoroughly. Dip in Batter for Frying (recipe 884). Brown in very hot shortening.

543. SALSIFY ROOTS IN SAUCE

PREPARATION TIME: 40 MIN.   COOKING TIME: 1½ HOURS.

Cut roots of 30 salsify into 2-in. slices. Cook 1½ hours

in white sauce for vegetables (see p. 161). Mix with 2 cups White (recipe 8 or 9) or Poulette (recipe 15) Sauce.

544. SAUERKRAUT À L'ALSACIENNE
PREPARATION TIME: 10 MIN. COOKING TIME: 3½-4 HOURS.

2 lbs. fresh sauerkraut
2 small onions
1 cup white wine
⅔ cup lard
¾ lb. bacon

½ lb. sausages
1 lb. potatoes, peeled, cut in pieces
6 slices ham, cooked

Add onions and sauerkraut to melted lard. Moisten with white wine, season with salt and pepper; cook 2½ hours over low flame. Add bacon; continue cooking 1 hour. Add sausages and potatoes; continue cooking 30 min. Serve sauerkraut on platter, garnished with sliced bacon, sausages and ham.

545. SPINACH
Remove stems. Wash leaves in several changes of water. Cook uncovered for 15 min. in large quantity of boiling salted water (about 3 qts. water for 2 lbs. spinach). Drain, squeeze to remove all water; rub through sieve or food mill.

Recipes for Chicory in Meat Sauce (recipe 472), Chicory in White Sauce (recipe 473) and Chicory Loaf à l'ancienne (recipe 475) may also be applied to spinach.

546. FLORENTINE RICE LOAF
PREPARATION TIME: 45 MIN. COOKING TIME: 1 HOUR.

2 lbs. spinach, cooked, chopped
¾ cup Rice, cooked (recipe 579)
2 eggs

2 cups Béchamel Sauce (recipe 10)
2 tbsp. butter

Mix sauce with spinach. Add eggs to rice. Place layer of rice in buttered mold or pan; add layer of spinach. Continue until all ingredients have been used. Dot with butter. Bake 20 min. in hot oven.

547. SPINACH SUBRICS

PREPARATION TIME: 20 MIN. COOKING TIME: 5 MIN.

1 lb. spinach, cooked	6 tbsp. butter
1 cup Béchamel Sauce	2 eggs, well beaten
(recipe 10)	¾ cup grated Gruyère

Mix spinach with Bechamel Sauce; rub through sieve or food mill. Add eggs and cheese. Melt butter in skillet; when hot, drop in spoonfuls of mixture. Brown on both sides. Serve with additional sauce.

548. STRING BEANS À L'ANGLAISE

PREPARATION TIME: 30 MIN. COOKING TIME: 20 MIN.

2 lbs. string beans	chopped parsley
5 tbsp. butter	

Cut off ends of beans pulling downward on both sides to remove strings along bean. Wash in warm water; plunge immediately into boiling salted water and cook for 15 min. Add butter and chopped parsley.

If desired, add pinch of bicarbonate of soda to water to preserve green color.

549. STRING BEANS À LA CRÈME

PREPARATION TIME: 30 MIN. COOKING TIME: 30 MIN.

2 lbs. string beans, cooked	2 tbsp. butter
2 cups cream	

Place beans in pot with butter. Heat cream; add to string beans and simmer 15 min.

550. STRING BEANS À LA NIÇOISE

PREPARATION TIME: 30 MIN. COOKING TIME: 40 MIN.

2 lbs. string beans, cooked	Chopped parsley
2 cups Tomato Purée	
(recipe 876)	

Simmer beans and tomato purée together for 20 min. Add chopped parsley just before serving.

551. SWISS CHARD

Remove green leafy part. Peel and scrape white ribs; cut in 1½-in. pieces. Cook 25 min. in boiling salted water. Drain and serve with one of following sauces: White (recipe 8 or 9), Mornay (recipe 14), Cream (recipe 11), Poulette (recipe 15).

TOMATOES À L'ANTIBOISE: See recipe 611.

TOMATOES WITH EGGPLANT: See recipe 482.

552. FRIED TOMATOES
PREPARATION TIME: 5 MIN. COOKING TIME: 8 MIN.

1 lb. tomatoes, sliced   6 tbsp. oil

Heat oil in skillet and brown tomato slices on both sides. Season to taste.

FRIED TOMATOES WITH EGGS: Break an egg on top of each slice when almost cooked; continue cooking 4 min. Season to taste. Serve immediately.

553. STEWED TOMATOES
PREPARATION TIME: 10 MIN. COOKING TIME: 1¼ HOURS.

2 lbs. tomatoes   4 tbsp. butter
4 cloves garlic, chopped   salt, pepper

Plunge tomatoes into boiling water for 2 min. Remove skins; cut in quarters. Place in casserole with butter and garlic, season to taste. Simmer gently 1 hour.

554. BAKED STUFFED TOMATOES
PREPARATION TIME: 35 MIN. COOKING TIME: 40 MIN.

6 large Tomatoes   salt
Duxelle (recipe 865)   fine bread crumbs
2⅔ tbsp. butter

Cut a slice from stem end of each tomato. Scoop out interior with spoon. Sprinkle with salt; turn tomatoes upside down and let stand for 30 min. so that liquid will drain out.

Stuff with duxelle; dot with butter, and replace slice. Bake 40 min. in slow oven.

555. STUFFED TOMATOES WITH RICE

PREPARATION TIME: 35 MIN. COOKING TIME: 25 MIN.

6 large tomatoes	fine bread crumbs **or**
¾ cup Rice, cooked (recipe 579)	1½ cups grated Gruyère
2 hard-boiled eggs, chopped	
chopped parsley, leeks	
chervil	

Hollow out tomatoes; drain. Stuff with mixture of rice, herbs, chopped egg. Sprinkle with bread crumbs or Gruyère. Bake 25 min. in hot oven.

STUFFED TOMATO SALAD: See recipe 612.

556. TURNIPS

Peel turnips; slice, quarter or dice, as desired. Cook 20 min. in boiling salted water. Serve with Maître d'hôtel Butter (recipe 4).

557. TURNIPS AU GRATIN

PREPARATION TIME: 30 MIN. COOKING TIME: 1 HOUR

2 lbs. turnip, peeled, thinly sliced	2 cups milk
1 qt. Stock (recipe 69)	6 tbsp. butter
½ cup flour	fine bread crumbs

Melt 4 tbsp. butter; sauté turnip slices. Moisten with stock; cook gently 45 min. Prepare a Béchamel Sauce (recipe 10) with remaining butter, flour, milk. Place cooked turnips in flat baking dish; nap with sauce and sprinkle with bread crumbs. Bake 15 min. in hot oven.

558. TURNIP PURÉE

PREPARATION TIME: 30 MIN. COOKING TIME: 20 MIN.

1 lb. turnips, peeled, sliced	4 tbsp. butter
1 lb. potatoes, peeled	salt, pepper

Cook turnips and potatoes together for 20 min. in boiling

salted water. Mash; rub through sieve or food mill. Beat in
butter, season. Add a little milk, if desired.

559. SAUTÉED ZUCCHINI AUX FINES HERBES
PREPARATION TIME: 15 MIN. COOKING TIME: 10 MIN.

4 zucchini	flour
5 tbsp. butter	chopped parsley, chervil, tarragon

Peel, seed and dice zucchini; dredge in flour. Brown 10
min. in butter. Sprinkle with chopped herbs.

560. VEGETABLE GALANTINE
PREPARATION TIME: 35 MIN. COOKING TIME: 2 HOURS.

1¾ cups bread crumbs	1 small onion, browned in
¼ lb. fresh haricot beans, cooked	3½ tbsp. butter
¾ cup Tomato Purée	6⅔ tbsp. milk
(recipe 876)	chopped parsley, chervil,
¼ lb. macaroni, cooked	fines herbes
1 hard-boiled egg	salt, pepper
1 raw egg	

Soak bread crumbs in milk. Chop all vegetables together;
mix with raw egg, purée, bread crumbs, chopped hard-boiled
egg, seasonings. Turn mixture into buttered earthenware terrine; cover. Bake 2 hours in slow oven. Set aside for 12 hours
before unmolding.

561. MACEDOINE OF VEGETABLES

Cook together for 30 min. in boiling salted water a mixture
of shelled peas, diced carrots, turnips, haricot beans, diced
potatoes, cauliflowerets, in desired quantities. Drain. Sauté
in small quantity of butter.

562. VEGETABLE PIE (FLAN AUX LEGUMES)
PREPARATION TIME: 45 MIN. COOKING TIME: 45 MIN.

Pie Pastry (recipe 796)	bread crumbs
¼ lb. string beans	Béchamel Sauce (recipe 10)
¼ lb. peas	3½ tbsp. butter
¼ lb. carrots	½ cup grated Gruyère
¼ lb. potatoes	

Line a pie tin with pastry; bake 15 min. in hot oven. Cook vegetables 15-20 min. in boiling salted water; dice, sauté in butter. Cover bottom of pie shell with layer of Béchamel Sauce, top with vegetables, finish with sauce. Sprinkle with grated Gruyère. Bake about 30 min. in hot oven.

Macaroni, Noodles, Rice

N.B.: All recipes serve 6, unless otherwise indicated.

How to cook pasta:

Use 2 tbsp. salt and at least 3 qts. of water for every half-lb. of pasta. Throw product into boiling salted water; bring water quickly back to boiling point so that pasta does not sink to bottom of pot. Do not cover. Cooking time (counted from moment water returns to boiling point): macaroni, 14 min.; spaghetti, 11 min.; noodles, 11 min.; spaghetti and spaghettini, 4 min.; vermicelli, 3 min.

Mix cooked pasta with butter, meat juice, or grated Gruyère or Parmesan. Or mix with one of following sauces: White (recipe 8 or 9), Béchamel (recipe 10), Poulette (recipe 15), Maître d'hôtel Butter (recipe 4), Brown Butter (recipe 6), Brown (recipe 40), Financière (recipe 32). Brown for a few minutes in hot oven, if desired.

Pasta may be used instead of bread in soups and stews. Use vermicelli or thin noodles for this purpose.

How to make your own noodles:

Sift 1 lb. flour onto board. Break 5 eggs into it. Knead quickly, adding sufficient water to form a firm and elastic dough. Roll out on floured board to thickness of ⅛ in. Set aside for 3 hours. With sharp knife, cut dough into thin strips. Dry for 30 min. on a white cloth. If stored in cool place, noodles will keep for 2 to 3 days.

563. FRIED MACARONI
COOKING TIME: 25 MIN.

½ lb. macaroni
   shortening for frying

salt, pepper
fried parsley (recipe 874)

Cook macaroni 15 min. in boiling salted water. Drain thoroughly. Fry until brown in smoking hot shortening, small portions at a time. Remove and drain, season to taste. Garnish with fried parsley.

564. MACARONI À LA NAPOLITAINE
PREPARATION TIME: 15 MIN. COOKING TIME: 20 MIN.

½ lb. macaroni
1 cup grated Gruyère

salt, pepper, nutmeg
Tomato Sauce (recipe 31)

Cook macaroni 15 min. in boiling salted water. Add cheese, salt, pepper, nutmeg. Add Tomato Sauce just before serving.

565. MACARONI NIÇOIS
PREPARATION TIME: 30 MIN. COOKING TIME: 25 MIN.

½ lb. macaroni, cooked
¾ tsp. Meat Extract
   (recipe 880)
¾ cup grated Parmesan
1 tbsp. flour
¼ lb. mushrooms, peeled, cut
   in pieces
   truffles

3 eggplants, peeled, thinly
   sliced
3 tomatoes, peeled, thinly
   sliced
⅔ cup butter
¾ cup diced ham
   garlic, salt, pepper
   shortening for frying

Sprinkle eggplant and tomato slices with salt; let stand 30 min. Drain. Dredge eggplant slices in flour; fry. Make a sauce by cooking together tomatoes, mushrooms, ham and truffles in butter; add meat extract and Parmesan. Mix sauce with macaroni; season to taste. Garnish with eggplant slices.

MACARONI À LA CÉVENOLE: See recipe 902.

566. MILANESE TIMBALE
PREPARATION TIME: 30 MIN. COOKING TIME: 25 MIN.

½ lb. macaroni
1 cup Light Brown Sauce
   (recipe 30)
6 tbsp. Tomato Sauce
   (recipe 31)

½ cup grated Gruyère
4 tbsp. butter
¼ cup grated Parmesan
   salt, pepper, *bouquet garni*

As desired:

truffles
ham
Chicken Quenelles (recipe 872)

mushrooms
calf's brains
sausages

Cook macaroni in boiling salted water; drain. Add butter
and cheese. Cook remaining ingredients (except Tomato
Sauce) with *bouquet garni* in Light Brown Sauce for 20
min.; add Tomato Sauce, salt and pepper during last 5 min.
Place layer of macaroni in buttered dish (or baked pastry
shell, if preferred); top with layer of sauce. Repeat until all ingredients have been used, finishing with sauce. Bake 20 min.
in moderate oven.

566A. *NEAPOLITAN TIMBALE:* Add ¼ lb. mushrooms
to basic recipe. Add shrimp, mussels, other shellfish, etc.,
as desired.

567. *MACARONI LOAF*
PREPARATION TIME: 20 MIN. COOKING TIME: 2 HOURS.

½ lb. macaroni, cooked
1 cup mixed grated Gruyère
  and Parmesan
¼ lb. cooked ham, chopped
⅓ lb. mushrooms

⅓ cup butter
1 cup cream
6 eggs, separated
salt, pepper, nutmeg

Mix macaroni with egg yolks, cheese, ham, half the mushrooms; season to taste. Fold in stiffly beaten egg whites. Turn
into well-buttered mold. Place mold in pan of water; bake
1½ hours in moderate oven. Mince remaining mushrooms;
cook uncovered for 10 min. in butter. Season to taste; add
cream. Pour over unmolded macaroni loaf.

568. *NEAPOLITAN CROQUETTES*
PREPARATION TIME: 20 MIN. COOKING TIME: 25 MIN.

½ lb. macaroni, cooked
2 cups grated Gruyère
2 eggs, separated
salt, pepper

1½ cups cooked chopped ham
1 whole egg
fine bread crumbs
shortening for frying

Combine all ingredients except egg whites; season to taste.

Form mixture into balls; roll first in beaten egg whites, then in bread crumbs. Brown in very hot shortening.

MACARONI SALAD: See recipe 605.

569. STUFFED MACARONI
PREPARATION TIME: 20 MIN.   COOKING TIME: 15 MIN.

½ lb. macaroni, cooked
¼ lb. cooked ham, chopped
¼ lb. mushrooms, sliced
1 onion, minced

leftover chopped meat
6 tbsp. Tomato Sauce
   (recipe 31)
¾ cup grated cheese
3½ tbsp. butter

As desired:

meat extract (recipe 880)

salt, pepper, parsley

Combine chopped ham and leftover meat. Cook mushrooms and onion 5 min. in butter; add to meat. Moisten with Meat Extract and Tomato Sauce, season to taste. Place layer of macaroni in buttered baking dish; top with layer of meat mixture; finish with macaroni. Sprinkle with grated cheese, dot with butter. Brown 7-8 min. in very hot oven.

570. STEWED MACARONI
PREPARATION TIME: 20 MIN.   COOKING TIME: 25 MIN.

½ lb. thin macaroni, cooked
¼ lb. mushrooms
¼ cup diced tongue
⅓ cup diced ham
salt, pepper

½ cup grated Gruyère
4½ tbsp. butter
2¼ tbsp. Tomato Purée
   (recipe 876)
3 tbsp. Madeira

Cook mushrooms 6-7 min. in butter. To cooked macaroni add mushrooms and their cooking liquor, tongue, ham, cheese, tomato purée. Sauté mixture quickly in a little butter; add Madeira, season to taste. Serve very hot.

571. SHELLS À LA REINE
PREPARATION TIME: 15 MIN.   COOKING TIME: 15 MIN.

½ lb. shells, cooked
   leftover roast chicken
1 cup Béchamel Sauce
   (recipe 10)
6 tbsp. Meat Extract
   (recipe 880)

⅔ cup butter
1¼ cups grated Gruyere
salt, pepper

Add butter and cheese to cooked macaroni. Crush left-over chicken; moisten with sauce and meat extract. Add to macaroni; season to taste.

572. NOODLES RÉGENCE
PREPARATION TIME: 5 MIN. COOKING TIME: 30 MIN.

½ lb. noodles
2 cups grated Gruyère

6⅔ tbsp. butter
½ cup fine bread crumbs

Cook noodles 12 min. in boiling salted water. Spread layer of cooked noodles in buttered baking dish; top with layer of cheese, dot with butter. Repeat until all ingredients have been used, finishing with layer of cheese. Sprinkle with bread crumbs. Bake 15 min. in slow oven.

573. NOODLE SOUFFLÉ
PREPARATION TIME: 30 MIN. COOKING TIME: 40 MIN.

½ lb. noodles
2 qts. water
3½ tbsp. butter
2 cups milk

3 tbsp. cream of rice
6 eggs, separated
salt, pepper

Cook noodles 15 min. in mixture of milk and water. Blend cream of rice with a little cold water; add sufficient cooking liquid from noodles to make a sauce, thicken over heat. Mix in noodles, add butter. Chill mixture. Fold in egg yolks and stiffly beaten egg whites, season to taste. Turn mixture into baking dish; bake 25 min. in slow oven. Serve immediately.

CROSETS: See recipe 922.

574. CANNELONI
PREPARATION TIME: 30 MIN. COOKING TIME: 25 MIN.

Noodle dough (see p. 193)
⅔ cup chopped cooked meat
¼ lb. sausage meat
½ lb. Spinach Puréed
    (recipe 545)
1 whole egg

¼ cup grated Gruyère
1 egg yolk
salt, pepper, nutmeg
Tomato Sauce (recipe 31)

Roll dough out very thin; cut into 12 3-in. x 3-in. squares.

Cook 12 min. in boiling salted water. Combine all remaining ingredients except Tomato Sauce; season to taste. Place small quantity of mixture on each cooked square; roll up lengthwise. Arrange rolls on baking dish. Cover with tomato sauce; sprinkle with additional grated Gruyère, if desired. Bake 10 min. in hot oven.

575. RAVIOLI
PREPARATION TIME: 50 MIN. COOKING TIME: 10 MIN.

Noodle dough (see p. 193)
¼ lb. chopped cooked meat
chopped parsley
salt, pepper

Roll out dough very thin; cut into large circles. Combine remaining ingredients. Place small quantity of mixture on each circle; moisten edges of dough slightly, fold and seal. Poach 10 min. in boiling salted water or stock. Serve as garnish for soup, meat or vegetables, or as a separate course with butter and grated Parmesan.

576. SPAGHETTI WITH NUT SAUCE
PREPARATION TIME: 30 MIN. COOKING TIME: 25 MIN.

½ lb. spaghetti, cooked
2 tbsp. olive oil
1 clove garlic
8 walnuts, shelled
1 cup grated Parmesan
salt, pepper, chopped parsley

Crush together garlic, nuts, parsley; add oil drop by drop. Season to taste. Drain spaghetti; mix with grated cheese, season. Cover with nut mixture.

577. PROVENÇAL TIMBALE
PREPARATION TIME: 30 MIN. COOKING TIME: 40 MIN.

½ lb. spaghetti, cooked
4 oz. black olives, pitted
1 cup grated Parmesan
¼ lb. mushrooms
2 or 3 small onions
⅔ cup butter
Tomato Sauce (recipe 31)

Heat butter; sauté onions and mushrooms. Simmer 5 min. Add to Tomato Sauce together with spaghetti, olives, cheese. Simmer for several minutes. Serve very hot.

578. GNOCCHIS
PREPARATION TIME: 20 MIN. COOKING TIME: 25 MIN.

Cream-puff Paste (recipe 790)   3½ tbsp. butter
2 cups Béchamel Sauce with
   cheese (recipe 10)

Set pastry aside for 2 hours before using. Form into small balls about size of a walnut; poach for 15 min. in boiling salted water. Arrange gnocchis in flat buttered baking dish; cover with Béchamel Sauce, dot with butter. Bake 10 min. in very hot oven.

Rice

Wash rice very thoroughly before cooking. The best way is to place it in a fine colander or sieve and hold it for several minutes under running cold water, stirring with hand. Washing removes the starch which would otherwise form a sticky paste during cooking.

Rice cooks quickly, so watch it closely.

579. RICE À L'INDIENNE
PREPARATION TIME: 3 MIN. COOKING TIME: 30 MIN.

1½ cups rice   3 qts. water
  1 tbsp. salt   6⅔ tbsp. butter

Throw rice into boiling salted water; cook 10 min. Drain. Mix in butter; cover and cook over very low flame 25 min.

579A. RICE WITH BUTTER: Mix in 4 tbsp. melted butter before serving. Serve immediately.

579B. RICE FINANCIÈRE: Mix rice with 2 cups Financière Sauce (recipe 32). This is a good accompaniment for a boiled fowl.

580. CREOLE RICE
PREPARATION TIME: 3 MIN. COOKING TIME: 10 MIN.

1½ cups rice   1 tbsp. salt
  3 qts. water   2 tbsp. butter

Throw rice into boiling salted water; cook uncovered over high flame for 10 min. or until rice is no longer brittle. Drain in collander or sieve, wash rapidly in cold running water. Drain and reheat immediately in butter. Season to taste.

581. FRIED RICE
PREPARATION TIME: 5 MIN. COOKING TIME: 15 MIN.

1½ cups rice	1 qt. water or stock
3½ tbsp. butter or chicken fat	salt, pepper

Melt butter in skillet; brown rice. Cook 4-5 min., stirring constantly. When grains are brown, pour in water or stock, season to taste. Cook 15 min.

582. RICH RICE
PREPARATION TIME: 5 MIN. COOKING TIME: 15 MIN.

1½ cups rice	3½ tbsp. butter or chicken fat
1 qt. stock	salt, pepper, *bouquet garni*
1 onion	

Throw rice into boiling stock together with onion, butter and seasonings. Cook uncovered over low flame for 15 min. Serve alone or as accompaniment for poultry or other white meat.

583. RICE À L'ITALIENNE
PREPARATION TIME: 7 MIN. COOKING TIME: 15 MIN.

1½ cups Rice, cooked (recipe 579)	3½ tbsp. butter
½ cups grated Parmesan	pepper, nutmeg

Add cheese, butter and seasoning to cooked rice just before serving.

583A. RICE À LA TOMATE:
Cook rice in 2 instead of 3 qts. water. Add to cooked rice ¾ cup Tomato Purée (recipe 876), ¼ cup grated Gruyère, ⅓ cup grated Parmesan.

584. RICE PEASANT-STYLE
PREPARATION TIME: 10 MIN. COOKING TIME: 15 MIN.

1⅓ cups rice
⅔ cup lard
1 onion, minced
⅓ cup diced fresh pork fat or
  blanched bacon

¾ cup grated Gruyère
2 qts. stock
bouquet garni, salt, pepper

Cook diced fat or bacon in lard. Add rice; cook, stirring constantly, 2-3 min. Moisten with stock, add seasonings. Cook 12-15 min. Add Gruyère just before serving.

585. RICE CROWN WITH MAYONNAISE
PREPARATION TIME: 10 MIN. COOKING TIME: 15 MIN.

1½ cups Rice, cooked
  (recipe 579)

1 cup Mayonnaise (recipe 60)
  Vinaigrette Sauce (recipe 56)

Pack cooked rice into ring mold; chill. Unmold onto serving dish. Fill center with mayonnaise. If desired, garnish with tomato slices and chopped parsley. Sprinkle with Vinaigrette Sauce.

586. RICE À LA REINE
PREPARATION TIME: 15 MIN. COOKING TIME: 15 MIN.

1⅓ cups rice
1½ cups Béchamel Sauce
  (recipe 10)
  leftover chicken or poultry,
  crushed

1½ qts. chicken stock
¼ lb. mushrooms
⅓ cup cream
  Quenelles (recipe 871)
  salt, pepper

Cook rice in stock following recipe 579. Use some of stock to prepare the Béchamel Sauce. Add mushrooms, quenelles and chicken to sauce; boil 20 min. Add cream, then drained cooked rice. Season to taste.

FLORENTINE RICE LOAF: See recipe 546.

587. RICE JAMBALAYA
PREPARATION TIME: 15 MIN. COOKING TIME: 25 MIN.

1½ cups rice
  1 lb. cooked meat or fish
  3 small onions, minced
  ¼ lb. ham, diced
  ¼ lb. fresh pork fat or
    blanched bacon, diced

1 qt. boiling water or stock
  salt, pepper, *fines herbes*
  Cayenne pepper

Brown diced onion and pork fat in skillet; remove. Brown meat or fish; add onion, pork fat, ham, stock or water. Cook 15 min. Add rice and seasonings; cook 10 min.

588. RICE AND ASPARAGUS CREAM
PREPARATION TIME: 30 MIN. COOKING TIME: 20 MIN.

1⅓ cups Rice, cooked
  (recipe 579)
  1 small bunch asparagus
  ½ lb. white bread, sliced

6⅔ tbsp. butter
  3 tbsp. cream of rice
  ¾ cup cream
  salt, pepper

Cook asparagus in boiling salted water until very tender; rub through sieve or food mill. Heat 4 tbsp. butter; add cream of rice, moisten with a little warm water. Add cream and asparagus purée, season to taste. Mix rice with sauce. Cut bread into fancy shapes; brown in remaining butter. Arrange around serving dish; place some of the rice mixture on each slice; heap remaining rice in center.

589. RICE WITH ARTICHOKES
PREPARATION TIME: 25 MIN. COOKING TIME: 30 MIN.

1⅓ cups Rice, cooked
  (recipe 579)
  4 tbsp. butter
  1 cup grated Parmesan
  1 medium onion, chopped

4 Artichoke Hearts, cooked
  (recipe 444), diced
1 lb. tomatoes, washed and
  quartered

Cook onion, artichoke hearts and tomatoes in butter for 20 min. Add rice and Parmesan. Serve piping hot.

590. CURRIED RICE
PREPARATION TIME: 5 MIN. COOKING TIME: 15 MIN.

2 med. onions, minced
1 qt. stock
4 tbsp. butter

1½ cups rice
salt, pepper
curry powder to taste

Brown onion thoroughly in 2 tbsp. butter. Add rice and seasonings; mix thoroughly. Moisten with stock. Cook 15 min. over low flame. Add remaining butter just before serving.

590A. PAPRIKA RICE: Substitute paprika for curry powder.

590B. SAFFRON RICE: Use only one onion; substitute saffron for curry powder. Add 6 tbsp. tomato purée (recipe 876) a few minutes before cooking is finished.

591. RICE PILAF
PREPARATION TIME: 5 MIN. COOKING TIME: 20 MIN.

1½ cups long-grain rice
3½ tbsp. butter

¾ cup boiling water or stock
salt, pepper

Heat butter; mix in rice, but do not brown. Add boiling liquid. Bring to boil, season to taste. Cover and cook over low flame until liquid is absorbed. Uncover and cook a little longer to dry rice.

592. MOTHER MARY'S LETTUCE
PREPARATION TIME: 30 MIN. COOKING TIME: 45 MIN.

¾ cup chopped cooked veal
or chicken
1 head lettuce, separated
⅓ cup rice

1 egg
salt, pepper
¾ cup cream

Mix chopped meat, rice, egg; season. Form mixture into small balls. Place one ball on each lettuce leaf (scald leaves 1 min. in boiling water so that they will roll easily); roll up and secure with toothpick or string. Place rolls in baking dish; cover with cream. Bake 45 min. in moderate oven.

Salads

N.B.: All recipes serve 6, unless otherwise indicated.

593. TOSSED GREEN SALAD

Salad greens should be thoroughly washed and dried (water on leaves prevents dressing from coating them properly), and wilted and damaged leaves should be removed. Tear greens into large pieces; toss with vinegar-and-oil dressing until thoroughly coated. Serve immediately.

594. VINEGAR-AND-OIL DRESSING

The classic French dressing for tossed green salad. (Our bottled "French" dressing is an American invention, not very popular with French visitors to our shores!)

For 2 med. heads of letture, or 1 large head escarole, or endive	4 tbsp. oil, 2 tbsp. vinegar, salt, pepper
For romaine	5 tbsp. oil, 2 tbsp. vinegar, salt, pepper
For 1 large head chicory	3 tbsp. oil, 2 tbsp. vinegar, salt, pepper
For watercress	1-1½ tbsp. oil, 2 tbsp. vinegar, salt, pepper

Add salt and pepper to taste to vinegar. Gradually beat in oil until dressing is smooth. A finely minced clove of garlic, 1 tsp. mustard, or chopped *fines herbes* may be added to vinegar before beating in oil, if desired. Add salad greens, toss.

594A. *CREAM DRESSING:* Substitute 3 tbsp. cream for oil; use ¾ tsp. vinegar or lemon juice.

594B. *RICH DRESSING:* Replace oil with fat obtained by melting bits of fresh pork fat or blanched bacon over low heat.

595. NINON SALAD
PREPARATION TIME: 10 MIN.

3 endive, washed and dried	6 tbsp. Rémoulade Sauce
1 head chicory	(recipe 58)
3 hard-boiled eggs	

Separate chicory and endive leaves; cut leaves which are too large. Season with sauce. Chop egg yolks, slice whites in strips; use to garnish salad.

596. PASTOURELLE SALAD
PREPARATION TIME: 20 MIN.   COOKING TIME: 30 MIN.

10 small onions	1 tbsp. capers
2 gherkins	10-15 olives, pitted
6 anchovy fillets, cut in	chopped *fines herbes*
thin strips	vinegar-and-oil Dressing
yolks of 6 hard-boiled eggs	

Cook onions 30 min. in boiling salted water, or in stock if available. Chill. Mince gherkins. Combine all ingredients; toss in dressing. Garnish with *fines herbes* and halved egg yolks.

597. ANDREA SALAD
PREPARATION TIME: 20 MIN.   COOKING TIME: 30 MIN.

1 head celery	4 hard-boiled eggs
½ lb. string beans	3 tbsp. Vinaigrette Sauce
4 tomatoes, halved	(recipe 56)
½ lb. potatoes	Mayonnaise (recipe 60)

Cook potatoes and string beans 30 min. in boiling salted water; peel potatoes. Scald celery for 2 min. in boiling water; peel. Cut potatoes and celery in thin slices; add string beans. Season with Vinaigrette Sauce. Garnish with eggs and tomato halves filled with mayonnaise.

598. *RACHEL SALAD*
PREPARATION TIME: 20 MIN.

2 med. apples
1 stalk celery
2 endive

¼ lb. cooked, sliced beets
12 walnuts, shelled, quartered
    vinaigrette sauce (recipe 56)

Peel apples, cut in thin slices. Slice celery, marinate for 2 hours in sauce. Add nuts, apple slices; mix well. Garnish with endive leaves and beet slices.

599. *YVETTE SALAD*
PREPARATION TIME: 25 MIN.   COOKING TIME: 20 MIN.

2 small heads celery
1 lb. potatoes
4 hard-boiled eggs, quartered

Vinaigrette Sauce (recipe 56)
Mayonnaise (recipe 60)

Boil potatoes; scald celery 2-3 min. in boiling water. Peel vegetables, cut into small slices. Add eggs. Season with sauce; nap with mayonnaise.

600. *TOURANGELLE SALAD*
PREPARATION TIME: 10 MIN.   COOKING TIME: 25 MIN.

½ lb. string beans
½ lb. new potatoes
1 head lettuce, washed and dried
  juice of 1 lemon

2 tomatoes, sliced
⅔ cup cream
salt, pepper

Cook string beans and potatoes in boiling salted water. Chill. Cut in small pieces; combine with lettuce leaves, lemon juice, salt and pepper, mix thoroughly. Garnish with tomato slices.

601. *RUSSIAN SALAD* (SALADE RUSSE)
PREPARATION TIME: 45 MIN.

Use the following cooked, chilled, diced vegetables, in amounts desired:

artichoke hearts
string beans
haricot beans
turnip
carrots
peas

cauliflower
2 tomatoes, sliced
7 or 8 olives, pitted
1 head lettuce
2 hard-boiled eggs, sliced
2 cups Mayonnaise (recipe 60)

Combine vegetables; dress with mayonnaise. Heap in salad bowl; garnish with sliced tomatoes, eggs, olives, lettuce leaves.

602. *CAULIFLOWER À LA MAYONNAISE*
PREPARATION TIME: 30 MIN. COOKING TIME: 30 MIN.

1 head cauliflower
½ lb. tomatoes, sliced
3 hard-boiled eggs
6 slices ham

Mayonnaise (recipe 60)
Mayonnaise Mousseline
  (recipe 60A)

Cook cauliflower according to recipe 459; chill. Heap up cauliflowerets on serving dish; garnish with 2 eggs rubbed through sieve. Surround with sliced tomatoes. Roll ham slices into horns; fill with mayonnaise. Arrange around outside. Garnish with Mayonnaise Mousseline.

603. *CUCUMBER À L'ANTIBOISE*
PREPARATION TIME: 45 MIN. COOKING TIME: 10 MIN.

1 cucumber, peeled, seeded,
  sliced
½ lb. tuna
½ lb. butter

2 cups Mayonnaise (recipe 60)
3 tbsp. Tomato Purée
  (recipe 876)
chopped parsley

Scald cucumber slices 10 min. in boiling salted water. Cream tuna with butter; season to taste. Blend tomato purée with mayonnaise. Arrange cucumber slices on serving dish; fill centers with tuna mixture. Spread with mayonnaise. Serve very cold.

604. *LENTIL SALAD*

Cook lentils (see page 161); chill. Season with Vinaigrette Sauce (recipe 56).

605. *MACARONI SALAD*
PREPARATION TIME: 1 HOUR. COOKING TIME: 25 MIN.

10 oz. macaroni, cooked
  several artichoke hearts
1 hard-boiled egg, chopped

4 tbsp. tomato paste
  salt, pepper, chopped parsley
  Mayonnaise (recipe 60)

Cook artichoke hearts according to recipe 444; chill and dice. Combine macaroni, diced artichoke hearts, hard-boiled egg, parsley. Season with mayonnaise mixed with tomato paste. Serve cold or slightly warm.

606. *MUSHROOM SALAD I* (Cooked)
PREPARATION TIME: 25 MIN. COOKING TIME: 3 MIN.

½ lb. mushrooms, peeled
½ cup oil
1 egg yolk

juice of 1 lemon
Mayonnaise (recipe 60)

Cook mushrooms 3 min. in boiling salted water seasoned with half the lemon juice. Drain; chill. Cut in small pieces. Combine with mayonnaise seasoned with remaining lemon juice.

607. *MUSHROOM SALAD II* (Uncooked)
PREPARATION TIME: 10 MIN.

⅓ lb. mushrooms, peeled, thinly
  sliced
juice of 1 lemon

2 tbsp. oil
salt, pepper, chopped parsley

Make a dressing with lemon juice, oil, salt and pepper; mix with sliced mushrooms. Garnish with chopped parsley. Serve immediately.

608. *MUSHROOMS À LA GRECQUE*
PREPARATION TIME: 10 MIN. COOKING TIME: 8 MIN.

1 lb. small mushrooms
6⅔ tbsp. white wine
3 tbsp. oil
  juice of 1 lemon

1 tbsp. tomato paste
salt, pepper, *bouquet garni*,
  coriander

Heat oil in skillet. Place in mushrooms. Add remaining ingredients. Cook uncovered over high heat for 7-8 min. Chill in cooking liquid. Serve very cold, as an hors-d'oeuvre.

609. *POTATO SALAD*
Cook potatoes according to recipe 521. Peel, slice thinly. Season with Vinaigrette Sauce (recipe 56). Add chopped onion, parsley, beets, hard-boiled eggs, etc., as desired. Place a little stock or milk in bottom of salad bowl so that salad won't be too dry.

619. MUSSELS À LA MAYONNAISE

Cook mussels according to recipe 171. Remove from shells; chill. Mix with Mayonnaise (recipe 60). Serve in scallop shells or small dishes.

620. TUNA FISH WITH OLIVES
PREPARATION TIME: 25 MIN.

1 lb. canned tuna	¼ lb. olives
6⅔ tbsp. butter	Mayonnaise (recipe 60)

Cream tuna and butter together into smooth paste. Add mayonnaise. Heap up on serving dish in shape of dome or loaf. Garnish with pitted olives.

621. SHELLS À LA MAYONNAISE
PREPARATION TIME: 20 MIN.

½ lb. cooked fish	1 hard-boiled egg, sliced
cooked mussels and shrimp	Mayonnaise (recipe 60)

Combine fish and mayonnaise. Fill 6 scallop shells or small dishes with mixture. Top with additional mayonnaise and slices of egg.

COLD MEAT SALADS

622. BEEF and LAMB

Arrange thin slices of cold cooked meat on serving dish. Serve with Tartare Sauce (recipe 63) or Mayonnaise (recipe 60).

623. VEAL and PORK

Arrange thin slices of cold cooked meat on serving dish. Garnish with parsley and gherkins; serve with Mayonnaise (recipe 60).

624. HAM WITH GHERKINS

Arrange thin slices of cold cooked ham on serving dish.

Garnish with chopped Meat Jelly (recipe 881) and sliced gherkins.

625. HAM AUX HERBES

Arrange slices of cold cooked ham on serving dish. Garnish with sorrel, spinach and salad greens.

626. HAM HORNS

Roll slices of cooked ham into horns. Fill with vegetable Macedoine (recipe 561) dressed with mayonnaise. Arrange on oval serving dish; garnish with sliced tomatoes and hard-boiled eggs; mayonnaise, chopped meat jelly.

627. POULTRY

Arrange cold slices of meat on platter; garnish with parsley and sliced hard-boiled eggs. Serve with mayonnaise.

Combine thin slices of meat, lettuce leaves, quartered hard-boiled eggs. Season with Vinaigrette Sauce (recipe 56). Serve mayonnaise separately.

628. TRIPE

Cut cooked Tripe (recipe 349) into thin slivers. Season with Vinaigrette (recipe 56), Ravigote (recipe 56) or Deviled (recipe 68) Sauce.

629. TROTTERS

Cut cold Trotters (recipe 352) in pieces. Season with Ravigote Sauce (recipe 56).

Fruit

630. BAKED APPLES
PREPARATION TIME: 5 MIN. COOKING TIME: 35 MIN.

Place 6 large apples in baking dish; add 1 tbsp. water. Prick apples in several places with fork, to prevent them from bursting. Bake about 35 min. in slow oven.

631. APPLES CHÂTELAINE
PREPARATION TIME: 30 MIN. COOKING TIME: 30 MIN.

6 apples, peeled, cored, halved
½ cup sugar
1 cup water

1 pinch of vanilla powder
juice of 1 lemon

Place apples cut side up in enameled casserole with sugar, water, vanilla. Cover and cook over moderate heat 8-10 min., or until fruit becomes transparent. Turn apples carefully, cook uncovered about 30 min. Drain. Arrange fruit in serving dish. Reduce syrup by boiling 7-8 min. over high flame; add lemon juice and pour over apples. Chill.

632. STUFFED APPLES
PREPARATION TIME: 20 MIN. COOKING TIME: 45 MIN.

6 large apples
4 oz. candied fruit
4 tbsp. butter

4 tbsp. sugar
¾ tsp. rum

Peel and core apples, removing sufficient fruit from center to enlarge opening to about 1¼ in. Remove bits of apple from around core; chop with candied fruit; add rum. Stuff holes in apples with mixture; sprinkle with a little water. Top with bit of butter, sprinkle with sugar. Bake 45 min. in hot oven, basting occasionally with syrup.

633. APPLES IN BUTTER
PREPARATION TIME: 15 MIN. COOKING TIME: 40 MIN.

6 large apples	6 thin slices stale white bread
6 tbsp. water	pinch of vanilla powder
¾ cup powdered sugar	butter

Peel and core apples. Fill centers with butter. Butter slices of bread on both sides; place in bottom of baking dish. Top each slice with an apple; sprinkle with sugar and vanilla powder. Add water. Bake 40 min. in very slow oven.

634. APPLESAUCE
PREPARATION TIME: 15 MIN. COOKING TIME: 15 MIN.

1 lb. apples, quartered	¾ cup water
¼ tsp. grated lemon peel	sugar to taste

Cook apples, covered, 15-20 min. in enameled casserole. Rub through fine sieve. Add lemon peel and sugar; mix well. Serve cold.

APPLESAUCE WITH CROUTONS: Add 3½ tbsp. butter to hot applesauce. Garnish with small slices of white bread fried in butter. Serve hot.

APPLESAUCE MERINGUE: Spread applesauce in buttered baking dish. Cover with 3 stiffly beaten egg whites, sprinkle with ¼ cup sugar. Bake 15 min. in very slow oven.

635. APPLE ASPIC
PREPARATION TIME: 15 MIN. COOKING TIME: 3 HOURS.

2 lbs. apples, peeled, thinly sliced	juice of 1 lemon
2 cups sugar	pinch of vanilla powder
1⅔ tbsp. butter	Vanilla Cream, flavored with kirsch if desired (recipe 687A)

Place apples in enameled casserole with sugar, vanilla, lemon juice; cook 3 hours over very low flame (watch carefully to see that fruit does not stick.) Rub through fine sieve; add butter in small quantities, stirring constantly. Turn mixture into buttered mold; chill overnight. Unmold and serve plain or with vanilla cream.

636. APPLE COMPOTE
PREPARATION TIME: 15 MIN. COOKING TIME: 15 MIN.

1 lb. apples, peeled, cored, quartered	sugar, as desired
1 cup water	vanilla extract or grated lemon rind

Combine all ingredients in enameled casserole. Cook 15 min. over high flame. Serve warm or cold.

637. FLAMING APPLES
PREPARATION TIME: 10 MIN. COOKING TIME: 20 MIN.

6 apples, peeled and cored	3 tbsp. rum
1 cup water	pinch of vanilla powder
⅔ cup sugar	

Place apples in enameled casserole with water, sugar, vanilla. Cover and cook 15-20 min. over low flame. Remove and drain apples; place in serving dish and keep warm. Reduce syrup by boiling; add 2 tbsp. rum, pour over apples. Heat remaining rum; ignite and pour over apples.

638. APPLES WITH RICE
PREPARATION TIME: 10 MIN. COOKING TIME: 30 MIN.

⅔ cup rice	1⅓ tbsp. butter
2 cups milk	1 cup water
6 apples, peeled and cored	pinch of vanilla powder
⅔ cup sugar	

Cook rice with milk, 4 tbsp. sugar and vanilla, according to recipe 722. Spread in buttered baking dish. Place apples in enameled casserole with water and 4 tbsp. sugar; cover and cook 10-15 min., or until tender but still whole. Remove from syrup; arrange on top of rice, sprinkle with remaining sugar. Bake 15-20 min. in slow oven. Serve hot.

639. APPLE-RICE CHARLOTTE
PREPARATION TIME: 10 MIN.

1 cup rice, cooked (recipe 722)	lady fingers
apple compote (recipe 636)	Custard Cream (recipe 687) or
3 tbsp. water, sweetened	apricot or currant jam

Line a round mold on sides and bottom with lady fingers cut in triangular shapes and soaked, flat side down, in sweetened water. (Cut side of lady fingers should face in.) Fill with alternating layers of rice and applesauce. Finish with scraps of lady fingers. Cover with plate and several weights. Chill overnight. Unmold and serve with custard cream or jam.

640. APPLE TIMBALE
PREPARATION TIME: 10 MIN. COOKING TIME: 1 HOUR.

1 lb. apples, peeled, cored, sliced crosswise	1¼ cups powdered sugar
¼ lb. thinly sliced white bread, stale	6 tbsp. water
	Custard Cream (recipe 687), optional
¼ lb. butter, or less if desired	

Line bottom of buttered mold with slices of bread; top with layer of apple slices, sprinkle with sugar and dot with butter. Repeat until all ingredients have been used. Sprinkle with water. Bake 1 hour in slow oven. Unmold and serve plain or with Custard Cream.

641. APRICOT COMPOTE
PREPARATION TIME: 10 MIN. COOKING TIME: 10 MIN.

1½ cups water	¾ cup sugar
2 lbs. apricots	

Following recipe 890, prepare a glazing syrup (large thread stage—219° F.) with sugar and water. Wash apricots, halve, remove pits. Boil 10-12 min. in syrup. Serve fruit covered with syrup.

642. DRIED APRICOT COMPOTE
COOKING TIME: 1 HOUR.

⅔ lb. dried apricots	2 cups water
½ cup sugar	

Soak apricots 1 day in advance. Cook with sugar and water for 1 hour.

643. *APRICOT MOUSSE*
PREPARATION TIME: 10 MIN.

½ lb. apricots ½ cup sugar
1 cup cream, whipped

Proceed as for Peach Mousse (recipe 663).

644. *APRICOT CONDÉ:* Proceed as for Banana Condé (recipe 650).

645. *EGG SURPRISE*
PREPARATION TIME: 10 MIN. COOKING TIME: 20 MIN.

12 large apricots, halved and pitted 2 cups Rice, cooked (recipe 722)
½ cup cream ½ cup sugar
6 tbsp. water

Prepare a syrup (recipe 890) with sugar and water. Add a few kernels from apricot pits; boil 10-12 min. Poach apricot halves 5-6 min. in boiling syrup; drain, chill. Spread rice on round serving dish; cover with cream. Top with apricot halves, cut side down. Serve cold.

646. *BANANA COMPOTE*
PREPARATION TIME: 3 MIN. COOKING TIME: 20 MIN.

6 bananas ½ cup sugar
1 cup water

Peel and slice bananas; remove fibers. Place sugar and water in pot; bring to boil. Add banana slices. Cook 20 min. over low heat, stirring frequently.

647. *FLAMING BANANAS*
PREPARATION TIME: 5 MIN. COOKING TIME: 5 MIN.

6 bananas pinch of vanilla powder
⅔ cup sugar 1½ tsp. rum

Prepare a syrup with water, sugar, vanilla. Peel bananas; poach 3-4 min. in boiling syrup. Drain; arrange on serving dish. Add rum to syrup; pour over bananas and ignite. Serve flaming.

648. FRIED BANANAS
PREPARATION TIME: 3 MIN. COOKING TIME: 3 MIN.

6 bananas   3 tbsp. sugar
4½ tbsp. butter

Peel bananas, halve lengthwise. Heat butter in skillet; fry bananas 2-3 min. each side. Sprinkle with sugar. Serve very hot. If desired, serve on bed of hot Rice with Milk (recipe 722).

649. BANANA MOUSSE
PREPARATION TIME: 10 MIN.

6 bananas   1 cup cream, whipped
¼ cup sugar

Proceed as for Peach Mousse (663).

650. BANANA CONDÉ
PREPARATION TIME: 15 MIN. COOKING TIME: 5 MIN.

6 bananas   candied or canned cherries
2 oranges   6 tbsp. water
2 tangerines   6 tbsp. sugar
2 apples   1-2 tbsp. apricot jam, if desired
2 cups Rice, cooked (recipe 722)

Fill a ring mold with cooked rice; chill. Peel bananas; cut in half crosswise, then again lengthwise. Combine sliced or quartered oranges, apples, tangerines. Place water and sugar in pot and bring to boil; poach bananas 3-4 min. Remove and drain. Poach remaining fruit 3-4 min. Unmold rice onto serving dish; surround with bananas. Fill center of ring with mixed fruit. Garnish with cherries; sprinkle with syrup mixed with jam, if desired.

651. BANANA SOUFFLÉ
PREPARATION TIME: 20 MIN. COOKING TIME: 10 MIN.

6 bananas	3 eggs, separated
¼ cup sugar	6 tbsp. warm milk
⅓ cup flour	pinch of salt
1⅓ tbsp. butter	pinch of vanilla powder

Hollow out bananas in form of a boat. Make a White Sauce (recipe 8 or 9) with butter, flour, warm milk; add mashed bananas, egg yolks, vanilla powder. Fold in stiffly beaten egg whites. Heap mixture into banana boats. Bake 6 min. in hot oven.

652. CHERRY COMPOTE
PREPARATION TIME: 15 MIN. COOKING TIME: 10 MIN.

2 lbs. cherries, pitted	1¼-1½ cups powdered sugar
¾ cup water	

Place cherries in pot with sugar and water. Bring to boil; cook 10 min. Chill.

653. CHERRIES DUCHESS
PREPARATION TIME: 20 MIN. COOKING TIME: 15 MIN.

1 lb. cherries, with stems	1⅓ cups powdered sugar
2 egg whites	

Wash and dry cherries. Beat egg whites 5 min. with fork. Roll cherries in egg white, then in powdered sugar. Arrange on plate sprinkled with sugar; heat in slow oven for 15 min. May be served hot, cold or slightly warm.

654. MELON COMPOTE
PREPARATION TIME: 10 MIN. COOKING TIME: 35 MIN.

3 small melons, not quite ripe	3 cups powdered sugar
3 tbsp. vinegar	

Peel melons; cut into thin slices. Cook with sugar and vinegar for 30-35 min. in enameled casserole.

655. MELON SURPRISE
PREPARATION TIME: 15 MIN.

1 large, ripe melon
1 cup powdered sugar
3 tbsp. kirsch

butter
1⅓ cups strawberries

Cut melon in half; carefully scoop out fruit without destroying rind. Cut pulp in small pieces; mix with strawberries, sugar, kirsch. Fill melon shells with mixture; tie two halves together, plaster crack over with butter. Chill 24 hours. Serve very cold.

656. ORANGE SURPRISE
PREPARATION TIME: 30 MIN.

6 oranges
1 pear, peeled, cut in pieces
1 apple, peeled, cut in pieces
2 bananas, peeled, sliced

candied cherries
raisins
½ cup sugar

Cut small section from top of each orange; carefully remove fruit without destroying rind. Cut fruit in small pieces; combine with remaining ingredients. Fill orange shells with fruit; replace top slice. Chill before serving.

657. ORANGES TAHITIAN
PREPARATION TIME: 20 MIN.

6 oranges, peeled
6 pineapple slices

4 oz. candied fruits, chopped
currant jelly

Arrange pineapple slices on serving dish; place an orange on each slice. Cover with currant jelly; surround with candied fruit. Serve chilled.

658. ORANGE ASPIC
PREPARATION TIME: 20 MIN.

juice of 12 oranges
juice of 3 lemons
1 lb. sugar

6 tbsp. gelatin
2½ cups warm water

Dissolve sugar and gelatin in water. Add grated rinds of 2 oranges, orange juice, lemon juice. Strain through fine strainer. Pour mixture into round mold; chill.

659. ORANGE SOUFFLÉ
PREPARATION TIME: 15 MIN. COOKING TIME: 20 MIN.

6 tbsp. flour
1⅔ tbsp. butter
4 egg yolks
5 egg whites
¾ cup warm milk

⅔ cup powdered sugar
1 oz. candied orange peel,
    chopped
grated rind of 2 oranges

Blend flour with 3 tbsp. milk; pour into remaining milk, thicken over heat. Away from heat, add butter, sugar, egg yolks, grated rind, candied peel, stiffly beaten egg whites. Pour into buttered mold. Bake 20 min. in slow oven.

660. PEACHES IN WINE
PREPARATION TIME: 10 MIN.

6 peaches
6 tbsp. powdered sugar

1 cup champagne or sparkling
    white wine

Peel and quarter peaches; arrange on serving dish or in bowl. Sprinkle with wine and sugar; set aside for 2 hours. Serve cold.

661. PEACHES COLOMBINE
PREPARATION TIME: 20 MIN. COOKING TIME: 30 MIN.

6 peaches
1 cup Rice, cooked (recipe 722)
½ cup sugar

candied fruit
1 cup Sabayon (recipe 818)

Heap rice in balls in center of serving dish. Poach whole peaches 5 min. in sweetened boiling water. Drain, peel, cut in half and remove pits. Stuff each half wtih a little rice then replace halves together. Arrange peaches around rice "eggs." Garnish with candied fruit and nap with Sabayon.

662. PEACHES MELBA STYLE
PREPARATION TIME: 30 MIN. COOKING TIME: 25 MIN.

6 peaches
5 egg yolks
¼ cup chopped roasted almonds
2 cups milk

¾ cup sugar
2 cups water
currant jelly

Peel peaches; poach in syrup made with water and ½ cup sugar. Arrange peaches in cups; cover with currant jam, sprinkle with almonds. Prepare a Custard Cream (recipe 687) with milk, egg yolks, remaining sugar. Chill. Pour sauce around peaches. Chill for several hours.

663. PEACH MOUSSE
PREPARATION TIME: 10 MIN.

3 peaches, peeled
½ cup sugar

1 cup cream, whipped
lady fingers

Rub peaches through a hair sieve. Add sugar; carefully fold in whipped cream. Arrange on serving dish; surround with lady fingers.

664. PEACH CONDÉ
PREPARATION TIME: 15 MIN.   COOKING TIME: 5 MIN.

Proceed as for Banana Condé (recipe 650), using 6 large peaches, peeled and halved, and filling center of ring with mixture of peaches, apricots and plums.

665. PEAR COMPOTE
PREPARATION TIME: 15 MIN.   COOKING TIME: 30 MIN.

1 lb. pears, peeled, cored, quartered
6 tbsp. sugar

1 cup water
grated rind of 1 lemon or
1 tsp. vanilla extract

Place pears in enameled casserole with water, sugar, lemon rind or vanilla extract. Cook 30 min. or until fruit is tender. Serve cold.

666. PEARS IN WINE
PREPARATION TIME: 15 MIN.   COOKING TIME: 30 MIN.

1 lb. small, firm pears with stems, peeled
6 tbsp. red wine
1 cup sugar

1 clove
¼ tsp. cinnamon
¼ tsp. nutmeg

Place whole pears in enameled casserole with wine and

spices; cook 30 min. Stand pears upright on serving dish; cover with syrup.

667. *PEARS À LA CRÈME*
PREPARATION TIME: 10 MIN. COOKING TIME: 35 MIN.

12 small, firm pears with stems, peeled	pinch of vanilla powder
1 cup water	1 cup Custard Cream
½ cup sugar	(recipe 687)

Cook pears 30-35 min. in syrup made of water, sugar, vanilla. Remove and drain pears; arrange on serving dish. Reduce syrup by boiling; pour over pears. Nap with Custard Cream.

668. *PEAR CONDÉ*
PREPARATION TIME: 15 MIN. COOKING TIME: 15 MIN.

Proceed as for Banana Condé (recipe 650), using 6 pears. Halve, core and peel fruit; poach 10-15 min. Fill center of ring with mixture of currants, raspberries and strawberries.

669. *PEAR ÉMINCÉ*
PREPARATION TIME: 10 MIN. COOKING TIME: 10 MIN.

6 pears, peeled, cored, sliced	6 small slices white bread, fried
4½ tbsp. butter	in butter
1¼ cups powdered sugar	

Heat butter in enameled casserole; sauté pear slices, being careful not to burn them. Arrange on slices of bread; sprinkle with powdered sugar. Serve very hot.

670. *PINEAPPLE WITH KIRSCH*
PREPARATION TIME: 5 MIN.

1 fresh pineapple, peeled and sliced or	3½ tbsp. kirsch
1 can sliced pineapple	¾ cup Light Sugar Syrup (recipe 890)

Macerate pineapple slices for 1 hour in mixture of syrup and kirsch. Serve very cold. Champagne, rum or other liqueur may be substituted for kirsch.

671. *PINEAPPLE COMPOTE*
PREPARATION TIME: 10 MIN. COOKING TIME: 35 MIN.

1 fresh pineapple, peeled, cut in
  pieces, or
1 can pineapple chunks
2 oranges, peeled, quartered

¾ cup sugar
1 cup water
3 tbsp. maraschino

Place water and sugar in casserole; bring to boil. Add pineapple and orange quarters; boil 35 min. Remove from heat; add maraschino.

672. *PINEAPPLE MOUSSE*
PREPARATION TIME: 10 MIN.

4 slices pineapple
1 cup cream, whipped

⅓ cup sugar

Proceed as for Peach Mousse (recipe 663).

673. *PINEAPPLE CROWN*
PREPARATION TIME: 15 MIN. COOKING TIME: 45 MIN.

1 cup rice
6 tbsp. sugar
3 cups milk
1 can sliced pineapple

pinch of salt
⅔ cup strawberries, crushed
  (optional)

Cook rice with milk, sugar and vanilla, following recipe 722. Pour into ring mold; chill. Unmold onto serving dish. Cut pineapple slices in half; arrange around rice crown. Reduce pineapple syrup; add crushed strawberries, if desired, and boil 10-15 min. over high heat. Pour into center of rice crown. Chill before serving.

674. *PRUNES*

Wash and soak prunes for several hours in cold water. Cook with sugar and water (1¼ cups powdered sugar and 1⅓ cups water to 1 lb. prunes) for 1 hour over low heat. Serve cold.

675. *PRUNES IN TEA*
PREPARATION TIME: 10 MIN.

¾ lb. prunes
2 cups hot tea

6 tbsp. sugar
pinch of vanilla powder

Wash prunes; soak for 2 hours in cold water. Drain; place in bowl. Cover with boiling tea; add vanilla, sugar. Chill 2-3 hours.

676. PRUNES IN WINE
PREPARATION TIME: 10 MIN.

¾ lb. prunes
6⅔ tbsp. red Bordeaux wine
6 tbsp. sugar

2 cups water
1 lemon, sliced
¼ tsp. cinnamon

Wash prunes; soak 2 hours in cold water. Drain, arrange on serving dish. Boil together remaining ingredients; pour over prunes. Macerate 2-3 hours.

677. RHUBARB COMPOTE
PREPARATION TIME: 10 MIN. COOKING TIME: 25 MIN.

2 lbs. rhubarb, cut in ½-in. pieces   ⅓ cup sugar

Place fruit and sugar in enameled casserole. Cook 25 min. over low flame, stirring frequently. Serve cold.

678. STRAWBERRIES À L'ITALIENNE
PREPARATION TIME: 10 MIN.

2⅔ cups strawberries
6 tbsp. sugar

juice of 2 lemons
2 tbsp. kirsch

Place strawberries in bowl; sprinkle with sugar, lemon juice, kirsch. Chill 2 hours.

679. RICE IN TANGERINES

6 tangerines
4 oz. orange peel, finely chopped

Rice in Milk (recipe 722)

Peel back section of rind at top of tangerines; remove fruit, leaving rind intact. Mix orange peel and rice. Fill tangerine shells with rice. Heap any remaining rice in center of serving dish; surround with tangerine shells and garnish with tangerine sections.

680. FOUR-FRUIT ASPIC
PREPARATION TIME: 25 MIN.

1 cup raspberries	juice of 2 oranges
¾ cup red currants	juice of 1 lemon
1 cup strawberries	¾ cup water
⅓ lb. cherries	7 tbsp. gelatin
2 cups sugar	grated orange peel

Squeeze berries in muslin cloth to extract juice. Add orange and lemon juice, a little grated orange peel. Prepare a light syrup (recipe 890) with sugar, water, gelatin; add to fruit juice. Filter through fine strainer; chill. Pour chilled mixture into round mold; chill until firm.

681. FRUIT COMPOTE
PREPARATION TIME: 30 MIN. COOKING TIME: 6 MIN.

½ lb. peaches	2⅔ cups raspberries
½ lb. apricots	1 cup strawberries
½ lb. cherries	1 cup sugar
2 bananas, peeled, sliced	2 cups water

Bring water and sugar to boil. Add peeled, pitted apricot quarters; cook 3 min. Add peeled, quartered peaches; cook 3 min. Add pitted cherries. Remove from heat, add remaining fruit. Chill.

682. FRUIT MACEDOINE
PREPARATION TIME: 30 MIN.

2 bananas, peeled and sliced	⅔ cup raspberries
½ lb. cherries, pitted	juice of 1 lemon
¼ lb. grapes, pitted	powdered sugar
1 cup strawberries	peaches, pears, etc., as desired

Wash fruit, peel where necessary. Place fruit in bowl; sprinkle with lemon juice and sugar. Chili if desired.

683. MADEIRA TART (CROÛTE AU MADÈRE)
PREPARATION TIME: 45 MIN.

2 cups mixed fresh or canned fruit, with syrup	12 slices white bread, or
6 slices canned pineapple, or	12 ½-in. slices brioche
1 small fresh pineapple, peeled, sliced	apricot jam
	1 cup Madeira wine
3½ tbsp. butter	candied cherries

Fry brioche or bread on both sides in butter. Spread apricot jam on one side of each slice; arrange slices on serving dish in form of ring, separating slices with half-slices of pineapple. Drain mixed fruit, reserving syrup; macerate in Madeira.

Combine 6 tbsp. apricot jam with ¾ cup syrup from mixed fruit and pineapple; boil 2-3 min., then strain. Add half of sauce to macerated fruit; set aside 6-7 hours. Pour remaining sauce over brioche ring; decorate with candied cherries. Just before serving, pour mixed fruit into center of ring.

May be served warm, if desired, by heating brioche crown 7-10 min. in slow oven, and heating mixed fruit (do not boil) before pouring into ring.

683A. *PORTUGUESE TART* (CROÛTE PORTUGAISE):

Proceed as for Madeira Tart, substituting Malaga wine for Madeira and 3 oranges, quartered, and 6 bananas, sliced, for mixed fruit.

684. *ICED FRUIT CUP*
PREPARATION TIME: 30 MIN.

Fruit Macedoine (recipe 682)
6⅔ tbsp. maraschino, kirsch or brandy, or 1 cup red or white wine, or ½ bottle champagne

Combine fruit macedoine and desired liqueur; chill 2-3 hours on crushed ice. Serve very cold.

685. *DRIED FRUIT COMPOTE*
PREPARATION TIME: 1½ HOURS. COOKING TIME: 1 HOUR.

½ lb. prunes
½ lb. dried figs
¾ cup seedless raisins
¾ cup golden raisins
½ cup sugar

1 cup water
pinch of vanilla powder
almonds, pistachio nuts, blanched hazelnuts

Wash fruit; soak for 2 hours in cold water. Cook gently for 1 hour with sugar, vanilla, water. Chill. Garnish with nuts.

Desserts

686. SWEET CREAM CAKE
PREPARATION TIME: 10 MIN. COOKING TIME: 20 MIN.

3 cups milk
3 tbsp. gelatin
1 cup cream, whipped

½ cup sugar
¼ cup sugar for caramel
any desired flavoring extract

Add sugar and flavoring to milk; scald. Soften gelatin in a little cold water; add to milk, cook 5 min. Blend in whipped cream. Pour mixture into caramelized mold (recipe 891). Chill.

687. CUSTARD CREAM (CRÈME ANGLAISE)
PREPARATION TIME: 5 MIN. COOKING TIME: 40 MIN.

1 qt. milk
½ cup sugar

6 egg yolks or
4 whole eggs

Add sugar to milk; scald. Beat egg yolks or eggs, gradually adding hot milk. Thicken mixture in top of double boiler (be careful not to let it boil).

687A. VANILLA CREAM: Add vanilla extract or a vanilla bean to milk before scalding.

687B. ORANGE or LEMON CREAM: Add orange or lemon rind, grated, to milk before scalding.

687C. COFFEE CREAM: Add 2 tsp. Coffee Extract (recipe 887) to egg yolks.

687D. *BANANA CREAM:* Rub 6 peeled bananas through sieve or food mill; add to cream while still warm. Serve chilled.

687E. *APRICOT CREAM:* Add ¼ lb. dried cooked apricots, puréed, to warm cream.

687F. *CHOCOLATE CREAM:* Melt 7 squares chocolate in hot milk. Use 5 egg yolks; omit sugar.

687G. *CARAMEL CREAM:* Make a caramel (recipe 891) with ¾ cup sugar. Carefully stir in hot milk. Strain milk through a fine strainer; continue with recipe.

687H. *VENETIAN CREAM:* Add stiffly beaten egg whites to warm cream. Mix well. Serve hot or cold.

687J. *PINEAPPLE CREAM:* Flavor custard cream with kirsch. Add 1 cup crushed pineapple.

687K. *PRUNE CREAM:* Mix crushed cooked prunes into cream.

688. HEDGEHOGS
PREPARATION TIME: 30 MIN. COOKING TIME: 40 MIN.

12 small Madeleines (recipe 762)	⅓ cup slivered, roasted almonds
3 cups milk	5 egg yolks
¾ cup rum	⅔ cup sugar

Soak Madeleines in mixture of rum, 3 tbsp. sugar, 3 tbsp. water. Stick slivers of almonds into Madeleines. Prepare a Custard Cream (recipe 687) with remaining ingredients. Garnish with Madeleines.

689. VANILLA BAVARIAN CREAM
PREPARATION TIME: 20 MIN. COOKING TIME: 40 MIN.

2 cups milk	vanilla flavoring
1 cup cream	2½ tbsp. gelatin, soaked in
6 egg yolks	3 tbsp. cold water
1 cup sugar	

Prepare a Custard Cream (recipe 687) with milk, egg yolks, sugar, vanilla. Before thickening, add gelatin soaked in water. Strain through fine strainer; chill. Whip cream; fold into custard when thick but not firm. Pour mixture into buttered mold; chill.

690. CHOCOLATE BAVARIAN CREAM
PREPARATION TIME: 25 MIN.   COOKING TIME: 30 MIN.

2 cups milk	5 egg yolks
7 squares chocolate	2½ tbsp. gelatin, softened in
1 cup cream, whipped	3 tbsp. cold water

Prepare a Chocolate Custard Cream (recipe 687F) with milk, chocolate, sugar, egg yolks. Add gelatin before thickening. Strain through fine strainer; chill. Fold in whipped cream before custard cream sets. Pour mixture into buttered mold. Chill.

691. COFFEE BAVARIAN CREAM
PREPARATION TIME: 5 MIN.   COOKING TIME: 40 MIN.

2 cups milk	1 tbsp. Coffee Extract (recipe
1½ cups powdered sugar	886)
5 egg yolks	2½ tbsp. gelatin, softened in
1 cup cream, whipped	3 tbsp. cold water

Proceed as for Chocolate Bavarian Cream (recipe 690).

692. FRUIT BAVARIAN CREAM
PREPARATION TIME: 25 MIN.   COOKING TIME: 45 MIN.

2 cups milk	1 cup cream, whipped
5 egg yolks	3½ tbsp. gelatin, softened in
⅔ cup sugar	4 tbsp. cold water
3 cups fruit—strawberries, raspberries, etc.	

Proceed as for Chocolate Bavarian Cream (recipe 690). Rub fruit through sieve or food mill; pour juice over unmolded cream.

693. CHOCOLATE MOUSSE
PREPARATION TIME: 20 MIN.

6 egg whites, stiffly beaten	7 squares chocolate
2 tbsp. water	

Melt chocolate in water. Mix gently into stiffly beaten egg whites. Serve immediately.

694. COFFEE MOUSSE
PREPARATION TIME: 10 MIN.

6 egg whites, stiffly beaten   2 tbsp. Coffee Extract (recipe 886)
6 tbsp. sugar

Add coffee extract to stiffly beaten, sweetened egg whites. Serve immediately.

695. STRAWBERRY MOUSSE
PREPARATION TIME: 15 MIN.

2 egg whites, stiffly beaten   1¾ cups strawberries
   sugar to taste

Crush berries in sieve or food mill. Mix gently into stiffly beaten, sweetened egg whites. Serve immediately.

696. MOUSSE À LA CRÈME CHANTILLY
PREPARATION TIME: 20 MIN.

4 egg whites, stiffly beaten   Chantilly Cream (recipe 889)
   sugar to taste   any desired flavoring extract

Blend sugar into beaten egg whites; fold into Chantilly Cream. Add flavoring. Serve immediately.

697. JAM MOUSSE

6 egg whites, stiffly beaten   any desired jam or jelly

Rub jam or jelly through sieve. Mix gently into beaten egg whites. Serve immediately.

698. FLOATING ISLAND
PREPARATION TIME: 20 MIN.   COOKING TIME: 45 MIN.

6 eggs, separated   3 cups milk
1 cup sugar   any desired flavoring

Add flavoring to egg whites; beat until stiff. Sweeten with 6 tbsp. sugar. Caramelize a mold (recipe 891) with 5 tbsp. sugar. Pour egg white mixture into mold. Set mold in pan of water; bake 45 min. in slow oven. Chill. Unmold onto

serving dish; cover with Custard Cream (recipe 687) made
with milk, egg yolks, remaining sugar.

698A. *RICHELIEU CREAM:* Add 10 finely crushed almonds and a drop of red food coloring to beaten egg whites.

699. *MACARONETTE*
PREPARATION TIME: 25 MIN. COOKING TIME: 45 MIN.

12 macaroons, crushed	1 qt. milk
6 eggs separated	¾ cup sugar

Beat egg whites until stiff; fold into macaroons. Caramelize
a mold (recipe 891) with 4½ tbsp. sugar; pour in egg white
mixture. Place mold in pan of water; bake 45 min. in slow
oven. Unmold and nap with Custard Cream (recipe 687)
made with egg yolks, milk, remaining sugar.

700. *LEMON MOUSSE*
PREPARATION TIME: 20 MIN. COOKING TIME: 8 MIN.

juice of 2 lemons	½ cup sugar
grated rind of 2 lemons	3 tbsp. water

Combine sugar, egg yolks, water, lemon juice and rind.
Thicken mixture about 5 min. in double boiler. Chill. Beat egg
whites; fold into chilled lemon mixture. Serve immediately.

700A. *ORANGE MOUSSE:* Use juice of 5 oranges, grated
rind of 3; use 6 tbsp. sugar.

701. *VALENCIAN CREAM*
PREPARATION TIME: 25 MIN.

6 egg yolks	¾ cup sugar
4 egg whites, stiffly beaten	5 tbsp. gelatin, softened in
juice of 6 oranges	3 tbsp. warm water
juice of 1 lemon	

Beat egg yolks with sugar until smooth; gradually add juice
and gelatin. When mixture begins to thicken, add stiffly
beaten egg whites. Pour into buttered mold. Chill overnight.

702. BALANCÉS
PREPARATION TIME: 25 MIN.

6 eggs, separated   6 squares chocolate

Soften chocolate in double boiler. Blend in egg yolks, then stiffly beaten whites. Pour into small buttered individual molds. Chill for several hours.

702A. MARIE-LOUISE CREAM: Melt chocolate over very low flame in 6 tbsp. very strong coffee.

703. BACCHUS CREAM
PREPARATION TIME: 15 MIN.

6 eggs, separated   3 tbsp. rum
½ cup sugar

Beat egg yolks vigorously with sugar and rum until foamy. Fold in stiffly beaten egg whites. Serve immediately.

704. RUSSIAN CREAM
PREPARATION TIME· 15 MIN.

6 eggs, separated   1 cup cream, whipped
½ cup sugar   2 tbsp. kirsch

Beat egg yolks with sugar until pale. Add cream and kirsch. Serve cold.

705. BAKED CUSTARD I (OEUFS AU LAIT)
PREPARATION TIME: 15 MIN. COOKING TIME: 45 MIN.

1 qt. milk   4 eggs
⅔ cup sugar   any desired flavoring

Add sugar and flavoring to milk; scald. Beat eggs; gradually stir into milk. Pour into baking dish. Bake 45 min. in slow oven.

705A. INDIVIDUAL BAKED CUSTARDS: Use 5 eggs. Pour mixture into small individual custard cups. Place cups in pan of hot water; bake 25 min.

706. BAKED CUSTARD II (CRÈME RENVERSÉE)
PREPARATION TIME: 15 MIN. COOKING TIME: 45 MIN.–1 HOUR.

1 qt. milk	1 cup sugar
6 eggs	any desired flavoring

Prepare custard as for Baked Custard I, using ¾ cup sugar. Caramelize a mold (recipe 891) with remaining sugar; pour in custard. Set mold in pan of water; bake 45 min.–1 hour in hot oven. Chill.

706A. APRICOTS VIENNOISE: Flavor custard with vanilla; bake in a caramelized ring mold. Chill. Unmold; fill center with ½ lb. cooked dried apricots.

707. BAKED CUSTARD "BELLE ET BONNE"
PREPARATION TIME: 1½ HOURS. COOKING TIME: 1¼ HOURS.

Baked Custard 1, baked in ring mold	½ cup sugar
6 med. pears	1¾ cups red wine
4 small pears	¾ cup cream, whipped

Dice 4 small pears; cook with sugar and wine for 30 min. Drain. In same syrup, cook 6 medium pears, halved lengthwise, for 40 min. Unmold chilled custard; fill center with diced pears. Surround custard ring with pear halves; garnish with whipped cream.

708. FRUIT CUSTARD
PREPARATION TIME: 20 MIN. COOKING TIME: 1 HOUR.

3 cups warm sweetened milk	3-4 lady fingers
4 eggs, beaten	candied cherries
3 tbsp. rum or kirsch	apricot jam, currant jelly, etc.
½ cup sugar	

Soak lady fingers in milk; add eggs. Rub mixture through sieve. Add sugar, rum or kirsch, some candied cherries. Pour into buttered mold. Set mold in pan of water; bake 1 hour in slow oven. Chill. Unmold and spread with jam or jelly.

709. BLANC MANGE
PREPARATION TIME: 1 HOUR.

3 cups (1 lb.) almonds, blanched	7 tbsp. gelatin
6 bitter almonds, blanched	2 cups sugar
2½ cups water	¾ tsp. any flavoring extract

Crush almonds in a mortar, gradually adding water. Place mixture in cloth and squeeze over bowl to extract juice. Dissolve gelatin in small quantity warm milk; add to almond liquid. Add sugar and flavoring extract. Strain through piece of muslin. Pour mixture into mold; chill for several hours.

710. CHESTNUT CAKE
PREPARATION TIME: 45 MIN. COOKING TIME: 1½ HOURS.

1 lb. chestnuts	vanilla extract or powder
1 cup milk	2 cups custard cream (recipe
4 egg whites	687)
½ cup sugar	

Split chestnuts (see recipe 468) and boil 30 min. in water. Remove shells. Cook meats 15 min. in milk, vanilla and sugar; rub through sieve. Add stiffly beaten egg whites. Pour mixture into a caramelized mold (recipe 891); bake 1½–1¾ hours in very slow oven. Serve with Custard Cream.

711. DIPLOMAT PUDDING
PREPARATION TIME: 20 MIN.

lady fingers	diced candied fruit
apricot jam	2 cups Custard Cream (recipe 687)
muscat raisins	3 tbsp. rum

Soak lady fingers, flat side down, in rum mixed with a little water. Place layer of lady fingers in bottom of a round mold. Spread with thick layer of apricot jam; sprinkle with raisins and candied fruit. Repeat, alternating layers until mold is full, finishing with layer of lady fingers. Cover with heavy dish or weight. Chill 24 hours. Unmold and serve with Custard Cream.

712. MONT-BLANC
PREPARATION TIME: 30 MIN.

1 lb. chestnuts   ¾ cup vanilla-flavored sugar*
1 cup cream

Prepare a sweetened chestnut purée, following recipe 470. Pile on serving dish in a pyramid; cover with cream. Serve very cold.

713. CHOCOLATE CHESTNUT PAVÉ
PREPARATION TIME: 30 MIN.

1 lb. chestnuts   2 egg yolks
5 squares (5 oz.) chocolate   ¼ cup sugar
¼ lb. butter, creamed   3 tbsp. kirsch
3 tbsp. cream   24 tea biscuits

Prepare a chestnut purée according to recipe 470. Soften chocolate in a little water. Beat egg yolks with sugar until pale and foamy. Add chocolate; blend in butter. Gradually add chestnut purée to mixture; finish with cream and kirsch. Line bottom and sides of cake pan with biscuits. Pour in layer of filling; top with layer of biscuits. Repeat. Cover with waxed paper; place a weight on top. Chill for 12 hours. Serve plain or with Custard Cream or Rum Sauce (recipe 817).

714. CHESTNUT VERMICELLI
PREPARATION TIME: 45 MIN. COOKING TIME: 30 MIN.

1 lb. chestnuts   1 cup Chantilly Cream (recipe
1½ cups powdered sugar   889)

Boil chestnuts 30 min. in water. Remove shells; rub nutmeats through coarse sieve held over serving dish. Sprinkle with sugar. Top with Chantilly Cream.

---

* Combine sugar with a few slivers of vanilla bean, finely pounded; press through very fine sieve.

715. YULE LOG (BÛCHE DE NOËL)
PREPARATION TIME: 40 MIN.

2 lbs. chestnuts
8 oz. chocolate
6⅔ tbsp. butter
3 tbsp. milk or water

1 cup Chantilly Cream (recipe 889)
sugar flowers for decorating

Prepare a chestnut purée according to recipe 470. Blend in butter. Over low heat, soften chocolate in milk or water; blend thoroughly into chestnut purée. Chill for several hours. Shape mixture into a log; decorate with sugar flowers and garnish with Chantilly Cream.

716. FRANGIPANE CREAM
PREPARATION TIME: 15 MIN.   COOKING TIME: 20 MIN.

5⅔ tbsp. sugar
1 cup + 2 tbsp. flour
6 tbsp. butter
⅓ cup crushed almonds

1⅓ cups milk, scalded
2 egg yolks
2 whole eggs
1 pinch salt

Combine sugar, eggs, egg yolks, flour, 4 tbsp. butter. Add milk. Place over heat; cook, stirring constantly, until mixture thickens. Add 2 tbsp. butter, almonds. Stir constantly until mixture cools.

717. PARISIENNE PUDDING
PREPARATION TIME: 10 MIN.   COOKING TIME: 45 MIN.

2½ cups flour
½ cup sugar
4 eggs

1 qt. milk, flavored with vanilla
2 tbsp. butter, melted

Place flour in bowl. Make depression in top; pour in sugar. Break eggs into sugar. Mix well. Add melted butter. Gradually add milk; beat until smooth. Pour mixture into buttered mold; bake 45 min. in hot oven. Serve cold.

718. PINEAPPLE PUDDING
PREPARATION TIME: 15 MIN.   COOKING TIME: 1 HOUR.

1 2-lb. can pineapple
6 eggs
½ cup flour

1¾ cups sugar
juice of 1 lemon
2¼ tsp. kirsch

Add 6 tbsp. sugar to syrup from pineapple; crush ¾ of pineapple, add to syrup, boil 5 min. Dice remaining pieces of pineapple, add to crushed mixture; continue cooking 5 min. Break eggs into bowl; add flour, lemon juice, kirsch, pineapple. Pour mixture into mold caramelized (recipe 891) with remaining sugar. Set mold in pan of water. Bake 1 hour in slow oven. Chill overnight.

719. CHOCOLATE SOUFFLÉ
PREPARATION TIME: 10 MIN. COOKING TIME: 30 MIN.

1¾ cups milk	5 eggs, separated
5 squares chocolate	3 tbsp. flour
6 tbsp. powdered sugar	

Add chocolate to milk; scald. Beat egg yolks; gradually add milk, stirring constantly. Blend flour with a little cold milk; add to egg mixture together with powdered sugar. Fold in stiffly beaten egg whites. Bake 10 min. in very slow oven. Increase heat to 425-450°F.; continue baking 20 min. Serve immediately.

720. VANILLA SOUFFLÉ
PREPARATION TIME: 10 MIN. COOKING TIME: 35 MIN.

6⅔ tbsp. butter	1¾ cups milk
⅔ cup flour	½ cup sugar
5 eggs, separated	vanilla extract

Add sugar and vanilla extract to milk; scald. Make a White Sauce II (recipe 9) with flour, milk, butter; add egg yolks. Chill. Gently fold in stiffly beaten egg whites. Bake 35 min. in slow oven. Serve immediately.

720A. LEMON SOUFFLÉ: Substitute grated rind of 1 lemon for vanilla.

721. CHESTNUT SOUFFLÉ
PREPARATION TIME: 30 MIN. COOKING TIME: 1¼ HOURS.

1 lb. chestnuts	2 tbsp. butter
4 eggs, separated	pinch of vanilla powder or
2 cups milk	¼ tsp. vanilla extract
½ cup sugar	

Split chestnuts (see recipe 468); boil 30 min. in water. Shell. Cook chestnuts with milk, vanilla and sugar for 15 min.; rub through fine sieve. Add egg yolks, beating constantly, then fold in stiffly beaten whites. Pour mixture into buttered baking dish; bake 25 min. in very slow oven.

722. RICE WITH MILK
PREPARATION TIME: 5 MIN. COOKING TIME: 20 MIN.

1 cup long-grain rice
1 qt. milk, scalded
¾ cup powdered sugar

1½ qts. boiling water
vanilla extract or powder

Cook rice 3 min. in boiling water; drain. Cook, covered, in scalded milk for 15 min. Remove from heat; stir in sugar and vanilla with fork.

723. RICE PUDDING
PREPARATION TIME: 20 MIN. COOKING TIME: 20 MIN.

1 qt. milk, scalded
1 cup rice
⅔ cup sugar
½ cup golden raisins

2 eggs, separated
pinch of salt
vanilla extract

Cook rice with milk, vanilla, ¼ cup sugar, salt, about 15 min. Add egg yolks, raisins, stiffly beaten egg whites. Pour into caramelized mold (recipe 891) with remaining sugar. Bake 6 min. in hot oven. Chill. If desired, serve flamed with rum, or napped with a Custard Cream (recipe 687).

724. RICE À L'IMPÉRATRICE
PREPARATION TIME: 1½ HOURS. COOKING TIME: 35 MIN.

⅓ cup rice
3 cups milk
1 qt. boiling water
¼ lb. candied fruit, diced, macerated in kirsch
⅔ cup powdered sugar

⅔ cup Chantilly Cream (recipe 889)
1 tbsp. gelatin, softened in 3 tbsp. warm water
2 cups Custard Cream (recipe 687)

Cook rice 5 min. in boiling water; drain. Cook gently with sugar and milk until milk has been absorbed. Add gelatin to Custard Cream; add Custard Cream to rice together with raisins and macerated candied fruit. Chill mixture slightly. While still warm, fold in Chantilly Cream. Pour mixture into buttered mold; chill overnight. Unmold and serve with whipped cream or currant jam; or nap with a kirsch-flavored Custard Cream.

724A. APRICOT CROWN: Chill rice mixture in a ring mold. Fill unmolded rice ring with ½ lb. cooked dried apricots. (Other canned or cooked fresh fruit may be substituted.)

725. BREAD PUDDING
PREPARATION TIME: 20 MIN. COOKING TIME: 1 HOUR.

1 lb. stale bread, coarsely crumbed	3 eggs, beaten
2 cups milk	¼ lb. candied fruit, chopped
¾ cup sugar	4 tbsp. butter

Add ½ cup sugar to milk; scald. Add beaten eggs. Pour over bread crumbs; add candied fruit. Caramelize a mold (recipe 891) with remaining sugar; pour in pudding mixture. Bake 1 hour in slow oven. If desired, candied fruit may be replaced by vanilla, grated lemon rind, pitted cooked prunes, etc.

726. JAM PUDDING
PREPARATION TIME: 20 MIN.

8 oz. lady fingers	apricot jam
¾ cup rum	2 cups Custard Cream (recipe 687)
6 tbsp. water	

Soak each lady finger in mixture of rum and water; use to line sides and bottom of a mold, cut side facing in. Fill mold with alternating layers of jam and lady fingers, finishing with layer of lady fingers. Chill for at least 4 hours. Unmold and nap with custard cream.

727. BUTTER PUDDING
PREPARATION TIME: 35 MIN.

yolks of 4 hard-boiled eggs
1 cup powdered sugar
¼ lbs. butter
Vanilla or Coffee Extract
   (recipe 886)

lady fingers
¾ cup rum
6 tbsp. water
2 cups Custard Cream (recipe
   687)

Crush egg yolks; beat together with butter and sugar. Add flavoring. Soak lady fingers one by one in mixture of water and rum; use to line bottom and sides of a mold. Pour pudding into mold; top with layer of lady fingers. Chill for 12 hours. Serve with Custard Cream.

728. ROYAL PUDDING
PREPARATION TIME: 35 MIN. COOKING TIME: 40 MIN.

4 oz. dry crackers, crushed
4 oz. macaroons
4 oz. lady fingers
4 oz. candied cherries
1 cup sweetened whipped cream

4 tbsp. butter
2 cups milk
4 eggs, beaten
¾ cup rum

Crush crackers; add to milk. Add butter, eggs, rum, a few candied chopped cherries. Butter a mold; fill with alternating layers of lady fingers soaked in rum and water, pudding mixture, macaroons, cherries. Set mold in pan of water; cover and bake 30 min. in slow oven. Uncover; bake 10 min. longer. Chill overnight. Unmold and garnish with whipped cream.

729. CHOCOLATE PUDDING
PREPARATION TIME: 35 MIN.

4 oz. lady fingers
6 tbsp. sugar
4 eggs, separated

6 squares chocolate
4 tbsp. butter
2 cups Custard Cream (recipe 687)

Melt chocolate in small quantity of water. Add egg yolks, sugar, stiffly beaten egg whites, butter. Line bottom and sides of mold with lady fingers. Pour in pudding; line with layer of lady fingers. Chill overnight. Unmold and serve with Custard Cream.

730. OMELET WITH RUM

PREPARATION TIME: 5 MIN. COOKING TIME: 7 MIN.

6 eggs pinch of salt	3 tbsp. warm rum, sweetened with 3 tbsp. sugar

Make an Omelet (recipe 197) with eggs and salt. Turn onto serving dish. Sprinkle with sweetened rum; ignite and serve.

730A. JELLY OMELET:

Omit salt. Fill with any desired jam or jelly before folding; slide onto serving dish and sprinkle with 3 tbsp. sugar.

731. APRICOT OMELET

PREPARATION TIME: 10 MIN. COOKING TIME: 5 MIN.

6 eggs 3½ tbsp. butter	5 tbsp. powdered sugar apricot jam

Make an Omelet according to recipe 197, adding small pinch sugar. Before folding, fill with apricot jam or Apricot Compote (recipe 641), sweetened. Slide omelet onto baking dish; sprinkle with sugar. Brown for a few minutes in hot oven.

NORMAN OMELET: See recipe 913.

732. SOUFFLÉED OMELET

PREPARATION TIME: 10 MIN. COOKING TIME: 22 MIN.

5 eggs, separated 1½ cups powdered sugar	1⅔ tbsp. butter any desired flavoring extract

Beat egg yolks with sugar until smooth; add flavoring. Mix in ¼ of stiffly beaten egg whites; then fold in remaining whites all at one time. Pour mixture into buttered baking dish, smooth top with a knife blade. Sprinkle with sugar; make a slash with knife across top. Bake 20-22 min. in slow oven. Serve immediately.

733. DESSERT PANCAKES (CRÊPES)

PREPARATION TIME: 10 MIN. COOKING TIME: 3 MIN. EACH
PANCAKE.

2 cups milk
3 cups flour
2 eggs

1 tbsp. butter (or oil, if desired)
any desired flavoring extract
pinch of salt

Place flour in bowl. Make a depression in top, break in
eggs. Add salt, oil or butter, a little milk. Beat vigorously
until light and fluffy. Gradually add sufficient milk to make a
batter which spins a ribbon when dropped from spoon. Add
flavoring. Set aside for 1 hour. (If batter thickens, it may
be thinned before cooking with a little water or milk.) Heat
a very small quantity of oil in skillet. Pour in small quantity
of batter, shaking skillet so that it spreads evenly. When crêpe
is golden and can be detached easily from pan, turn and
brown other side. Sprinkle with sugar. Serve very hot. If
desired, spread crêpe with spoonful of jam, Custard Cream,
Frangipane Cream, or whipped cream; roll up.

734. FLUFFY DESSERT PANCAKES

PREPARATION TIME: 10 MIN. COOKING TIME: 3 MIN. FOR
EACH PANCAKE.

3 cups flour
5 eggs, separated
6⅔ tbsp. butter
1⅓ cups milk

¾ cup warm water
grated lemon rind
pinch of salt

Combine flour, milk, water; add 1 tbsp. butter, salt. Set
aside for 1 hour. Add egg yolks, grated lemon rind, remaining butter (slightly softened). Fold in stiffly beaten, slightly
salted egg whites. Batter should be smooth and light. Proceed
as for recipe 733. Sprinkle with sugar before serving.

735. FRUIT FRITTERS

Roll cored and sliced peaches, apple slices, strawberries,
etc. in a Batter for Frying (recipe 885) or Dessert Pancake
Batter (recipe 733). Brown in hot shortening. Drain and
sprinkle with sugar. Serve hot.

736. RICE CROQUETTES
PREPARATION TIME: 15 MIN. COOKING TIME: 30 MIN.

⅔ cup rice
2 cups milk or 1 cup milk +
    1 cup water
2 eggs

4½ tbsp. sugar
vanilla extract or grated lemon
    rind
shortening for frying

Cook rice according to recipe 579, adding pinch of salt and vanilla or lemon rind to milk. Chill slightly. Add 2 eggs. When mixture is completely cold, form into small oblong rolls. Dredge in flour or egg white; brown in very hot shortenin. Sprinkle with sugar.

737. CHOCOLATE BÉCHAMEL
PREPARATION TIME: 10 MIN. COOKING TIME: 10 MIN.

8 squares chocolate (8 oz.)
4 tbsp. butter

½ cup flour
3 cups warm milk

Melt chocolate in milk. Melt butter in casserole; stir in flour. Gradually add chocolate milk. Cook 10 min., stirring constantly. Serve cold.

738. MARQUISE AU CHOCOLAT
PREPARATION TIME: 15 MIN.

8 squares (8 oz.) chocolate
⅔ cup butter, creamed
¼ cup sugar

4 eggs, separated
Vanilla Cream (recipe 687A)

Break chocolate in pieces; soften over low flame in a little water until it forms a smooth, thick paste. Chill. Blend in sugar, egg yolks, creamed butter; mix well. Add stiffly beaten egg whites. Pour into mold; chill. Unmold and nap with Vanilla Cream.

739. BLACK-AND-WHITE PUDDING (NÉGRE EN CHEMISE)
PREPARATION TIME: 25 MIN.

6 squares chocolate
¾ cup butter

4 eggs, separated
1 cup cream, whipped

Soften chocolate in double boiler; beat with butter. Add

egg yolks and beaten whites. Pour into buttered mold; chill overnight. Unmold and garnish with whipped cream.

740. FROZEN FRUIT MOUSSE

2 cups Sugar Syrup, thread stage (recipe 890)
8 egg yolks

any desired fruit
1 cup cream, whipped (optional)

Beat egg yolks vigorously; slowly add hot syrup. Thicken mixture in double boiler. When firm, beat until cool. Add desired fruit and cream. Pour into freezing tray and freeze.

741. COFFEE ICE (CAFÉ GLACÉ)

1 qt. boiling water
5 tbsp. ground coffee

1 cup sugar
1 pint cream, whipped

Make strong Coffee (recipe 839); sweeten with sugar. Freeze until mushy. Just before serving, fold in whipped cream.

742. FRUIT SUNDAE (COUPE JEANNETTE)

¼ lb. grapes
½ lb. pineapple
1 apricot
1 peach
⅔ cup strawberries

1 banana
2 tbsp. kirsch
⅔ cup powdered sugar
vanilla and strawberry ice cream

Dice fruit and mix with powdered sugar; macerate for 30 min. in kirsch. Place spoonful of fruit at bottom of each serving dish; cover with ice cream.

743. PEACH MELBA

6 large peaches
⅓ cup almonds, blanched and slivered
2 cups water

vanilla ice cream
½ cup sugar
2 cups currant or fruit syrup
1 cup cream, whipped

Cook whole peaches in water and sugar for 15 min. Peel and chill. Place scoop of ice cream in each individual dish; top with 2 peach halves. Cover with syrup, sprinkle with almonds. Garnish with whipped cream.

Cakes, Icings, Cookies, Pastry

CAKES

744. APPLE CAKE (FLAN AUX POMMES)

PREPARATION TIME: 25 MIN. COOKING TIME: 40 MIN.

6 apples, peeled, thinly sliced
¼ cup sugar
3½ tbsp. butter

Pancage Batter (recipe 733)
grated rind of 1 lemon

Combine apples, grated lemon rind and pancake batter. Pour mixture into well-buttered baking dish. Dot with butter, sprinkle with sugar. Bake 40 min., gradually increasing temperature from 300 to 425°F.

745. BABA

PREPARATION TIME: 30 MIN. COOKING TIME: 30 MIN. FOR LARGE BABAS, 15-20 FOR SMALL BABAS.

3 cups flour
6⅔ tbsp. butter
2 tbsp. sugar
3 eggs
½ cup seedless raisins

1½ tsp. salt
3½ tbsp. warm milk
2 pkg. (about ½ oz.) dry granular yeast
Sauce for Baba (recipe 817)

Sift flour into bowl. Make a depression in top; pour in yeast blended with milk. Add eggs; mix well. Beat with hand for several minutes, or until dough pulls away from hand. Cover bowl; set aside in warm place until mixture has doubled in volume. Blend in softened butter, sugar, salt; add raisins. Pour into well-buttered baba mold. (Mold should be ⅔ full.) Bake 30 min. in hot oven (less time for small babas). While still warm, sprinkle with sauce.

746. QUICK BABA
PREPARATION TIME: 10 MIN. COOKING TIME: 15 MIN.

1¼ cups flour
½ cup sugar
3 eggs, separated

½ cup seedless raisins
2¼ tsp. baking powder
Sauce for Baba (recipe 817)

Combine egg yolks and sugar. Add stiffly beaten egg whites, flour, raisins. Heat a ring mold; butter well. Pour in batter. Bake 15 min. in hot oven. Sprinkle with sauce while still warm. If desired, fill center with Pastry Cream (recipe 816).

747. BRIOCHE
COOKING TIME: 30 MIN.

3 cups flour
¼ lb. butter
3 tbsp. powdered sugar
1 tsp. salt

1 pkg. dry granular yeast, blended with small quantity warm milk
3 eggs

Combine yeast with small quantity of flour. Place in floured bowl; set aside for 6 hours, or until dough has doubled in volume. Knead with palm of hand while adding flour, salt, eggs, butter. Set aside for 12 hours in warm place. Fold sides of dough in toward center; repeat several times, as for Puff Paste (recipe 800). Place ¾ of dough in buttered mold; top with smaller ball of remaining dough. Bake 30 min. at 325°F.

748. QUICK BRIOCHE
PREPARATION TIME: 10 MIN. COOKING TIME: 45 MIN.

2¼ cups flour
2⅓ tbsp. sugar
¾ cup cream

2 eggs
pinch of salt
2¼ tsp. baking powder

Blend cream with flour. Add 1 beaten egg, sugar, salt. Pour into buttered mold lined with waxed paper. Brush with remaining egg, beaten. Bake 45 min. in very slow oven.

CLAFOUTI (Limousin Cherry Cake): See recipe 908.

FAR (Breton Cake): See recipe 897.

KUGELHOPF (Alsatian Tea Cake): See recipe 893.

749. SAVARIN
PREPARATION TIME: 30 MIN. COOKING TIME: 30 MIN.

3 cups flour
¼ lb. butter
3 pkg. dry granular yeast,
   blended with
   3½ tbsp. warm milk

2 tbsp. sugar
3 eggs
1½ tsp. salt
Sauce for Baba (recipe 817)

Proceed as for Baba (recipe 745). Turn dough into buttered ring mold. Bake 30 min. in hot oven. While cake is still warm, sprinkle with sauce.

750. QUICK SAVARIN
PREPARATION TIME: 10 MIN. COOKING TIME: 15 MIN.

1¼ cups flour
½ cup sugar
3 eggs, separated

2¼ tsp. baking powder
Sauce for Baba (recipe 817)

Proceed as for Quick Baba (recipe 746).

751. WAFFLES
PREPARATION TIME: 30 MIN. COOKING TIME: 10 MIN.

3 cups flour
6 cups warm milk
⅔ cup sugar
1 pkg. dry granular yeast

2 eggs
dash of bicarbonate of soda
1 tsp. rum

Blend yeast with milk; blend into flour. Set aside in warm place for 6 hours. Knead while adding eggs, sugar, butter, rum, bicarbonate. Set aside for 2 hours. Heat waffle iron over low heat; grease with pork fat. Pour in small quantity of batter; close iron. Cook 5 min. each side.

HONEY WAFFLES: See recipe 895.

752. SPICE CAKE (PAIN D'ÉPICES)
PREPARATION TIME: 10 MIN. COOKING TIME: 1½ HOURS.

2¾ cups flour
1 tbsp. sugar
6 tbsp. warm water
½ cup honey

1 tsp. bicarbonate of soda
1 tsp. powdered aniseed
1 tsp. grated orange peel

Over heat, combine sugar, honey, water, bicarbonate of soda. Add remaining ingredients. Pour batter into well-buttered cake pan. Cover and bake 1½ hours in very slow oven.

NANCY CAKE: See recipe 911.

753. MOUSSELINE CAKE
PREPARATION TIME: 20 MIN. COOKING TIME: 45 MIN.

⅓ cup cornstarch
⅓ cup sugar

5 eggs, separated
grated lemon rind

Beat together sugar and egg yolks. Stir in cornstarch, grated lemon rind, stiffly beaten egg whites; mix well. Pour batter into buttered cake pan. Bake 45 min. in very slow oven.

754. SPONGE CAKE (GÂTEAU DE SAVOIE)
PREPARATION TIME: 20 MIN. COOKING TIME: 20 MIN.

½ lb. powdered sugar
¼ cup potato starch
4 eggs, separated

½ cup flour
vanilla extract or grated lemon rind

Beat together egg yolks and sugar until white and foamy. Add flour, potato starch, vanilla or lemon rind, stiffly beaten egg whites. Pour into well-buttered cake pan. Bake 20 min., increasing temperature gradually from 300 to 450°F.

755. ALMOND CAKE
PREPARATION TIME: 20 MIN. COOKING TIME: 45 MIN.

2 cups flour
1½ cups sugar
4½ tbsp. butter, melted
⅓ cup crushed almonds

1 whole egg
3 eggs, separated
flavoring extract

Beat together crushed almonds, sugar, whole egg, egg yolks. Add flour, melted butter, flavoring and stiffly beaten egg whites. Bake 45 min. in slow oven.

756. ORANGE CAKE
PREPARATION TIME: 20 MIN. COOKING TIME: 40 MIN.

⅔ cup sugar
1 cup crushed almonds
¼ cup cornstarch
3 eggs, separated

2 tbsp. butter
juice and grated rind of 1
    orange

Beat egg yolks; add remaining ingredients and stiffly beaten egg whites. Pour into cake pan which has been buttered and lined with waxed paper. Bake 40 min. in slow oven.

757. FOUR-PART CAKE (QUATRE QUARTS)
PREPARATION TIME: 20 MIN. COOKING TIME: 40–50 MIN.

3 large eggs, separated
¾ cup flour
3 tbsp. sugar

4 tbsp. butter, softened
grated lemon rind

Beat egg yolks with sugar into thin white batter. Blend in flour and butter, alternating. Add lemon rind; fold in stiffly beaten egg whites. Pour into buttered cake pan. Bake 40–50 min. in slow oven.

758. GENOA CAKE (PAIN DE GÊNES)
PREPARATION TIME: 25 MIN. COOKING TIME: 45 MIN.

1¼ cups flour
¼ lb. butter
1½ cups sugar

2 cups finely chopped almonds
2 tbsp. kirsch
4 eggs

Cream butter with sugar. Add eggs one by one, then almonds, flour, kirsch. Pour batter into buttered pan lined with waxed paper. Bake 45 min. in slow oven.

759. ENGLISH CAKE
PREPARATION TIME: 15 MIN. COOKING TIME: 20 MIN.

1⅔ cups rice flour
⅔ cup sugar
¼ lb. butter, softened
2 eggs, separated

candied peel of 3 oranges
vanilla extract
Kirsch Icing (recipe 809)

Beat butter until foamy. Gradually add, in alternating quantities, sugar, flour, orange peel. Gently fold in egg yolks and stiffly beaten whites. Pour batter into well-buttered pan.

Bake 20 min. in hot oven. Unmold, chill. Ice with Kirsch Icing.

760. *CHOCOLATE CAKE*
PREPARATION TIME: 20 MIN. COOKING TIME: 50 MIN.

1 cup flour	1 tbsp. flavoring (rum, kirsch,
5 squares chocolate	etc.)
⅔ cup sugar	Chocolate Icing (recipe 810)
4 tbsp. butter	candied fruit for garnish
4 eggs, separated	

Break up chocolate; melt in butter over very low heat. Add egg yolks one by one, flour, sugar. Fold in stiffly beaten egg whites, flavoring. Pour into well-buttered pan; bake 50 min. in very slow oven. Ice and decorate.

761. *NUT GRENOBLOIS*
PREPARATION TIME: 30 MIN.

5⅓ cups powdered sugar	4 egg yolks
6⅓ tbsp. butter	2 egg whites
3 tbsp. brandy	Coffee Cream (recipe 687C),
¾ cup crushed nuts	optional
28 plain biscuits	
6⅔ tbsp. Coffee Extract (recipe 886)	

Cream butter. Beat egg yolks with sugar until white and foamy. Add butter, nuts, 3 biscuits crushed to a powder. Fold in stiffly beaten egg whites. Soak biscuits in mixture of brandy and coffee extract. Line a loaf pan with waxed paper. Cover bottom of pan with biscuits; spread with layer of cream mixture. Repeat until all ingredients have been used, finishing with layer of biscuits. Cover with waxed paper, place several weights on top. Chill overnight. Unmold and serve plain or with a Coffee Cream.

762. *MADELEINES*
PREPARATION TIME: 20 MIN. COOKING TIME: 8–10 MIN.

2 cups flour	2 large eggs
¼ lb. butter, softened	vanilla or lemon extract
¾ cup sugar	

Beat eggs with sugar until white. Gradually add flour, butter, flavoring. Pour into well-buttered Madeleine molds.° Bake 8–10 min. in hot oven.

763. ALMOND CAKES (VISITANDINES)
PREPARATION TIME: 25 MIN. COOKING TIME: 30 MIN.

1⅔ cups flour
¼ lb. butter, softened
1¼ cups sugar

¾ cup crushed almonds
5 egg whites, stiffly beaten
grated rind of ½ lemon

Combine all ingredients, adding butter last. Pour into well-buttered muffin tins. Bake 30 min. in very slow oven.

COOKIES

764. SUGAR COOKIES I (SABLÉS)
PREPARATION TIME: 20 MIN. COOKING TIME: 30 MIN.

3 cups flour
½ cup sugar
¼ lb. butter
1 egg

pinch of salt
vanilla extract or grated lemon
rind or pinch of cinnamon

Beat egg with sugar and salt. Add flour; mix well. Place mixture on floured board; knead in butter and flavoring. Roll out; cut in desired shapes. Place on buttered cookie tin. Bake 30 min. in slow oven.

765. SUGAR COOKIES II
PREPARATION TIME: 15 MIN. COOKING TIME: 20 MIN.

3 cups flour
2½ tbsp. milk
¼ lb. butter

½ cup sugar
pinch of bicarbonate of soda
vanilla

Beat together sugar, vanilla, milk, bicarbonate of soda. In separate bowl, work butter into flour. Combine all ingredients. Roll out; cut in desired shapes. Place on buttered cookie sheet. Bake 20 min. in hot oven.

° Special cookie tins shaped like small scallop shells. Small muffin tins may be substituted.

766. *CRISP SUGAR COOKIES* (SABLÉS CROQUANTS)
PREPARATION TIME: 10 MIN.   COOKING TIME: 10 MIN.

3 cups flour
1 cup sugar

1½ tsp. rum
2 eggs

Combine all ingredients. Drop mixture by spoonfuls onto buttered cookie sheet. Bake 10 min. in hot oven.

767. *NORWEGIAN KNOTS*
PREPARATION TIME: 25 MIN.   COOKING TIME: 30 MIN.

yolk of 1 hard-boiled egg
2 eggs, separated
¼ lb. butter

2½ tbsp. sugar
3 cups flour
powdered sugar

Crush yolk of hard-boiled egg; beat together with 2 egg yolks. Fold in sugar, beat 15 min. Add half the flour, then butter. Add remaining flour; knead dough with hands. Divide mixture into small balls about the size of a walnut. Roll out into thin ribbons; form into knots. Roll knots in egg whites beaten with fork, then in powdered sugar. Place on buttered cookie sheet. Bake 30 min. in hot oven.

768. *WHITE-WINE CAKES*
PREPARATION TIME: 10 MIN.   COOKING TIME: 20 MIN.

3 cups flour
⅔ cup sugar

½ cup butter
1 tsp. white wine

Combine ingredients; knead on board. Roll out and cut into desired shapes. Bake 20 min. in hot oven.

769. *ORANGE GALETTES*
PREPARATION TIME: 15 MIN.   COOKING TIME: 25 MIN.

3¾ cups flour
¾ cup sugar
⅔ cup butter

2 eggs
2 oz. chopped candied orange peel

Knead all ingredients together on board. Roll out; cut into circles. Bake 25 min. in hot oven.

770. ANISEED GALETTES

PREPARATION TIME: 35 MIN. COOKING TIME: 20 MIN.

3 cups flour
1 cup sugar
2 eggs

1 tbsp. aniseed
pinch of bicarbonate of soda

Beat together sugar and eggs. Add flour, aniseed, bicarbonate of soda; knead. Roll out; cut into circles. Bake 35 min. in slow oven.

771. TANGERINE GALETTES

PREPARATION TIME: 15 MIN. COOKING TIME: 35 MIN.

1 cup flour
1 cup finely chopped almonds
½ cup sugar
1 whole egg

rind of 2 tangerines, finely chopped
1 egg, separated
food coloring

Beat together all ingredients, folding in stiffly beaten egg white last. Drop by spoonfuls onto buttered cookie sheet. Bake 20 min. in hot oven.

772. CHOCOLATE GALETTES

PREPARATION TIME: 25 MIN. COOKING TIME: 25 MIN.

4 squares chocolate, slivered
⅔ cup sugar

¾ cup crushed almonds
1 egg

Beat together all ingredients. Roll out; cut into circles. Bake 25 min. in slow oven.

773. NANTES GALETTES

PREPARATION TIME: 25 MIN. COOKING TIME: 25 MIN.

1⅔ cups flour
4 tbsp. butter
4½ tbsp. sugar
2 egg yolks

¼ cup powdered almonds
⅓ cup blanched almond halves
1 egg, beaten with 1 tbsp. water
pinch of salt

Beat together flour, powdered almonds, butter, sugar. Roll out dough and cut into circles. Place on buttered cookie sheet. Score tops; brush with beaten egg, decorate each cookie with an almond half. Bake 25 min. in hot oven.

774. SOUVAROFFS

PREPARATION TIME: 10 MIN. COOKING TIME: 5 MIN.

3 cups flour
¾ cup butter
½ cup sugar
  vanilla powder

pinch of salt
powdered sugar
currant or raspberry jam

Knead together butter, sugar, flour; add vanilla powder and salt. Roll out carefully into thin sheet; cut into circles. Bake 5 min. in hot oven. When cold, spread half the rounds with jam; cover with remaining rounds. Sprinkle with powdered sugar.

775. ALMOND CRESCENTS

PREPARATION TIME: 25 MIN. COOKING TIME: 25 MIN.

3½ cups flour
¾ cup butter

½ cup crushed almonds
½ cup sugar

Combine all ingredients. Form mixture into small crescents; place on buttered cookie sheet. Bake 25 min. in hot oven. Sprinkle with additional sugar while still warm.

776. CINNAMON STICKS

PREPARATION TIME: 20 MIN. COOKING TIME: 20 MIN.

2¾ cups flour
¾ cup almonds
¼ lb. butter
⅔ cup sugar

1 egg
1 tsp. cinnamon
1 egg yolk, beaten

Finely chop almonds. Combine all ingredients; set aside for 1 day. Form mixture into small sticks; brush with egg yolk. Bake 20 min. in hot oven.

777. CROQUIGNOLES

PREPARATION TIME: 15 MIN. COOKING TIME: 20 MIN.

2 egg whites
2¼ cups powdered sugar

2½ cups flour

Combine all ingredients; knead thoroughly. Form into small cakes about the size of a quarter. Place on buttered cookie sheet. Bake 20 min. in slow oven.

778. SATURN RINGS
PREPARATION TIME: 20 MIN. COOKING TIME: 3 MIN.

2½ cups sugar
4½ tbsp. butter
3 eggs
1 cup cream
pinch of salt

pinch of bicarbonate of soda
flour
grated lemon rind
shortening for frying

Beat together eggs, sugar and salt until foamy. Add cream, butter, rind, bicarbonate of soda. Add sufficient flour to form a thick batter. Roll out to thickness of about ½ in.; cut in rings. Fry rings in very hot shortening until brown. Drain and sprinkle with additional sugar.

779. RIGOLOTS
PREPARATION TIME: 10 MIN. COOKING TIME: 10 MIN.

3 cups flour
1 cup sugar

3 eggs

Beat eggs and sugar until foamy; add flour. (If batter is too dry, add a little milk.) Drop by spoonfuls onto greased cookie sheet. Bake 10 min. in very hot oven.

780. LADY'S QUOITS (PALETS DE DAME)
PREPARATION TIME: 15 MIN. COOKING TIME: 25 MIN.

2 cups flour
2 eggs
¼ lb. butter

⅔ cup sugar
1 tbsp. rum
¼ cup seedless raisins

Cream butter and sugar. Add eggs one by one; add flour all at once. Add raisins soaked in rum. Drop by spoonfuls onto buttered cookie sheet. Bake in slow oven for 25 min., or until brown around edges.

781. DOLLARS
PREPARATION TIME: 10 MIN. COOKING TIME: 20 MIN.

¾ cup butter
⅔ cup sugar
1½ tsp. rum

2 cups flour
1 egg

Beat egg with rum; add remaining ingredients. Drop mixture by spoonfuls onto buttered cookie sheet. Bake 20 min. in hot oven.

782. CONGOLESE CAKES
PREPARATION TIME: 10 MIN. COOKING TIME: 45 MIN.

1½ cups sugar
⅔ cup shredded coconut

5 egg whites
vanilla extract

Combine sugar and egg whites; heat. When mixture is very hot, add coconut and vanilla. Drop by spoonfuls onto waxed paper. Bake 45 min. in very slow oven.

783. ALMOND MACAROONS
PREPARATION TIME: 25 MIN. COOKING TIME: 25 MIN.

1¾ cups crushed almonds
2⅓ cups sugar

3 egg whites

Gradually blend egg whites into crushed almonds. Add sugar; mix thoroughly. Form mixture into small balls; flatten slightly, place on waxed paper. Bake 25 min. in moderate oven.

783A. HAZELNUT MACAROONS: Substitute 1¾ cups crushed hazelnuts for almonds. Decrease sugar to 1¼ cups; use 2 egg whites, stiffly beaten.

784. LADY FINGERS (BISCUITS À LA CUILLÈRE)
PREPARATION TIME: 25 MIN. COOKING TIME: 15 MIN.

1 cup flour
⅓ cup sugar
3 eggs, separated

flavoring extract
powdered sugar

Beat sugar with egg yolks until pale and foamy. Add a few drops of flavoring, then stiffly beaten egg whites and flour. Form mixture into thin oblongs; place on buttered cookie sheet. Sprinkle with powdered sugar. Bake (do not let brown) 15–20 min. in slow oven.

785. TILES
PREPARATION TIME: 10 MIN. COOKING TIME: 10 MIN.

⅔ cup sugar
1 cup cream

1⅔ cups flour
4 egg whites, stiffly beaten

Combine sugar and flour; fold stiffly beaten egg whites into cream. Beat all ingredients together. Drop by spoonfuls onto buttered cookie sheet; bake in very slow oven 5 min., or until cookies spread, then increase heat to 425-450° F. and bake 5 min. longer. Remove from oven; while still hot, roll cookies around neck of bottle to give them shape of roof tiles. Store in metal box to conserve their freshness.

786. ALMOND TILES

PREPARATION TIME: 10 MIN. COOKING TIME: 10 MIN.

1 cup powdered sugar
1⅓ tbsp. cornstarch
2 egg whites
1 egg yolk

⅓ cup coarsely chopped almonds
pinch of salt
vanilla powder

Combine almonds, 1 egg white, sugar, salt, cornstarch. Add egg yolk, then remaining egg white. Drop by small spoonfuls onto buttered cookie sheet. Bake 10 min. in hot oven. Remove from oven; while still hot, roll cookies around neck of bottle.

787. CAT'S TONGUES

PREPARATION TIME: 20 MIN. COOKING TIME: 20 MIN.

1 cup flour
5⅓ tbsp. butter

6 tbsp. sugar
2 eggs

Cream butter; add sugar, blend well. Blend in eggs, one by one, then flour. Drop mixture by spoonfuls onto buttered cookie sheet. Bake in hot oven 20 min., or until brown around edges but still pale in center.

788. PUFFS (PETITS SOUFFLÉS)

PREPARATION TIME: 30 MIN. COOKING TIME: 30 MIN.

½ cup sugar
1 egg white

flavoring—Coffee Extract
(recipe 886), powdered
chocolate, chopped almonds,
etc.

Mix egg white and sugar; beat with fork until mixture no longer spins a ribbon. Drop by spoonfuls, widely spaced, onto buttered cookie sheet. Bake 30 min. in very slow oven.

VIEUX GARÇONS (Brown Sugar Cookies): See recipe 898.

789. HAZELNUT COOKIES
PREPARATION TIME: 15 MIN. COOKING TIME: 30 MIN.

1 cup finely chopped hazelnuts	2 egg whites
⅔ cup sugar	powdered sugar

Combine all ingredients. Form mixture into small balls; roll in powdered sugar, place on buttered cookie sheet. Bake 30 min. in very slow oven.

PASTRY

790. CREAM-PUFF PASTRY (PÂTE À CHOUX)
PREPARATION TIME: 20 MIN.

⅔ cup water	1⅔ cups flour
2 tbsp. powdered sugar	6⅔ tbsp. butter
4 eggs	pinch of salt

Heat together water, sugar, butter, salt. When mixture begins to boil, pour in flour all at once. Lower heat, stir constantly until mixture forms a ball which pulls away from sides of pot. Blend in eggs one by one. Chill before using.

791. SOUFFLÉED FRITTERS (PETS DE NONNE)
PREPARATION TIME: 20 MIN. COOKING TIME: 5 MIN. (IN DEEP-FAT FRYER).

Prepare Cream-Puff Pastry (recipe 790). Drop by small spoonfuls into fairly hot shortening; increase heat as fritters swell. Remove when brown. Drain and sprinkle with sugar. If desired, serve with Vanilla Custard Cream (recipe 687A).

792. CHEESE PUFFS
PREPARATION TIME: 25 MIN. COOKING TIME: 20 MIN.

Substitute 1¼ cups grated Gruyère for sugar in Cream Puff Pastry recipe. Place egg-sized balls of mixture on floured cookie sheet; bake 20 min. in hot oven. Serve hot or cold.

GOUGÈRE (Cheese-flavored Pastry): See recipe 899.

793. CREAM PUFFS
PREPARATION TIME: 25 MIN. COOKING TIME: 20 MIN.

Place egg-sized balls of Cream-Puff Pastry on buttered cookie sheet. Bake in hot oven 20 min., or until puffy and brown. Serve hot or cold.

794. FILLED CREAM PUFFS
PREPARATION TIME: 30 MIN. COOKING TIME: 20 MIN.

Slash baked, chilled Cream Puffs crosswise near top. Fill with a thick Chantilly Cream (recipe 889) or Pastry Cream (recipe 816.)

795. ÉCLAIRS
PREPARATION TIME: 30 MIN. COOKING TIME: 20 MIN.

Form Cream-Puff Pastry into rolls about the thickness and length of finger. Bake 20 min. in hot oven. Chill. Slash lengthwise along one side; fill with any desired pastry cream. Cover with icing.

795A. CHOCOLATE ÉCLAIRS: Fill éclairs with chocolate-flavored Pastry Cream (recipe 816); ice with Chocolate Icing (recipe 810).

795B. COFFEE ÉCLAIRS: Fill éclairs with Coffee-flavored Pastry Cream (recipe 816) ice with Coffee Icing (recipe 811).

795C. ÉCLAIRS À LA FRANGIPANE: Fill éclairs with Frangipane Cream (recipe 716); ice with White Sugar Icing (recipe 809).

795D. ÉCLAIRS WITH PASTRY CREAM: Fill éclairs with Pastry Cream (recipe 816); ice with White Sugar Icing (recipe 809).

796. PIE PASTRY (PÂTE BRISÉE)

3 cups flour	water
¼ lb. butter, in small pieces	1½ tsp. oil or
pinch of salt	1 tbsp. lard

Heap flour on board. Make a depression in top of heap; place in oil, salt, butter. Work butter into flour lightly with fingers. Moisten with water, stirring with wooden spoon. Knead dough with palm of hand. Roll out dough to thickness of about ¼ in.; line pie tin or individual tart shells.

Entire operation should be performed very quickly; this results in a better crust. Less butter may be used if desired for reasons of economy.

Dough may be set aside for one day, if desired, before rolling out. Roll it up in a ball; cover with bowl.

When pre-baking an unfilled pie shell, prick bottom with fork and fill shell with clean gravel, stones, cherry pits etc., so that inside will remain white.

Leftover pastry may be cut in strips, baked separately, and used to garnish one-crust pies.

797. FRUIT PIES

Cooked fruit, fruit compotes, jam, etc.—Fill baked pie shell.

Strawberries, raspberries, currants, etc.—Fill baked pie shell with cooked fruit. Nap with Sugar Syrup (recipe 890) in which a few berries have been crushed, or spread with currant jam.

Apples, pears, blackberries—Fill unbaked pie shell with cored, sliced fruit. Cover with mixture of ¾ cup milk, 2 tbsp. sugar, 1 tbsp. flour, 1 egg. Bake 45 min. in hot oven.

Plums, apricots, cherries—Arrange sliced, pitted fruit in unbaked shell, starting from outside and working in toward center. Sprinkle liberally with powdered sugar. Bake 45 min. in hot oven.

798. ORANGE PIE

PREPARATION TIME: 20 MIN.   COOKING TIME: 25 MIN.

juice and grated rind of 1 orange	4½ tbsp. butter, melted
1 egg	1 unbaked pie shell, or
¾ cup sugar	individual tart shells

Combine egg, sugar, orange juice and rind; add butter.

Pour mixture into pie shell. Top with ½-in. strips of pastry. Bake 25 min. in hot oven.

798A. LEMON PIE: Substitute lemon for orange; use 4 tbsp. butter.

798B. PINEAPPLE PIE: Substitute 2 slices pineapple (one diced, the other crushed) for orange. Use 5⅓ tbsp. butter; add ¾ tsp. kirsch.

799. FRANGIPANE CREAM PIE
PREPARATION TIME: 20 MIN. COOKING TIME: 25 MIN.

Line buttered pie plate with Pie Pastry. Bake for 10 min. in hot oven. Fill crust with Frangipane Cream (recipe 716). Continue baking for 15 min. in hot oven.

TUTSCHE (Custard Pie): See recipe 907.

RAISIN PIE: See recipe 909.

800. PUFF PASTE (PÂTE FEUILLETÉE)
PREPARATION TIME: 2 HOURS.

1½ cups flour	6 tbsp. water (approx.)
6⅔ tbsp. butter	1 tsp. salt

Sift flour in a heap onto board. Make a depression in top; pour in water in which salt has been dissolved. Mix and knead with fingers or with spatula until a smooth, firm, elastic dough forms. Flour board; roll out dough in a square to thickness of about ¼ in. Dot with butter. Fold over 4 corners of dough; set aside for 10 min. in cool place. Flatten dough with rolling pin (do not let butter come out) into rectangular band about ¼ in. thick. Fold dough over three times, like a napkin; set aside for 15 min. in cool place. Roll out again. Repeat operation 6 times or more (the more often it is repeated, the lighter pastry will be).

The quantity of butter used may vary from an amount equal to that of the flour, to ⅓ of the quantity of the flour.

The greater the quantity of butter the more nourishing and expensive the pastry (and the more difficult to digest!). A proportion of ½ to 1 seems to be about the best.

801. *PALMS*
PREPARATION TIME: 2¼ HOURS. COOKING TIME: 20 MIN.

Sprinkle board with sugar. Roll out puff paste in oblong band, to about ¼ in. thick. Fold pastry lengthwise, folding sides into middle; repeat. Cut pastry into pieces about ¼ in. thick. Place on baking sheet which has been sprinkled with sugar. Bake 15-20 min. in hot oven, turning once.

802. *TEA CAKES*

Roll out Puff Paste very thinly. Cut into circles 1–1½ in. in diameter. Brush with egg yolk beaten with a little water; place on buttered baking sheet. Bake 25 min. in hot oven. Serve warm or cold.

803. *RISSOLES* (PETITS PÂTÉS)
PREPARATION TIME: 15 MIN. COOKING TIME: 25 MIN.

Roll out Puff Paste (recipe 800) to thickness of ¼ in.; cut into circles about 2 in. in diameter. Place spoonful of any desired stuffing on a circle; cover with another circle. Press edges together with a little water to seal. Brush with beaten egg yolk. Bake 25 min. in very hot oven, or fry in large quantity of very hot shortening.

804. *SOUFFLÉED RISSOLES* (PETITS PÂTÉS SOUFFLÉS)
PREPARATION TIME: 20 MIN. COOKING TIME: 30 MIN.

1⅔ cups flour	1 pkg. (about ¼ oz.) dry grandular yeast
4 tbsp. butter	
½ cup cream	3 eggs, separated
1 tsp. salt	¼ lb. sausage meat (or any desired filling)

Melt butter in top of double boiler. Remove from heat; gradually add flour by spoonfuls. Add egg yolks one by one, salt; beat well. Add cream, yeast, stiffly beaten egg whites. Set aside for 15 min. Fill buttered individual molds or pie plates with spoonful of batter; top with a little sausage meat or filling. Finish with another spoonful of batter (molds should be only ¾ full). Bake 30 min. in slow oven. Unmold and serve hot as an entrée.

805. HOUSEHOLD CAKE (GALETTE DE MÉNAGE)
PREPARATION TIME: 2 HOURS. COOKING TIME: 30 MIN.

Roll out Puff Paste (recipe 800) in circle, to thickness of ¾ in. Brush top with egg yolk beaten with a little water; score with tip of knife. Bake 30 min. in very hot oven.

806. CREAM HORNS (CORNETS À LA CRÈME)
PREPARATION TIME: 10 MIN. COOKING TIME: 30 MIN.

Puff Paste (recipe 800)
1 cup Pastry Cream (recipe 816) or Chantilly Cream (recipe 889)
1 egg yolk, beaten with 1 tbsp. warm water

Roll out pastry very thinly. Cut into bands about 1½ in. wide and long enough to spiral around buttered horn-shaped molds. Brush with egg yolk. Bake 30 min. in hot oven. Carefully remove horns from molds. When cold, fill with Pastry or Chantilly Cream. Makes about 1 doz. medium-sized horns.

807. APPLE TURNOVERS (CHAUSSONS AUX POMMES)
PREPARATION TIME: 10 MIN. COOKING TIME: 30 MIN.

Puff Paste (recipe 800)
thick Apple Compote (recipe 636)
4½ tbsp. sugar
1 egg yolk, beaten with a little water

Roll out puff paste very thin. Cut into circles about 4–4½ in. in diameter. Place spoonful of compote on one half of circle; fold over other half, pinching edges together with a little water to seal. Brush with egg yolk; sprinkle with sugar. Bake 30 min. in very hot oven.

807A. JELLY TURNOVERS:
Substitute any desired thick jam or jelly for Apple Compote.

808. PITHIVIERS CAKE

PREPARATION TIME: 2 HOURS.   COOKING TIME: 30 MIN.

Puff Paste (recipe 800)
¾ lb. almonds, blanched
 2 bitter almonds
¾ cup sugar
¾ cup butter, softened

3 eggs
 grated rind of ¼ lemon
1 egg yolk, beaten with a little
 water

Crush almonds in a mortar together with sugar and lemon rind. Add eggs one by one, butter; beat well. Line a buttered pie plate with half the pastry. Fill with almond mixture. Cover with remaining pastry, sealing edges with a little water. Score top crust with knife; brush with egg yolk. Bake 30 min. in slow oven.

ICINGS AND FILLINGS

809. KIRSCH ICING

1½ cups powdered sugar   kirsch

Moisten sugar with sufficient kirsch to make a smooth paste. Spread over cake.

810. CHOCOLATE ICING

2 squares chocolate
4 tbsp. butter

2 eggs, separated

Soften chocolate with butter. Beat in egg yolks. Fold in stiffly beaten egg whites. This icing hardens as it cools.

811. COFFEE FONDANT ICING

1¾ cups sugar
 10 drops lemon juice
 1 tbsp. glucose

2 tsp. Coffee Extract (recipe
 873)
6⅔ tbsp. water

Following recipe 890, prepare a sugar syrup (feather stage —232° F.) with sugar and water. Pour onto oiled slab of marble or enameled table top; cool. When cold, flatten with spatula; add lemon juice. Knead mixture with hands into a ball. Place over heat and melt (do not boil). Add coffee extract.

812. SAINT-HONORÉ CREAM

6 tbsp. flour
⅔ cup sugar
1 whole egg

3 eggs, separated
2 cups milk, scalded
vanilla powder

Beat together flour, sugar, egg, egg yolks, vanilla powder. Gradually beat in milk. Thicken mixture over low flame; cool slightly. While still warm, fold in stiffly beaten egg whites. Chill. Use immediately for filling and garnishing pastries.

813. BUTTER CREAM

PREPARATION TIME: 30 MIN. COOKING TIME: 10 MIN.

3 eggs
⅔ cup sugar

½ lb. butter
any desired flavoring

Beat eggs with sugar over low heat. Chill. Cream butter; add to egg mixture. Add flavoring. Use for garnishing and filling cakes and pastries.

814. CREAM-PUFF FILLING

¾ cup flour
¼ cup sugar
3 eggs
2 tbsp. butter

2 squares chocolate, melted in
2 cups milk
pinch of salt

Beat together flour, sugar, salt, eggs. Add milk; gradually blend in butter. Thicken over low heat; cook 1 min. Remove from heat; beat until mixture is cold.

815. CHEESE FILLING

¼ lb. butter
6 tbsp. flour
1¾ cups grated Gruyère

2 eggs, separated
¾ cup milk
salt, pepper

Prepare a Béchamel Sauce (recipe 10) with flour, milk, half the butter; cook 15 min. Away from heat, add cheese, egg yolks, stiffly beaten whites, remaining butter in small pieces. Beat well. Season.

Use for filling unsweetened cream-puffs, tart shells, small galettes.

816. PASTRY CREAM (CRÈME PATISSIÈRE)
PREPARATION TIME: 15 MIN. COOKING TIME: 10 MIN.

1 cup milk	1 whole egg
1½ cups powdered sugar	3 egg yolks
⅔ cup flour	vanilla

Beat together flour, sugar, eggs, vanilla. Gradually beat in milk. Heat mixture slowly, beating constantly. Remove from heat as soon as it begins to boil.

817. SAUCE FOR BABA (Rum Sauce)

2 cups water	¾ cup rum
⅔ cups sugar	

Combine ingredients; heat. Remove from heat when mixture begins to boil. Sprinkle over warm Baba or Savarin.

818. SABAYON
PREPARATION TIME: 10 MIN.

¾ cup Port, Sherry or Madeira wine	5 egg yolks
1 cup sugar	grated rind of 1 lemon
	pinch of vanilla powder

Beat together sugar, egg yolks, vanilla powder and lemon rind until white and smooth. Add wine. Place mixture in top of double-boiler; heat slowly, beating constantly. Serve separately, as a sauce, or use to nap hot puddings. May also be eaten alone as a custard.

Beverages

819. ALMOND MILK
PREPARATION TIME: 20 MIN.

1 qt. lukewarm water
¼ cup almonds, blanched

1½ tbsp. sugar
¾ tsp. flavoring extract

Macerate almonds 15 min. in water. Drain, reserving water. Crush almonds with sugar to form a paste. Gradually add water and flavoring. Strain.

Syrup concentrates for use with water:

820. RED FRUIT SYRUP

1 lb. red fruit—cherries, currants, raspberries, etc.

2 lbs. sugar

Squeeze fruit in cloth to remove juice. Set juice aside for 1 day; then strain. Place sugar and juice in deep, wide pan; bring to boil, then skim. Remove from heat, chill. Bottle syrup; seal.

Used in proportion of 1 part syrup to 4 or 5 parts cold water, this makes a very refreshing drink.

821. PINEAPPLE SYRUP

1 pineapple, peeled, sliced
3 cups water

2 lbs. sugar

Place fruit and water in pot; boil 40 min. Strain through cloth; set aside for 1 day. Place syrup and sugar in pot; bring to boil, then skim. Remove from heat; strain and chill. Bottle syrup and seal.

822. ORANGE SYRUP I

8 oranges
2 lbs. sugar cubes
2 cups water

½ lemon
½ tsp. citric acid

Wash and dry oranges. Rub sugar cubes individually on rind until cubes take on orange color. Add to cubes juice of oranges and lemon, citric acid. Pour in water, which has been boiled 2–3 min. Cover; set aside for 2 or 3 days, stirring frequently. Wash a strainer and several bottles and corks in boiling water. Pass mixture through strainer; bottle and seal. This syrup will keep for several months.

823. ORANGE SYRUP II

6 oranges
1 lb. sugar

1 cup water

Peel oranges, reserving peels. Prepare a syrup with sugar and water; cook 5 min. over high flame. Add orange juice; remove from heat. Wash peels, place in a strainer; pour boiling syrup over peels. Chill, then strain, bottle and seal.

823A. TANGERINE SYRUPS I and II: Use 10 tangerines, 1 cup water, 2¼ cups sugar.

823B. LEMON SYRUPS I and II: Use 6 lemons, 1 cup water, 1 lb. sugar.

824. LEMON SQUASH

juice of 4 lemons
1½ quarts water

1⅔ cups powdered sugar

Melt sugar in water; add lemon juice. Serve very cold.

824A. ORANGE SQUASH: Use juice of 6 oranges, 1½ quarts water, 2 cups powdered sugar.

824B. LEMON-ORANGE DRINK: Use juice of 3 lemons and 4 oranges, 2 quarts water, 1 cup granulated sugar.

825. STRAWBERRY LEMONADE

1 pint strawberries
2 lemons

3 cups boiling water
¼ lb. sugar cubes

Rub sugar cubes over lemon rinds until they take on yellow color. Crush strawberries in sieve; add juice of lemons. Pour liquid over sugar cubes. Pour in water; stir. Chill. Strain before bottling.

825A. RASPBERRY LEMONADE: Use 1¾ cups raspberries, ⅓ lb. sugar cubes, 1 lemon, 3 cups water.

825B. CURRANT LEMONADE: Substitute currants for strawberries.

825C. ORANGE LEMONADE: Use 2 oranges, ½ lemon, ¼ lb. sugar cubes, 3 cups water.

826. HOT WINE

3 cups wine
1½ cups water
2 sticks cinnamon

⅔ cup sugar
1 lemon, sliced

Boil together wine, water, sugar and cinnamon for 1 min. Serve very hot, with lemon slices.

827. CURRANT WINE

1 tsp. vinegar
1 cup sugar
5 lbs. currants

1 pkg. dry granular yeast
warm water

Boil currants in a little water. Add sufficient water to make 6 quarts, vinegar, sugar, yeast blended with a little warm water. Place mixture in large container, a barrel if possible. Expose to air for 4 days. Pour off liquid gently. Crush juice from currants; bottle and seal. Set bottles aside for 4 days before drinking. Makes about 6 quarts.

828. PUNCH

2 cups boiling tea
juice and rind of 1 lemon

1½ cups very hot rum
¾ cup sugar

Sweeten tea with sugar; pour over lemon rind. Add lemon juice. Add hot rum very slowly, so that it remains on surface of liquid. Ignite. Serve very hot.

829. GROG

Place 2 tbsp. brandy or rum in glass; fill glass with boiling water. Add 3 cubes sugar, slice of lemon. Serve very hot.

830. AMANDINE

½ lb. almonds	1½ cups alcohol (90%)
1¾ cups boiling water	2 cups sugar

Shell almonds. Soak shells for 3 days in alcohol (the nut-meats are not used). Melt sugar in water. Strain alcohol and water separately, then mix. Bottle and seal. Set aside 5–6 weeks before using.

831. CHERRY LIQUEUR

3 lbs. cherries, pitted	1½ cups kirsch
2½ lbs. sugar, approx.	

Cook cherries with sugar 35 min. Strain without pressing fruit. Add kirsch, mix well. Bottle.

832. CRÈME DE CACAO

1 oz. cocoa beans	1½ cups boiling water
1½ cups alcohol (90%)	¾ lb. sugar

Roast cocoa beans 10-12 min. in skillet; remove from fire, chill. Crush beans; macerate for 15 days in alcohol. Strain. Add water, which has been boiled 5–6 min., and sugar. Strain through paper filter. Bottle.

833. CRÈME DE CAFÉ

1¾ oz. coffee beans	1 cup boiling water
5 or 6 bitter almonds	1½ cups alcohol (90%)
1 lb. sugar	

Proceed as for Crème de Cacao.

834. *BLACK CURRANT LIQUEUR* (LIQUEUR DE CASSIS)

1 quart alcohol (40%)
2 lbs. black currants

¾ cup sugar
2 cups water

Wash currants and place in glass jar together with a few of their leaves. Cover with alcohol. Cover container; macerate 2–3 months. Remove fruit. Make a syrup of sugar and water, bring to boil, add to alcohol.

835. *HOT CHOCOLATE I*

FOR EACH SERVING:

1 oz. powdered chocolate, or 1
    square solid chocolate

1 cup water
a little vanilla flavoring

Melt chocolate in very small quantity water. When it forms a smooth paste, add remaining water, vanilla; cook 10–15 min. Beat with egg beater until foamy.

836. *HOT CHOCOLATE II*

FOR EACH SERVING:

1 oz. chocolate
1 cup milk

6 tbsp. water

Melt chocolate in water. When it forms a smooth paste, add milk; cook 10-15 min. Beat with egg beater until foamy.

837. *COCOA*

1 cup boiling water or
    scalded milk
2 tbsp. cocoa

6 tbsp. powdered sugar
6 tbsp. cold water

Blend cocoa and sugar in cold water. Gradually add milk or water, stirring constantly.

838. *SPANISH CHOCOLATE*

2 squares (2 oz.) chocolate
1 cup water

pinch of cinnamon
¼ tsp. vanilla extract

Melt chocolate in very small quantity water. Add remaining water; cook 8-10 min. over low flame. Add vanilla and cinnamon. Beat vigorously until foamy.

839. COFFEE (FILTERED)

Use 1 tbsp. ground coffee for each cup. Place coffee in filter; pack down. Gradually pour in desired quantity of boiling water.

840. TURKISH COFFEE

Use 1 tbsp. very finely ground coffee for each cup. Place in special copper pot. Add equal amount of powdered sugar; gradually blend in desired quantity of boiling water. Bring to boil. When coffee rises, remove from fire; set aside for 2 min. Reheat. When coffee begins to rise again, remove from fire. Pour in 1 tsp. cold water to make grounds fall. Serve immediately.

841. CAFÉ AU LAIT

First method: Add ordinary coffee, or preferably coffee extract, to scalded milk in desired quantity.

Second method: Proceed according to recipe for Filtered Coffee, but substitute scalded milk for water.

842. TEA

Rinse teapot in boiling water; drain. Use 1 tsp. tea for each cup, plus 1 tsp. "for the pot." Pour 1 cup boiling water into pot; let stand 5 min. Fill teapot with boiling water; cover and steep 7-8 min.

842A. MINT TEA: Add a few dried mint leaves to tea.

Candy

843. BARLEY SUGAR

1⅛ cups sugar   ¾ tsp. lemon juice
 6 tbsp. water

Combine ingredients in long-handled pan. Cook over high flame, stirring, until sugar is light brown in color. Pour mixture on greased marble slab or enamel table top, or into greased caramel mold. While still warm, cut into small squares.

843A. NOUGAT: Follow recipe 843, but add ¾ lb. mixed nuts (almonds, pistachio nuts, hazelnuts), which have been blanched, slightly toasted and coarsely chopped. When cool, cut into pieces.

844. HONEY NOUGAT

½ cup honey
 1 lb. mixed almonds, walnuts,
   pistachio nuts

Boil honey in pan for 10 min. Add nuts; cook, stirring constantly, until small quantity of syrup forms a small ball when dropped into cold water (246-252° F.). Remove from heat. Pour mixture on greased slab of marble. Smooth out surface with wooden spatula rubbed with lemon. Cover with waxed paper and place heavy weight on top. When cold, cut into pieces.

845. CHOCOLATE CARAMELS
PREPARATION TIME: 10 MIN. COOKING TIME: 15 MIN.

3 bars chocolate, slivered
6⅔ tbsp. butter
1¼ cups powdered sugar

3 tbsp. honey
⅓ cup cream

Combine chocolate, cream, honey, butter and sugar in pan. Cook 12-15 min. over low flame. Pour mixture into greased caramel mold. Makes 60 caramels.

846. COFFEE CARAMELS
PREPARATION TIME: 5 MIN. COOKING TIME: 15 MIN.

1 lb. sugar
¾ cup cream
½ tsp. milk

½ cup honey
2 tsp. Coffee Extract (recipe 887)

Combine sugar, cream and milk in pan; melt. Cook 15 min. over very low flame. Add coffee extract; mix well. Pour mixture into greased caramel mold. Makes 60 caramels.

847. PASTILLES
PREPARATION TIME: 10 MIN.

1 lb. sugar
4-5 drops flavoring—mint,
   lemon, etc.

¾ cup water

Make a thick paste of sugar and water; heat over very low flame (do not boil). Add desired flavoring extract; mix well. Pour mixture in drops on greased marble slab. When cool (about one hour), remove drops from marble.

848. TOFFEES
PREPARATION TIME: 20 MIN. COOKING TIME: 2¼ HOURS.

½ cup molasses or maple syrup
½ lb. butter

1 lb. light brown sugar

Heat molasses or syrup gently in pan; add brown sugar, butter. Let mixture stand for 2 hours near heat source (do not boil). Place over low flame; cook 15 min., stirring constantly. Mixture is cooked when small quantity dropped in cold water hardens immediately. Remove from heat and pour into greased caramel mold. Remove candies when cold.

849. *CHOCOLATE TRUFFLES*
PREPARATION TIME: 25 MIN.

½ lb. chocolate
2 tbsp. milk
2 eggs yolks

¼ cup butter
2 tbsp. powdered chocolate

Melt chocolate in milk over low flame; remove from heat when mixture forms a smooth paste. Add egg yolks, stirring, then butter in small pieces; beat 2–3 min. Chill 4–5 hours. Form mixture into small balls about the size of walnuts; roll in powdered chocolate. Keep cool until ready to serve. Must be eaten within 48 hours.

850. *GLAZED CHESTNUTS*
Shell 2 lbs. chestnuts, being careful not to break them. Place chestnuts in casserole, cover with cold water; heat, but do not let water boil. Cook gently 3 hours. Drain chestnuts; carefully remove skins. Soak chestnuts 12 hours in cold Sugar Syrup (recipe 890); then heat slowly in double boiler. Remove and drain chestnuts; heat syrup to large thread stage (219° F.) Replace chestnuts; let stand in syrup for 12 hours. Remove and drain; heat syrup to small pearl stage (220° F.). Replace chestnuts; let stand in syrup for 12 hours. Place chestnuts in wire basket; plunge for 1 min. into boiling syrup (crack stage, or 270° F.). Drain thoroughly. Dry for several hours in very slow oven.

851. *STUFFED WALNUTS*
PREPARATION TIME: 40 MIN.

24 large walnuts, halved
¼ lb. almonds, blanched
1¼ cups powdered sugar

2 squares chocolate, slivered
1 egg white

Crush almonds in mortar with egg white. Add sugar and chocolate; beat thoroughly. Form mixture into balls about size of walnuts. Place each ball between two walnut halves.

852. STUFFED FIGS

PREPARATION TIME: 35 MIN.

2 doz. large dried figs
4½ tbsp. butter
3 squares chocolate, slivered

1 tbsp. crushed almonds
4 hazelnuts, blanched, roasted

Remove stems from figs; slit along one side. Cream together butter, chocolate, almonds. Stuff figs with mixture. Close openings with sliver of hazelnut.

853. STUFFED DATES

PREPARATION TIME: 35 MIN.

2 doz. large pitted dates,
    slightly dry
1 cup powdered sugar

⅓ cup pistachio nuts, blanched
½ egg white

Crush pistachio nuts in mortar. Add sugar and egg white; work into firm, smooth paste. Slash dates along one side; stuff with nut mixture.

854. STUFFED PRUNES

PREPARATION TIME: 35 MIN.

1 lb. large prunes, pitted
¼ lb. mixed hazelnuts and
    almonds

⅓ cup pistachio nuts

Coarsely chop nuts and a few of the less presentable prunes. Fill prunes with mixture. Carefully close opening.

854A ORANGE-STUFFED PRUNES: Stuff prunes with mixture of orange marmalade and ½ cup coarsely chopped almonds.

Miscellaneous Preparations

MARINADES

855. INSTANT MARINADE

6⅔ tbsp. white wine	juice of 1 lemon
1 tbsp. oil	thyme, parsley, pepper

Combine all ingredients. Marinate meat for 2 hours, turning frequently. Use for small pieces of meat.

856. COOKED MARINADE, RED WINE

3 cups red wine	1 small onion, minced
3 tbsp. vinegar	1 clove garlic
1 small carrot, sliced	pepper, thyme, bay leaf
several cloves	

Combine all ingredients; cook for several minutes. Chill before marinating meat. Store in refrigerator.

857. COOKED MARINADE, WHITE WINE: Proceed as for marinade with red wine, substituting white wine for red.

858. UNCOOKED MARINADE

1 large carrot, sliced	small clove garlic
1 large onion, sliced	2 tbsp. oil
¾ cup vinegar	several cloves
2 tsp. minced shallot	salt, pepper, bay leaf

Used for changing flavor or tenderizing piece of meat. Cover meat with sliced carrot and onion, spices. Sprinkle with vinegar and oil. Marinate 3 or 4 days, turning meat daily.

859. SWEET MARINADE

¼ lb. bacon, diced	½ tsp. minced garlic
1 tbsp. chopped onion	3 tbsp. vinegar
1 tbsp. oil	salt, pepper
2 tsp. minced shallot	chervil and parsley

Used for meats which do not have a pronounced flavor of their own (e.g., veal). Chop together bacon, onion, shallot, garlic, parsley and chervil. Combine with oil, vinegar, salt and pepper.

STUFFINGS

860. STUFFING FOR CHICKEN, SQUAB, GOOSE

Chop together liver, heart and stomach of bird. Soak some bread crumbs in milk; drain, add to chopped meat. Add mushrooms cooked in butter, chopped parsley, salt and pepper. Amount of stuffing may be increased by adding small quantity of finely crushed sausage meat.

861. STUFFING FOR TURKEY

CHOP TOGETHER:

¼ lb. veal	2 oz. truffles
turkey liver	¼ lb. fresh pork fat or
1 lb. Cooked Chestnuts	blanched bacon
(recipe 468), mashed	

862. STUFFING FOR PHEASANT

CHOP TOGETHER:

½ lb. veal	1 lb. Cooked Chestnuts (recipe
¼ lb. fresh pork	468)

863. STUFFING FOR MEAT

CHOP TOGETHER:

¼ lb. fresh pork fat or	parsley
blanched bacon	brandy
¼ lb. pork	salt, pepper

864. STUFFING FOR FISH

2 cups thick White Sauce
(recipe 8 or 9)
2 hard-boiled eggs
1 lb. fish, preferably whiting
or hake

mushrooms or truffles, finely
chopped
crushed anchovies (optional)

Cook fish for 5 min. in a Court-bouillon (recipe 866 et seq.),
Remove skin, head, bones; crush meat into white sauce. Add
eggs, mushrooms or truffles, crushed anchovies.

865. DUXELLE (Meatless stuffing for vegetables)

2 tbsp. butter
1 tbsp. oil
1 med. onion
1 tsp. chopped shallot

¼ lb. mushrooms, finely
chopped
salt, pepper, nutmeg

Cook onion, shallot and mushrooms in butter until golden.
Add seasonings; cook until mixture thickens.

COURT-BOUILLON

Stock for cooking fish. Combine all ingredients, simmer for
1 hour. There should be enough liquid to cover fish completely.

866. COURT-BOUILLON WITH SALT

1 quart water   4 tsp. salt

For mackerel and mullet.

867. COURT-BOUILLON WITH VINEGAR

3 quarts water
1 med. carrot, sliced
1 clove
¾ cup vinegar

1 med. onion
1 sprig parsley
salt, pepper

For hake, pike, carp.

868. COURT-BOUILLON WITH WHITE WINE

2 quarts water
1 qt. white wine
1 med. carrot

1 med. onion
thyme, bay leaf, parsley
salt, pepper

For salmon and trout.

869. COURT-BOUILLON WITH RED WINE

Proceed as for Court-Bouillon with White Wine, but substitute 1 qt. red wine for white. For pike, carp, trout.

870. COURT-BOUILLON WITH MILK

3 quarts water
2 cups milk

lemon slices
salt, pepper

For halibut, catfish, sole.

QUENELLES

A kind of dumpling often served alone as an entree, or used as a garnish for stews and soups, blanquettes, vol-au-vent etc.

871. GODIVEAU (Batter for Quenelles)
PREPARATION TIME: 30 MIN. COOKING TIME: 10 MIN.

⅓ lb. veal
½ lb. fat from calf's kidney
2 eggs
small quantity of cream
chopped parsley and chives

¾ cup bread crumbs, soaked in small quantity of milk
salt, pepper, nutmeg
flour

Clean and chop fat; pound with veal. Rub through sieve or food mill. Add eggs one by one, chopped herbs, bread crumbs, sufficient cream to form a smooth paste. Spread mixture out in thin layer; set aside for several hours. Form mixture into oblong balls about length of pinky; dredge in flour. Poach 10 min. in "shivering" (not boiling) water. If desired, serve with a sauce.

After poaching, quenelles may be rolled first in beaten egg, then in fine bread crumbs, and fried in smoking hot shortening. Garnish with Fried Parsley (recipe 874).

In Northern France the quenelle mixture is often formed into round balls and added to a soup. These are called *fricadelles*.

871A. LIVER QUENELLES: Decrease fat to ⅓ lb.; substitute ¾ lb. calf's or chicken livers for veal.

871B. *BREAD CRUMBS QUENELLES:* Use 1 lb. slightly stale bread, crumbed and soaked in milk; combine with 4 eggs, chopped *fines herbes*, salt and pepper.

871C. *FLOUR QUENELLES:* Use 3 cups flour, 3½ tbsp. butter, 5 eggs, 2 tsp. milk, salt and pepper.

871D. *POTATO QUENELLES:* Use ¾ lb. potatoes, cooked and mashed, ⅓ cup cream, 5 eggs, separated, salt and pepper.

872. FISH QUENELLES

PREPARATION TIME: 40 MIN. COOKING TIME: 3 MIN.

1 lb. fish	3½ cups fresh bread crumbs,
½ lb. butter	soaked in small quantity of
4 eggs	milk
	salt, pepper

Crush fish, combine with butter and bread crumbs. Mix to form smooth dough. Add eggs one by one; season. Set aside for several hours. Proceed according to recipe 871.

873. QUENELLES À LA NANTUA

PREPARATION TIME: 2 HOURS. COOKING TIME: 25 MIN.

Fish Quenelles (recipe 872)	4 tsp. cream
⅔ cup flour	2 tbsp. shrimp butter
2 tbsp. butter	(see p. 31)
¾ cup white wine	1 tbsp. chopped onion
6⅔ tbsp. stock	salt, pepper, *bouquet garni*

Simmer together wine, stock, onion, seasonings and any leftover fish for 1 hour. Strain. Prepare a Light Brown Sauce (recipe 30) with flour, butter, strained liquid. Bind with cream and shrimp butter. Simmer quenelles 15 min. in sauce.

874. FRIED PARSLEY

Blanch whole or chopped parsley for several seconds in boiling shortening. Drain. Serve immediately.

875. *BÉARNAISE EXTRACT*
PREPARATION TIME: 20 MIN. COOKING TIME: 2 HOURS.

1 quart vinegar
1 lb. onions
¾ lb. shallots
generous handful of
tarragon

1⅓ cups white wine
pepper

Combine all ingredients; simmer 2 hours over low flame. Rub through sieve or food mill. Pour into small bottles and cork tightly. Use for flavoring sauces, soups, etc.

876. *TOMATO PURÉE*
PREPARATION TIME: 30 MIN. COOKING TIME: 2½ HOURS.

4 lbs. ripe tomatoes, quartered
1 large onion

salt, pepper, *bouquet garni*

Combine all ingredients; cook 45 min., stirring frequently. Rub through sieve. Pour into small bottles; seal. Sterilize 1½ hours in pressure cooker or other type of canner. Once seal on bottle is broken, use contents immediately.

877. *HERB COLORING* (VERT D'ÉPINARDS)
PREPARATION TIME: 5 MIN. COOKING TIME: 1 MIN.

⅓ lb spinach
⅓ lb. tarragon

¼ lb. chervil

Blanch ingredients for 1 min. in scalding water; plunge into cold water. Rub through sieve. Use for coloring sauces.

878. *MIREPOIX*
PREPARATION TIME: 15 MIN. COOKING TIME: 5 MIN.

¼ lb. carrots, diced
1 tsp. minced shallot
1 small onion

¼ lb. ham, diced
3½ tbsp. butter
thyme, parsley, bay leaf

Brown ingredients in butter; season. Add to sauce to improve its flavor.

879. FISH EXTRACT

PREPARATION TIME: 20 MIN. COOKING TIME: 2 HOURS.

1 qt. water	1 med. carrot
2 cups Chablis wine	1 small onion
2 lbs. mixed whiting and mullet	parsley
1/8 lb. turnip, peeled	salt, pepper, *bouquet garni*

Simmer all ingredients together for 2 hours. Strain liquid. Use to flavor sauces for fish.

880. MEAT EXTRACT

PREPARATION TIME: 30 MIN. COOKING TIME: 3 HOURS.

6 cups water	1 med. carrot
2 lbs. meat bones	1 small onion
1/8 lb. turnip, peeled	blanched bacon rinds and ends
1 ham bone	parsley, *bouquet garni*, pepper

Cook as for Stock (recipe 69). Strain liquid; do not skim. Pour into terrine; chill.

Canned consommé or bouillon may be substituted in recipes calling for meat extract, but they are not as good.

881. MEAT JELLY

PREPARATION TIME: 25 MIN. COOKING TIME: 4 HOURS.

6 cups water	1/3 lb. blanched bacon rind
2 lbs. veal knuckle	(remove fat)
1 calf's foot	2 onions
1 lb. beef shank (or soup bone)	1 carrot
1 chicken or turkey giblet	salt, pepper, *bouquet garni*

Combine ingredients. Bring to boil; skim. Lower heat until liquid is barely "shivering"; simmer for 4 hours. Chill; skim off grease.

882. TO CLARIFY MEAT JELLY

If liquid is very thin, warm slightly, then add 1 tbsp. of gelatin softened in a little cold water. Place liquid in pot; add 2 slightly beaten egg whites. Place pot over low heat; heat, beating constantly with wire whisk, until liquid begins to boil. Strain through wet muslin. If desired, add 6⅔ tbsp. Madeira wine. Chill until firm.

883. MUSHROOM FUMET
PREPARATION TIME: 10 MIN. COOKING TIME: 10 MIN.

½ lb. mushrooms, chopped juice of 1 lemon
4 tbsp. butter

Combine all ingredients; cook 10 min. Use resulting liquid
to flavor stocks and sauces.

884. BATTER FOR FRYING (PÂTÉ À FRIRE)
PREPARATION TIME: 8 MIN.

3 cups flour   1 egg white
1 pkg. dry granular yeast warm water
1 tbsp. oil

Place flour in mixing bowl. Make depression in top; place
yeast and oil in bowl. Gradually blend in sufficient warm
water to form a batter which spins a ribbon when dropped
from spoon. Add egg white beaten for 1 min. with fork. Set
aside for 2 hours before using.

Dessert Pancake Batter (recipe 733) may also be used for
frying, but it is less crusty.

885. TO CLARIFY BUTTER

When ordinary butter is heated until it liquefies, a milky
residue sinks to the bottom of the pan. The clear, yellow
liquid remaining on top is clarified butter, which burns less
easily than ordinary butter and can therefore be heated to the
high temperature necessary for frying and browning foods
properly.

Cut butter into pieces; place in saucepan over moderate
heat. When butter has melted, skim off foam. Strain clear yellow liquid into bowl.

Milky residue left in bottom of saucepan may be added to
soups and sauces to enrich them.

886. COFFEE EXTRACT

1¼ cups boiling water   ½ lb. ground coffee

Place half the coffee in water. Remove from heat, cover
and set aside until cold. Strain. Bring liquid to boil; pour

through filter containing remaining coffee. Bottle and seal tightly.

887. ALMOND PASTE
PREPARATION TIME: 30-35 MIN.

½ lb. sweet almonds
6 bitter almonds

1 cup powdered sugar
1 egg white

Blanch almonds. Crush in mortar with sugar and egg whites. Mix thoroughly.

888. SALTED ALMONDS

Blanch almonds. Roll in salt while still moist. Place on plate, heat for several minutes in hot oven. Remove excess salt.

889. CHANTILLY CREAM
PREPARATION TIME: 10 MIN.

1 cup heavy cream
powdered sugar

vanilla extract to taste

Beat cream until foamy and stiff. Add sugar and vanilla extract to taste. If cream is very thick, it may be thinned with 6⅔ tbsp. milk.

890. SUGAR SYRUP

Use 4 parts sugar to 3 parts water. Heat together to boiling point. Cook until desired stage is reached.

Large thread stage: Fairly long and strong threads form when syrup is dropped from spoon. 219° F.

Small pearl stage: Syrup falls in thick drops or small balls. 220° F.

Fillet: Small quantity of syrup taken between thumb and index finger forms a thread when fingers are stretched apart. 222° F.

Soufflé: Small balls detach themselves when skimming spoon dipped in syrup is blown through. 232° F.

Ball stage: Small quantity of syrup taken between 2 wet

fingers and dropped in glass of cold water forms a small ball. 230-250° F.

Hard crack stage: Small quantity of syrup dropped in cold water immediately shatters. 260-335° F.

891. *TO CARAMELIZE A MOLD*

Use 4 parts of sugar to 1 part of water. (One-half cup sugar to 2 tbsp. water is enough to caramelize a 6-cup mold.) Boil sugar and water together in mold until syrup turns first dark red, then brown (356°F.). Remove mold from heat; tilt and turn in hands until bottom and sides are covered with film of syrup. Let film harden before pouring in liquid.

A Gastronomic Tour of France

N.B.: All recipes serve 6, unless otherwise indicated.

Each of the French provinces has its own special regional dishes which have been handed down from mother to daughter for centuries. The following recipes can only hint at the richness of this culinary tapestry!

Alsace

892. POTATO FRITTERS
PREPARATION TIME: 15 MIN. COOKING TIME: 6 MIN.

2 lbs. potatoes, peeled, grated
5 eggs
  chopped *fines herbes*
salt, pepper
shortening for frying

Drain and dry grated potatoes. Beat eggs until foamy; add potatoes. Add chopped *fines herbes*, seasonings to taste. Drop mixture by spoonfuls into boiling shortening. Cook about 3 min. each side.

893. KUGELHOPF (Alsatian Tea Cake)
PREPARATION TIME: 30 MIN. COOKING TIME: 1 HOUR.

6¼ cups flour
6⅔ tbsp. butter
  2 eggs
¾ cup milk
¾ cup seeded raisins
  3 pkgs. dry granular yeast

Melt butter in milk, then add milk to flour and eggs and beat well. Blend yeast with a little milk; add to batter, together with pinch of salt. Knead dough with hands until it pulls away from sides of bowl. Add raisins. Line bottom of buttered Kugelhopf mold (or any deep ring-type cake pan) with almonds. Place dough in pan (pan should be only half full); set aside to rise for 6 hours. Bake for 1 hour, beginning with temperature of 250-275°F., gradually increasing heat to 425-450°F. Sprinkle with powdered sugar before serving.

894. DAMPFNOUDELN (Steamed Fritters)

10⅔ cups flour	7 pkgs. dry granular yeast
3¾ tbsp. sugar	4½ tbsp. lard
¼ lb. butter	salt
2 cups warm milk	

Melt butter in milk. Beat together flour, milk, sugar, pinch of salt. Knead dough with hands until it pulls away from side of bowl. Add yeast; mix well. Set aside to rise for 2 hours. Heat lard in heavy pot until smoking hot; drop in batter by spoonfuls. Cover pot, but leave small opening through which to pour in 6 tbsp. cold water; then cover pot tightly. (Upon contact with hot grease, cold water turns to steam and inflates fritters.) Sprinkle with sugar and serve hot, with a fruit compote.

Berry

895. HONEY WAFFLES

PREPARATION TIME: 15 MIN. COOKING TIME: 5 MIN. EACH WAFFLE.

6⅓ cups flour	5 eggs
¾ cup honey	1½ tsp. rum

Mix ingredients into smooth dough. Roll out on floured board; cut into pieces. Cook each waffle 5 min. in well-buttered waffle iron.

Brittany

896. POOR MAN'S MEAT PIE (PÂTÉ DE GUEUX)
PREPARATION TIME: 20 MIN. COOKING TIME: 25 MIN.

¼ lb. fatback, blanched bacon
    or blanched fat salt pork,
    cooked
¾ lb. leftover cooked meat
1 large onion

1 lb. potatoes, cooked
1 cup Stock (recipe 69)
1 tbsp. butter
salt, pepper, *fines herbes*

Mash potatoes with a little milk. Chop together cooked pork and meat, onion, *fines herbes*; mix with mashed potatoes. Beat mixture, gradually adding stock; season. Pour mixture into buttered pie plate. Bake 25 min. in hot oven.

897. FAR (Breton cake)
PREPARATION TIME: 20 MIN. COOKING TIME: 40 MIN.

3 cups flour
½ lb. sugar
1 quart milk
1 tbsp. butter

½ tsp. salt
4 eggs
½ lb. prunes, soaked overnight
1½ tsp. rum

Sift flour and salt into bowl. Break in eggs one by one; mix carefully so that no lumps form. Beat until light and fluffy. Add sugar, milk, rum, drained prunes. Pour mixture into buttered baking dish. Bake 40 min. in hot oven, decreasing temperature to moderate when cake begins to set.

898. VIEUX GARÇONS (Brown sugar cookies)
PREPARATION TIME: 20 MIN. COOKING TIME: 20 MIN.

3 cups flour
½ cup brown sugar

¼ lb. butter, softened
1 egg, separated

Heap flour on board. Make a depression in top; place in butter, sugar, egg white. Knead mixture quickly. Flatten slightly with rolling pin; knead again. (Keep board and dough well floured.) Roll out dough to thickness of about ⅓ in. Cut into circles with cookie cutter; brush with beaten egg yolk. Bake 20 min. in slow oven.

In Brittany these cookies are baked in an oven fired with furze branches, which gives them a distinctive flavor.

Burgundy

899. GOUGÈRE (Cheese-flavored pastry)
PREPARATION TIME: 15 MIN. COOKING TIME: 30 MIN.

Make a Cream-Puff Pastry, following recipe 790, but substitute 1 cup grated Gruyère for sugar. Shape dough into ring; place on buttered cookie sheet, and sprinkle with additional Gruyère. Bake 25-30 min. in very hot oven.

900. MEURETTE (Fish Stew)
PREPARATION TIME: 15 MIN. COOKING TIME: 30 MIN.

½ lb. eel, skinned	6⅔ tbsp. butter
½ lb. carp	6 tbsp. flour
½ lb. pike	1 onion
1 bottle red Burgundy	1 clove garlic
6 tbsp. brandy	bouquet garni, salt, pepper

Clean and dress fish; cut eel in pieces. Bring wine to boil; add fish, eel, onion, garlic, half the butter, seasonings. Cook 10 min. Add brandy; ignite. Simmer 15 min. Bind sauce with blended flour and remaining butter; cook 5 min.

900A. PAUCHOUSE

Substitute white wine for red. Bind sauce with mixture of ¾ cup cream, 6 tbsp. butter, 2 egg yolks.

901. MARZIPAN CAKES
PREPARATION TIME: 20 MIN. COOKING TIME: 30 MIN.

½ lb. sugar	2 egg whites
¼ lb. almonds, shelled and blanched	3 tbsp. flour
	grated rind of 1 lemon

Crush almonds with sugar and egg whites; mix into rather liquid paste. Add flour and lemon rind. Place small mounds of mixture on floured cookie sheets. Bake 30 min. in slow oven.

Cévennes

902. MACARONI À LA CÉVENOLE
PREPARATION TIME: 20 MIN.   COOKING TIME: 30 MIN.

½ lb. macaroni, cooked
1 lb. chestnuts
1 cup grated Gruyère

⅓ cup cream
4½ tbsp. butter
salt, pepper

Split and roast chestnuts; remove shells, halve chestnuts.
Mix cooked macaroni and chestnuts. Turn mixture into
buttered baking dish; sprinkle with Gruyère, dot with butter.
Pour cream over mixture; season. Bake 15-20 min. in slow
oven.

Dauphiné

903. GRATIN DAUPHINOIS
PREPARATION TIME: 15 MIN.   COOKING TIME: 1 HOUR.

2 lbs. potatoes, peeled,
   thinly sliced
1½ cups grated Gruyère
2 cups milk, scalded

1 egg, well beaten
3½ tbsp. butter
garlic, salt, pepper, nutmeg

Combine potatoes, milk, ¾ cup grated cheese, egg, salt,
pepper. Turn mixture into flame-proof baking dish which has
been rubbed with clove of garlic. Sprinkle with Gruyère; dot
with butter. Bring mixture to boil on top of stove; then place
in moderate oven, cover, bake 30 min.

Franche-Comté

904. CHICKEN À LA COMTOISE
PREPARATION TIME: 10 MIN.   COOKING TIME: 2½ HOURS.

1 chicken, 3-4 lbs. cut in
   pieces
1 medium onion
½ tsp. minced shallot
6⅔ tbsp. brandy
¼ tsp. minced garlic

4 tbsp. butter
1⅓ cups white wine
1⅓ cups Stock (recipe 69)
½ lb. mushrooms, cut in pieces
bouquet garni, salt, pepper

Brown chicken pieces thoroughly in butter. Sprinkle with brandy, ignite. Add onion, garlic, shallot, seasonings; moisten with wine and stock. Cook 1½ hours. Add mushrooms; continue cooking one hour.

905. FONDUE FRANC-COMTOISE
PREPARATION TIME: 5 MIN. COOKING TIME: 15–20 MIN.

6 eggs, well beaten
1 cup grated Gruyère
4 tbsp. butter

6⅔ tbsp. dry white wine
1 clove garlic
salt, pepper, nutmeg

Rub and crush garlic clove on bottom of earthenware skillet. Heat wine in skillet; add grated cheese, stirring constantly over low flame until creamy. Add beaten eggs, butter; thicken 7–8 min. Season. Serve on buttered hot plate.

906. TROUT À LA CRÈME
PREPARATION TIME: 15 MIN. COOKING TIME: 25 MIN.

6 small trout
¼ lb. butter
½ lb. mushrooms, peeled, finely chopped

2 egg yolks
⅔ cup cream
6 slices bread, fried in butter

Cook trout in butter (see recipe 122); arrange in baking dish. Cook chopped mushrooms in same butter; use to garnish fish. Blend cream and egg yolks, pour over fish. Bake 10 min. in hot oven. Serve on slices of bread.

907. TUTSCHE (Custard Pie)
PREPARATION TIME: 20 MIN. COOKING TIME: 30 MIN.

6⅓ cups flour
⅔ cup butter
3 pkgs. dry granular yeast
2 cups warm milk

1⅓ cups cream
2 eggs
salt

Knead together flour, 6 tbsp. butter, yeast blended in milk, pinch of salt. Set aside for 2 hours. Roll out dough to thickness of ½ in.; line a large pie plate. Mix cream, eggs, pinch of salt; pour into pie shell. Dot with butter. Bake 30 min. in hot oven.

Limousin

908. *CLAFOUTI (Cherry Cake)*
PREPARATION TIME: 30 MIN.   COOKING TIME: 35 MIN.

1¼ cups flour
½ cup sugar
6 eggs
1 cup milk

1¾ lbs. cherries, washed and
   pitted
⅓ cup kirsch
pinch of salt

Combine flour, eggs, salt. Add a little milk; beat mixture until light and fluffy. Gradually add remaining milk; beat until batter has the consistency of a pancake batter. Add cherries and kirsch. Pour batter into buttered baking dish. Bake 35 min. in hot oven. Serve cold, sprinkled with sugar.

Lorraine

909. *RAISIN PIE*
PREPARATION TIME: 20 MIN.   COOKING TIME: 45 MIN.

2 cups flour
raisins as desired, washed and
   dried
1 egg

⅓ cup crushed almonds
6⅔ tbsp. milk
3½ tbsp. sugar

Line a pie tin with pastry made with flour and butter (see recipe 796). Fill shell with raisins; cover with mixture of crushed almonds, milk, egg, sugar. Sprinkle with sugar. Bake 45 min. in very slow oven.

910. *QUICHE LORRAINE (Custard Tart)*
PREPARATION TIME: 20 MIN.   COOKING TIME: 40 MIN.

Pie Pastry (recipe 796)
½ lb. bacon, diced
2 cups cream

6⅔ tbsp. sour cream
4 eggs
salt, pepper

Line a pie plate with pastry. Cover bottom with diced bacon. Fill shell with mixture of beaten eggs, cream, seasonings. Bake 40 min. in slow oven.

911. NANCY CAKE

PREPARATION TIME: 25 MIN.   COOKING TIME: 45 MIN.

½ lb. chocolate	6 eggs, separated
⅔ cup sugar	1⅓ tbsp. butter
5 tbsp. cornstarch	6⅔ tbsp. milk
¼ lb. almonds, blanched, crushed	pinch of vanilla powder

Melt chocolate and vanilla powder in milk over low flame, stirring constantly until smooth. Add sugar and cornstarch; beat slightly. Mix crushed almonds with egg yolks; add to chocolate mixture. Add stiffly beaten egg whites. Beat batter vigorously 5-6 min. Pour into buttered cake pan (pan should be no more than ¾ full). Bake 45 min. in slow oven. Serve cold.

Morvan

912. POTATO CAKE

PREPARATION TIME: 15 MIN.   COOKING TIME: 45 MIN.

2 lbs. potatoes, cooked and mashed	2 eggs
1 cup flour	4 tbsp. butter
¾ cup milk	salt, pepper

Blend flour, milk and 1 egg into mashed potatoes; season to taste. Roll out mixture into a circle; trace diamond designs on top with knife. Brush with remaining beaten egg; dot with butter. Brown 15 min. in hot oven.

Normandy

913. NORMAN OMELET

PREPARATION TIME: 20 MIN.   COOKING TIME: 8 MIN.

1 lb. apples, peeled, thinly sliced	5⅓ tbsp. butter
5 eggs	sugar, salt

Cook apples in skillet with half the butter; remove. Beat eggs with pinch of salt until foamy. Heat remaining butter in skillet. Pour in half the beaten eggs; cover with apples; top with remaining egg. Cook 8 min. over low flame. Fold omelet. Sprinkle with sugar before serving.

Picardy

914. FLAMIQUE PICARDE (Picard Leek Pie)
PREPARATION TIME: 30 MIN. COOKING TIME: 1 HOUR.

10 large leeks (white portion only)	2 eggs, separated
¼ lb. butter	½ cup cream
3 cups flour	salt, pepper
3 whole eggs	

Peel and wash leeks; cut in thin slices. Place in casserole with 3½ tbsp. butter, salt, pepper to taste; cook 30 min. over low flame, stirring frequently. Prepare pie pastry (see recipe 796) with flour, remaining butter (softened), 3 whole eggs, 2 egg whites, pinch of salt. Knead dough with hand. Roll out thinly on well-floured board. Line buttered pie tin with half the pastry. Bind leek mixture with 2 egg yolks and cream, season to taste; pour into pie shell. Cover with remaining pie crust, sealing edges with a little water. Pierce upper crust in several places with knife. Bake 30 min. in very hot oven. Serve hot.

Provence

915. BOURRIDE (Provençal Fish Stew)
PREPARATION TIME: 30 MIN. COOKING TIME: 30 MIN.

1¾ lbs. white fish	thyme, bay leaf, salt, pepper
2 quarts water	2 onions
2 cups cream	Ailloli (recipe 60E)

Place fish in cold water with onions and seasonings. Heat slowly until water "shivers"; cook 30 min., keeping water just at "shivering" point. Strain liquid; blend very gradually into ailloli. Add cream. Pour mixture over thin slices of bread dried (not toasted) in oven. Serve fish separately.

922. CROSETS

PREPARATION TIME: 30 MIN. COOKING TIME: 25 MIN.

6¼ cups flour	6⅔ tbsp. Brown Butter (recipe
4 eggs	6) or Meat Extract (recipe
1 cup milk	880)
¾ cup grated Gruyère	pinch of salt

Make noodle dough (see page 193) with flour, eggs, milk, salt. Roll out on floured board; dice. Cook 20 min. in boiling salted water; drain. Sprinkle with Gruyère and brown butter or meat extract before serving.

Toulouse

923. MILLAS (Fried Porridge)

PREPARATION TIME: 10 MIN. COOKING TIME: 30 MIN.

½ lb. cornmeal	¼ lb. butter
2 cups boiling water	6⅔ tbsp. cream
2 cups milk	pinch of salt
3 eggs	

Blend cornmeal with a little cold water; then throw into boiling water; cook 20 min., stirring frequently. Drain. Place in casserole with milk; cook 10 min. Remove from heat, add eggs, half the butter, cream; place over heat and cook, stirring until smooth (mixture should not boil). Season with salt. Spread porridge in plate; chill. When cold, cut into circles and fry in remaining butter.

924. CASSOULET

PREPARATION TIME: 1 HOUR. COOKING TIME: 4 HOURS.

1 lb. white haricot beans	¼ lb. cooked sausages, cut in
5¼ oz. fatback or blanched fat	pieces
salt pork	2 medium onions
1¾ lbs. pork or lamb, cut in	several cloves garlic
pieces	⅓ cup tomato purée
1¼ lbs. *confit d'oie,** cut in	*bouquet garni,* salt, pepper,
pieces (optional)	a few cloves
1 carrot	oil or goose fat for frying

* *Confit d'oie*—portions of goose cooked in goose fat. Imported canned *confit* is available in specialty stores in this country.

Soak beans for several hours in cold water. Place drained beans in earthenware pot with carrot, one onion stuck with cloves, fatback or pork, *bouquet garni*, and about 4 quarts of water, or enough to cover generously. Cook one hour. Brown pieces of pork or lamb in goose fat or oil; add remaining onion, one or two cloves garlic, tomato purée and 2 cups cooking liquid from beans; cook 10 min. over medium heat. Remove carrot and onion from beans; add pork or lamb, sausage and *confit d'oie* if used; simmer one hour. (There should be just enough liquid in pot to cover meat and beans.) Place in heavy baking dish alternating layers of beans, meat and cooking liquid, finishing with layer of sausage and fatback or salt pork. Season. Bake 2 hours in very slow oven.

Index

301

Heloise's

Over 350,000 copies sold in the $3.95 edition
Now in one volume—the best of Heloise, whose column
is read daily by millions of women all over America.

* **Money-savers for all your housekeeping:**
shortcuts and tips that save on the family budget.

* **Speedier ways to get things done:**
quick tricks that save both time and effort.

* **Easier methods: new simplified**
how-to for almost every household task.

* **Unusual hints for every need:**
clever new uses for old standby items in your home.

50070 / 50¢